The Boys of St. Joe's '65
in the Vietnam War

The Boys of St. Joe's '65 in the Vietnam War

DENNIS G. PREGENT

McFarland & Company, Inc., Publishers
Jefferson, North Carolina

All images and documents are provided by the author
unless otherwise stated.

LIBRARY OF CONGRESS CATALOGUING-IN-PUBLICATION DATA

Names: Pregent, Dennis G., 1947– author.
Title: The boys of St. Joe's '65 in the Vietnam War / Dennis G. Pregent.
Description: Jefferson, North Carolina : McFarland & Company, Inc.,
Publishers, 2020 | Includes index.
Identifiers: LCCN 2019049531 | ISBN 9781476679716 (paperback : acid free paper) ∞
ISBN 9781476638157 (ebook)
Subjects: LCSH: Pregent, Dennis G., 1947—Friends and associates—
Biography. | Vietnam War, 1961–1975—Veterans—United States—
Biography. | Vietnam War, 1961–1975—Massachusetts—North Adams. |
Veterans—Massachusetts—North Adams—Biography. |
North Adams (Mass.)—Biography.
Classification: LCC DS557.5 .P74 2020 | DDC 959.704/3409227441—dc23
LC record available at https://lccn.loc.gov/2019049531

BRITISH LIBRARY CATALOGUING DATA ARE AVAILABLE

ISBN (print) 978-1-4766-7971-6
ISBN (ebook) 978-1-4766-3815-7

―

On the front cover: *clockwise from top left* Gary DeMastrie;
Bill Buzzell; Joe Daigneault; Russell Roulier; Dennis Pregent; Mike Gorman;
Jim Luczynski (all images courtesy of those shown)

Printed in the United States of America

*McFarland & Company, Inc., Publishers
Box 611, Jefferson, North Carolina 28640
www.mcfarlandpub.com*

To all the men and women who served in Vietnam.
You are not forgotten.

Acknowledgments

This book would have never reached the light of day had not my wife, Carol, encouraged me. She was the catalyst from my first inkling about writing of the war. It began when she said, "write your story first," then go on to others. She has been a resolute and confident cheerleader not only for the past several years but over a half-century of marriage.

I am forever grateful to my classmates. They allowed me into their lives again and again, spent hours of time with me on the phone and in person, answered innumerable questions, took me to old haunts, shared meals, and were just plain kind. All willingly referred me to family members and long-ago acquaintances, and smoothed the way with introductions. Everyone was willing to share pictures, award citations, and most importantly poignant, if dusty, memories.

I feel honored that both Senator Bob Dole and General John C. "Doc" Bahnsen, Jr., U.S. Army (Ret.) have provided their endorsements. Receiving tributes from two decorated and well-known soldiers was very gratifying.

My family has been supportive from the beginning, with my daughters and especially my granddaughter Cecelia who proofread, provided technical advice, offered ideas, and always gave strong encouragement.

A special thanks goes to Jane Hobson Snyder who worked diligently as a developmental editor, smoothing out my writing as well as providing inestimable guidance with the technical aspects of pulling all the pieces together.

Ed Palm, PhD, retired USMC Major, was a great help in critiquing all things military.

Charlie Perdue, acquisitions editor for McFarland, helped to initiate my understanding of the publishing process.

Thanks also to Richard T. Evans of Infodex Indexing Services, Inc.

My brother Jack was always there with encouraging words.

To everyone and anyone I may have missed, thank you for making this book possible.

Table of Contents

Where We Fought

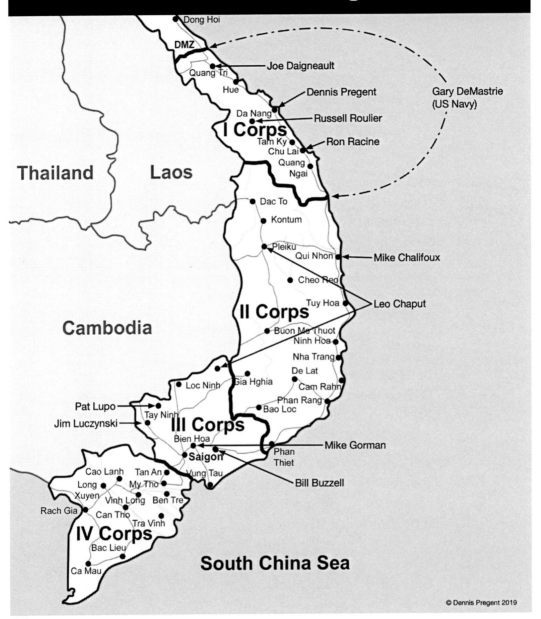

Dong Hoi

DMZ

Quang Tri — Joe Daigneault

Hue — Dennis Pregent

Da Nang — Russell Roulier

I Corps

Tam Ky — Ron Racine
Chu Lai
Quang Ngai

Gary DeMastrie (US Navy)

Dac To

Kontum

Pleiku
Qui Nhon — Mike Chalifoux

Cheo Reo

Tuy Hoa — Leo Chaput

II Corps

Cambodia

Buon Me Thuot
Ninh Hoa

Nha Trang
De Lat

Loc Ninh Gia Hghia Cam Rahn

Phan Rang
Bao Loc

Pat Lupo

Jim Luczynski

Tay Ninh

III Corps

Bien Hoa

Saigon

Phan Thiet — Mike Gorman

Thailand   **Laos**

Cao Lanh Tan An
Long   My Tho   Vung Tau — Bill Buzzell
Xuyen
         Vinh Long Ben Tre
Rach Gia
         Can Tho
              Tra Vinh
IV Corps

Bac Lieu

Ca Mau

South China Sea

© Dennis Pregent 2019

Corps Tactical Zones, 1963–1973

During the Vietnam War, South Vietnam was divided into four tactical zones, also called Military Regions. The four corps tactical zones were identified as I Corps (pronounced "eye" corps), II Corps, III Corps and IV Corps (pronounced as expected: two, three, and four corps).

I Corps was the northernmost Corps in the region closest to North Vietnam and adjacent to the DMZ (Demilitarized Zone). The area's five provinces reached from the DMZ southward slightly beyond Quang Ngai province, with Laos to the west. Its major cities were Hue and Da Nang. Marines fighting near the DMZ often encountered larger, well-trained NVA (North Vietnamese Army) forces.

II Corps, the Central Highlands military region, was the tactical zone encompassing the Highlands and contiguous lowlands. Its military and administrative headquarters were located in Pleiku. The western part of this region was bordered mostly by Cambodia, easterly by the South China Sea. U.S. troops often fought guerrilla forces and insurgents from Cambodia.

III Corps encompassed the densely populated fertile region between Saigon and the Highlands. It extended from the northern Mekong Delta to the southern Central Highlands. U.S. Army headquarters was based at Long Binh, just outside of Saigon. U.S. and Army of the Republic of Vietnam Troops provided security for Saigon. It was bordered exclusively by Cambodia on its western side.

IV Corps was the southernmost of the four tactical zones. Its headquarters were located in Can Tho in the Mekong Delta. The difficult, swampy terrain created geographical isolation from the rest of the country. Viet Cong guerrillas and small units challenged government forces; Cambodia on its west provided major supply arteries for the insurgents.

U.S. Armed Forces—
Organizational Structure

United States Army

The smallest unit is a **Team** of four soldiers, who are part of a 10-person **Squad.**
Three or four squads make up a 40+ person **Platoon** led by a lieutenant.
Four platoons make up a **Company,** and four companies equal a 1000-person **Battalion.**
A few battalions make up a **Brigade,** which is usually 3,000 to 5,000 soldiers.
(Some battalions are organized into Regiments, such as Armored Cavalry, Rangers, Special Forces, etc.)
Three or four brigades make a **Division** of about 10,000 to 15,000 soldiers.
Three-to-five divisions make a **Corps**, with 20,000 to 45,000 soldiers.
Two or more corps constitute a **Field Army.**
Four or five field armies make an **Army Group** of between 400,000 and 1,000,000 soldiers.

United States Marine Corps

USMC has a structure similar to the Army's, albeit on a smaller scale: It begins with a four-man **Fire Team,** and three fire teams make up a 12-person **Squad.** Three+ squads make up a 40+ person **Platoon.** Four platoons make up a 200-person **Company** and four companies equal a 1,000-person **Battalion.** Four battalions make up a **Regiment.** Three regiments make up a **Division** of between 10,000 and 20,000 persons. The Marines also have Air Wings and Marine Expeditionary Force (MEFs).
Note: In Vietnam, most infantry soldiers and Marines served in undermanned squads or platoons and had little knowledge of what was happening on the Company level or higher.

United States Navy

U.S. Navy organization is more complex and provides naval and aviation support to combat operations around the world. The Navy has numerous active fleets in operation.

In the Vietnam era, the Seventh Fleet was one of the largest, supported operations in the Pacific Theater. The fleet was home-based in San Diego, California, with its overseas headquarters at Subic Bay in the Philippines. The fleet consisted of hundreds of ships and aircrafts, ranging from carriers and destroyers to submarines and logistics support vessels. Thousands of sailors were assigned to the Seventh Fleet. The fleet provided amphibious support in situations ranging from air support, mining enemy harbors, and naval gunfire, to close-to-shore (a.k.a., "brown-water") operations that resupplied U.S. infantry units and interdicted enemy movement.

United States Air Force

One of the smallest units in the Air Force is a **Flight Group**, with two or more flights equaling a **Squadron**. Squadrons have several hundred air personnel. Two or more squadrons make up an **Air Group,** and several Groups form a **Wing,** which has a large formation of planes. The Seventh Air Force became the primary USAF command and control organization in Vietnam and was headquartered at Tan Son Nhut Air Base near Saigon. The Seventh Air Force and its thousands of air personnel supported large bombing operations that targeted rail lines, highways, bridges, petroleum sites, and supply lines. They also served an important role providing close air support for ground troops, aeromedical flights, and air-sea rescues.

Military Occupational Specialties

United States Army

The U.S. Army used alphanumeric codes to identify a soldier's Military Occupational Specialty (MOS). The MOS is a job in which the soldier has been schooled and is trained to perform. Enlisted soldiers' MOS codes are **five alphanumeric characters**. The first three characters indicated their *specific job*. The last two digits indicated their *rank*; e.g., 10—private or private first class, 20—corporal/specialist 4th class, 30—specialist 5 or sergeant, and 40—non-commissioned officer, sergeant, staff sergeant etc.

ENLISTED SOLDIERS

Example:

11B10: 11B = infantryman + 10 = infantryman private or private first class
11B20: 11B = infantryman + 20 = infantryman corporal
11B30: 11B = infantryman + 30 = infantryman sergeant
11C30: 11C = indirect fire (mortars) + 30 = indirect fire sergeant
67A20: 67A = aircraft maintenance + 20 = helicopter maintenance corporal
76P30: 76P = stock control + 30 = stock control/accounting sergeant

Mike Chalifoux, Leo Chaput, and **Pat Lupo** were 11B's=infantrymen (in military slang, called 11-Bravos). Leo was also a jump-qualified parachutist.

Ron Racine was an 11C30, a mortar sergeant.

Mike Gorman was a 67A20, helicopter maintenance specialist.

Bill Buzzell was a 76P30, stock control sergeant.

OFFICERS

Commissioned officers' MOS codes were all numeric, e.g., 1542—infantry officer.

A prefix number might be added for special qualification, e.g., 71542—jump-qualified infantry officer.

Jim Luczynski was 71542, a jump-qualified infantry officer.

United States Marine Corps

The Marine Corps MOS system categorizes career fields. All officer and enlisted Marines are assigned a **four-digit code** denoting their primary occupational field and specialty. Marines are schooled and trained to perform the job duties of their MOS. Occupational fields are identified in the **first two digits;** the **next two digits** relate to a specific job.

Occupational Field		Title	Job Code	Known as
Administration	01	Personnel Clerk	11	0111
Intelligence	02	Intelligence Specialist	31	0231
Infantry	03	Rifleman	11	0311
Infantry	03	Machine Gunner	31	0331
Infantry	03	Antitank Assault	51	0351
Logistics	04	Maintenance Spec	11	0411

There are close to 100 occupational fields and hundreds of individual job codes.

Joe Daigneault was designated an 0351, an anti-tank assaultman, when he was wounded.

Russell Roulier was designated an 0331, a machine gunner, when he was killed.

No matter their designations, Marine infantrymen (03's) are often placed in basic rifleman positions.

United States Navy

The Navy calls its enlisted jobs **ratings**. Ratings are very similar to military occupational specialties (MOSs). Ratings are placed in "communities" and grouped with similar jobs under administration, aviation, intelligence, submarine, surface combat ships, etc.

Rate is different from ratings, and equates to military pay grade. Petty officer second class (PO2) is a rate.

Under, for example, Surface Combat Ships, there are ratings (jobs) for boatswain's mate, gunner's mate, and quartermaster.

Boatswain's mates (BMs) direct and supervise the ship's maintenance, to include the ship's external structure, rigging, deck equipment and boats. Their tasks are varied and could include damage control, security, helmsman, etc.

Gary DeMastrie was a boatswain's mate second class (BM2).

1

Introduction:
The Boys of St. Joe's '65

Saint Joseph's High School's class of 1965 dispatched many of its boys to Vietnam. All served honorably, some heroically. In the years between 1965 and 1972, many were wounded, all affected, and one paid the highest price, killed in action defending his platoon.

While over three million Americans served in the Southeast Asia Theater, this book captures the stories of 11 young men and one young woman who came from two small, abutting New England towns in northwest Massachusetts. They all attended Saint Joseph's High School in North Adams and were members of the 1965 class. The high school, a large bunker-type building, was managed by the Order of Saint Joseph sisters from the time it was built in 1928 until its closure in 1974. The class of 1965 contained 80 young women and 66 young men.

I was one of them. We came of age during the mid–1960s, most of us still teenagers during the war's most fearsome years.

After 1977, I never returned to North Adams. I lost contact with my high school classmates. For nearly 50 years, in the back of my mind I wondered who else had served, and what had become of them. I recalled that Joe Daigneault and Russell Roulier had joined the Marine Corps on the "buddy system." I knew Mike Chalifoux and Leo Chaput had been Army infantrymen, and Mike Gorman had been a helicopter gunner with the Army.

I knew at the time that Russell had been killed and Joe had been grievously wounded, that Mike Gorman had been paralyzed, and it didn't take much research to discover that Mike Chalifoux and Leo Chaput were left with likely disabilities. Their sacrifices were extreme. Suddenly, in my retirement, I found myself compelled to find out who else was hurt in Vietnam, or merely hurt by Vietnam.

Initially, I was hesitant about writing anything down. I needed only to glance at my bookshelves to appreciate even a fraction of the officers, enlisted men, and capable news reporters who'd studied the war from all angles for many decades. Some carried weighty bylines by Ivy League alumni, generals, politicians, and war heroes.

I determined I would keep any writing to myself, a way to come to terms with my own experiences. Even now, a half-century after leaving Vietnam, I still have anxiety when talking about my time in-country. Although it doesn't usually stop me from talking with other veterans, I struggle being in large groups of people, especially when confined in a shopping mall, or unable to find a nearby exit.

Classmates' Time In-Country

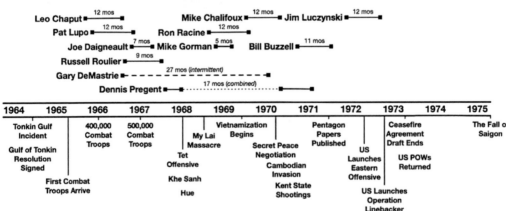

Leo Chaput ■—— 12 mos ——■		Mike Chalifoux ■—— 12 mos ——■ Jim Luczynski ■—— 12 mos ——■

Pat Lupo ■—— 12 mos ——■   Ron Racine ■—— 12 mos ——■

Joe Daigneault ■—7 mos—■ Mike Gorman ■—5 mos—■   Bill Buzzell ■—— 11 mos ——■

Russell Roulier ■—9 mos—■

Gary DeMastrie ■ - - - - 27 mos (intermittent) - - - - ■

Dennis Pregent ■—■····· 17 mos (combined) ·····■

1964	1965	1966	1967	1968	1969	1970	1971	1972	1973	1974	1975
Tonkin Gulf Incident		400,000 Combat Troops	500,000 Combat Troops	My Lai Massacre	Vietnamization Begins			Pentagon Papers Published	Ceasefire Agreement Draft Ends		The Fall of Saigon
Gulf of Tonkin Resolution Signed				Tet Offensive		Secret Peace Negotiation		US Launches Eastern Offensive	US POWs Returned		
	First Combat Troops Arrive			Khe Sanh		Cambodian Invasion					
				Hue		Kent State Shootings		US Launches Operation Linebacker			

(AP Images, copyright Associated Press)

More often lately, I'd noticed myself becoming enraged over perceived slights. My wife suggested I begin a personal blog, writing about my military service. The blog was accessible by my family exclusively, and it was the right place to start. As I recorded my story, my confidence grew. The first classmate I sought out was encouraging. Though he hadn't seen me since high school, he placed his hands on my shoulders and said, "Welcome home, Brother."

Somehow, these words had never been spoken to me, and I was affected. This veteran, 100 percent disabled, struggled fiercely with symptoms of PTSD, and at times he was judged to be a pugnacious and troubled personality. His words and kindness, in spite of the ravaging effects of his disability, were astounding.

As I began to research, I found that classmates were willing to talk openly about their Vietnam experiences, even sharing grainy black-and-white pictures and faded letters, in a way they might not have with just any historian. I received referrals and cooperation from family, friends, and military buddies. Maybe it was our shared history, the years with the sisters at St. Joe's, or maybe it was that after 50 years we all just figured, it's time. (Even St. Joe's itself had evolved: It's now a senior-living community containing more than 75 apartments.)

I soon ran across a website dedicated to a classmate who had been killed in the war. Early one morning in 1967, he had switched defensive positions with another Marine, his best friend, and been killed. The surviving Marine had penned a poignant tribute to the sacrifice. I arranged for him to talk to his friend's still-grieving mother, some 40-plus years after her son's death. This had become less about writing and more about healing.

Then came my 50th class reunion. I secured a copy of our yearbook and the last

St. Joseph's Court apartments, Eagle Street, North Adams, circa 2009. Looks just the same as it did in 1965 (photograph by Keith Bona).

known contact information for our classmates. I strove to find every Vietnam veteran of our class of 1965. I scoured the Internet, mailed letters, hired social media searchers, traveled across states, and over several years contacted many classmates. I identified more than 40 St. Joe's men and women with military service during the Vietnam era, either active duty or with participation in the Reserves or National Guard.

Often a conversation with one person would lead to further contacts. Initially I told everyone I spoke with that I was trying to identify those persons who had served in the military so I might create a testimonial to them. As the contacts accumulated, I began to realize that most people were unaware of others' stories of personal sacrifice, perilous situations, and resulting disabilities.

A number of classmates had passed away. Compiling life stories for each person meant interviewing mothers, children, wives, former wives, relatives, friends, comrades-in-arms, and other classmates. Some stories were uplifting and heartening, others deeply depressing. Of all the conversations over the many months, one mother's words continue to resound: "I sent my beautiful nineteen-year-old boy to Vietnam, and all I got back was a box. And I couldn't even look in it."

People shared their reddish, clay-tinged, sweat-stained letters from long ago; their old black-and-white 35-millimeter war pictures; blunt and terse Western Union grams notifying parents that their son had been killed or wounded; and copies of citations for exemplary or heroic actions.

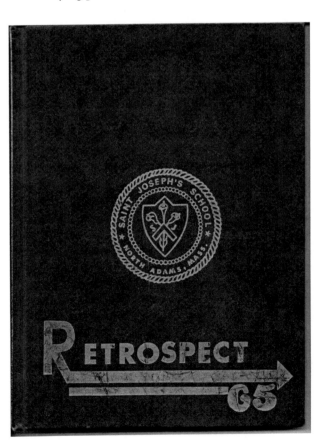

St. Joe's yearbook, 1965. Titled *Retrospect*.

I narrowed the group down to 11 male service members from our class (10 plus myself), and one female civilian who stayed behind and protested the war, as she witnessed our town's losses. Even after 50 years, my mind still pictured younger men and women. I discovered that we were grayer, heavier, slower, and wrinkled. Most everyone had hearing aids, eyeglasses, dentures, and heart or cholesterol considerations.

It was interesting how stories varied when different people recalled the same person or incident. Usually, certain threads in each interview were identical, but the height of the wall might be six feet in one story and fifteen in another.

I found that the experiences and injuries we incurred at a young age became increasingly bothersome at 70 years old. Fortunately, I also found that after 50 years we were able to talk candidly. Some of the interviews were disheartening. There were credible stories about killing innocent civilians that even after fifty years were difficult to talk about. People shared with me their difficult upbringings, some coping with horrible dads, who themselves had suffered undiagnosed issues from World War II.

Some gave testimonies about first-time exposure to drugs and alcohol in Vietnam, and how they brought these debilitating habits home, devastating their families before being able to bring addictions under control. In any case, I advised everyone that this book was not an exposé but would focus on sacrifices made after they enlisted or were drafted and how they led the rest of their lives.

All participants were from blue-collar families, usually with two parents and a stay-at-home mom. Dads were universally World War II veterans, patriotic, proud to have served, returning home with one idea—to get on with their lives.

Their sons joined up out of patriotic fervor, looking for a personal challenge, seeking independence—or, as they grew tired of college, the looming draft induced them to enlist while they could still select a specific job or branch of the service.

From the group of 11 men, an Army soldier and a Marine volunteered (or asked specifically to be sent to Vietnam) for a combat assignment. The others were assigned to units that were headed to combat or already there. All expected during the mid-to-late 1960s that Vietnam would be their destination, and they were right. It was obvious where soldiers were headed when they received orders to Tiger Land (Fort Polk, Louisiana) for jungle training; Marines receiving WestPac (Western Pacific) orders sent to staging battalions at Camp Pendleton, California, were ultimately going to Vietnam. The Navy man was assigned to an assault cargo ship being refitted; his return trip to Asia was almost imminent.

The cadre from St. Joe's distinguished itself, earning a total of four bronze stars, a Navy/Marine Corps medal, five combat infantrymen's badges, three combat action ribbons, more than 10 air medals, four purple hearts, many unit citations and a number of U.S. and Vietnamese commendation medals. We all fought in Vietnam sometime between 1965 and 1972, which means our ages at time of service ranged from 18 to 24, although most were 19 or 20. Those killed and wounded were either 19 or 20 years of age, and none were married except for the author.

We see now that our mostly idyllic Adams and North Adams childhoods intersected rudely with the Vietnam War. Classmates would describe their youth as "Tom Sawyer days," whether hiking the Appalachian Trail, bicycling, hunting, or playing pick-up sports miles from home when mom's only requirement was "be home when the street lights come on."

As you might expect from a small town, the interviews among St. Joe's class of '65 revealed any number of close connections. Joe Daigneault, Russell Roulier, and Gary DeMastrie were high school friends and enjoyed fishing, hiking, and hanging around together. Leo Chaput and Jim Luczynski spent a lot of time together at the YMCA, or hiking and target shooting. Both became accomplished parachutists. Ron Racine and Joe Daigneault played in a high school band together, and each still plays now and then. Mike Chalifoux and Mike Gorman spent years together and, postwar, cofounded the North Adams Vietnam Veterans Club. Bill Buzzell was friends with Mike Gorman in high school, and after the war Bill would accompany Mike and his wife when Mike received treatment for his paralysis. Ron Racine was in Cub Scouts with Russell Roulier.

Joe Daigneault and I worked at the Adams Supermarket. Carol Boucher's father, a

North Adams' Main Street, with Woolworth's, J.C. Penney's, two banks, and the beloved Mohawk Theater (North Adams Historical Society, Inc.).

President McKinley overlooks Park Street in Adams, anchored by the post office on one end and Notre Dame church on the other (Spylios Nikitas Collection—Adams Historical Society).

barber, cut the hair of some the participants. There were many other small town connections: Jean Daigneault, Joe's mom, worked with my mother at the local hospital and called her when Joe was wounded. My brother, Richard, served as an altar boy at the Requiem Mass for Russell Roulier's military funeral. Pat's mom worked at the Wall Streeter Shoe Company where my father-in-law worked.

Postwar, we and our families coped with the ongoing effects. Most went on to lead productive lives against a backdrop of sacrifice, sadness, courage, perseverance, and adjustment—all resulting from their service in Vietnam. I would like to say that all the endings are happy, but that would be untrue.

At a late stage in writing, I heard from a fellow Marine veteran who suggested that including a classmate who'd protested the war would provide good balance. I was nonplussed at first. After all the contacts, I had not come across anyone from our class who had been a war protester. I decided to contact Carol Boucher, who lives in North Adams, and is a great class historian, to see if she knew someone. She responded to my email with, "LOL … don't know how you would feel about this, BUT I was a protester, not against you, or the military, but the war itself." After many phone conversations, I added Carol's interesting story.

Everything is true to the best recollection of the participants. Some memories, of course, have faded over a half-century, and some details may have been repressed, pro-

Flapper Days, the sophomore year musical. Dennis is on the far left, Jim seated as grandpa, and Russ standing third from the right (St. Joseph's 1965 yearbook).

tecting the participants from painful truths. This is crucial: For the most part, during military operations they didn't know where they were on any given day, or where they'd be tomorrow. Even the stated goal of defeating Communism seemed murky in a triple-canopy jungle. They knew the war was opposed by many of their peers, which is why I've included the experiences of a classmate who protested the war. Yet they slogged on, won most battles, and came home to an unappreciative nation.

The stories herein are captivating, heartening, and occasionally discouraging, but necessary. Our war did not end when we left the battlefield. It continues today.

2

When Memory Invades

Only minutes ago we landed at a Marine Corps fire base. It was under attack, which meant so were we. Our critical mission was to pick up some seriously wounded and dead Marines and get out of there. The base radio operator announced one emergency medevac, a few priorities, and at least two "permanent routines." The operator also instructed our pilot to keep both his machine gunners "on their guns" since there were "gooks in the wires" which translates to: the enemy is about to penetrate the base perimeter.

I didn't know what to expect. It was my first nighttime medevac. When we received the call for medical assistance, we quickly left our staging area and flew to the fire base. Upon approach the pilot hovered, sized up the situation and descended, rapidly, towards the steel planking of the landing zone. He kept the helicopter's lights off until just before touching down, so as not to attract enemy fire. Adding to the confusion: our own engine noise, whirling rotor blades, and swirling dust.

We had strolled, casually, through the fuselage of a dark green CH-46 Sea Knight. That's all it took.

At the National Museum of the Marine Corps in Quantico, Virginia, the entryway to the Vietnam exhibit requires you to walk up the ramp and through the shortened fuselage of a tandem-rotor transport helicopter, just like the one I served on fifty years ago. I instinctively ducked my head to avoid hitting the helicopter's low ceiling. As I walked up the ramp and entered the rigid aluminum structure, I began to hear voice transmissions from the helicopter's overhead. My wife paused as she saw my face. It took a few seconds to realize the words were recordings and call signs of actual missions.

Instantly I felt transported to September 1970, when I was an aerial gunner with a HMM (Helicopter Marine Medium) Squadron 263. The overhead voices seemed to intensify. My heart beat wildly. I was there again.

We landed. The cool night air evaporated and was replaced by a heavy mugginess. The comfortable darkness we had at 2500 feet was replaced by a light-show of explosions and rifle fire. We could see crisscrossing lines of red and green tracers as Marines exchanged fire with the enemy. I knew the Viet Cong used green tracers and Americans used red. By the volume of green tracers, the base was under a concentrated attack.

As if by confirmation, I began seeing faint, ghostlike figures crawling in the barbed wire that encircled the fire base. I "charged" (loaded) my .50-caliber machine gun. The other gunner and I stood ready for action. Then we loaded our M-16 rifles as a preventive measure in case the enemy attempted to surge up our vulnerable ramp area, which could not be covered by machine guns.

As we stood by our guns, Marine infantrymen and corpsmen (medics) began loading casualties on the helicopter. The critically wounded Marine was brought on first, then the less wounded Marines either limped on or were helped aboard. Finally, the two dead, wrapped in ponchos, our "permanent routines," were placed on the ramp in the rear of the helicopter. Once everyone was onboard, our pilot raised the ramp and we departed for the nearest medical facility. I felt a sense of relief and security as we gained elevation, receding from the gunfire and explosions. The wind from the open windows also helped to cool the inside of the helicopter, and everyone's anxiety seemed to lessen.

A corpsman was checking the vital signs of the Marine in critical condition. He was unconscious, on a stretcher, and had been brought to the front near the gunner areas while the other Marines had been helped into the web seating on either side of the aisle.

Once we'd reached a certain height where we no longer needed to man our guns, the corpsman, via hand signals, indicated that I should hold the unconscious Marine's head motionless while he examined the head wound. The task was not difficult since the Marine, lying on a damp, bloody stretcher, was almost lifeless. As I held his fractured head the corpsman quickly checked him over.

He determined that the Marine needed help breathing and signaled that I should maintain my position. Then he cut a slit in the young man's throat and inserted some sort of breathing tube. The emergency tracheotomy took just seconds, and the young Marine did

My position at the .50-caliber machine gun, just behind the pilot.

not react. I came to realize that my hands were sticky with his blood, and the skull I had been holding was in pieces. How had he received such a catastrophic wound?

I'd volunteered for an aerial gunner position with Marine Air Group 16 on my second tour, about five months after returning in-country. Living at 1st Marine Wing Headquarters barracks, I'd felt very far from the war and uninvolved while some of my buddies, who I'd come overseas with, were already in the action. A number had been wounded. I knew I did not want to be a grunt (infantryman) and doubted my commanding officer would ever release me for that type of position anyway. I did understand some Marine squadrons were looking for aerial gunners and thought this would put me closer to the action and allow me to earn Aircrew Wings and Air Medals. So I volunteered.

I was somewhat concerned about passing an eye exam, but a corpsman was very "helpful" and, as long as I could see the eye chart (if not the letters), I passed the test. I thought there must be a serious need for gunners. The only other prerequisite was a familiarization flight over the South China Sea, and firing our .50-caliber machine guns at a yellow dye marker.

Once the procedure had been completed, the corpsman remained with the critically wounded Marine, and I checked on the others, who seemed to have superficial wounds. I had never seen a dead Marine so I wandered to the rear of the ship to look at the two bodies in the ramp area. One had a poncho over his head that covered his torso to his waist. The other Marine's poncho had been blown aside by air turbulence allowing me to see his face. I drew closer to him and found myself staring

Preparing to board with the .50 caliber. I also carried an M-16 rifle and a .38-caliber pistol on missions.

into a young Hispanic man's face. He looked peaceful, with his eyes wide open and a small bullet hole in the center of his forehead.

I have often wondered what his name was, where was he from, what his family was like, was he an only child, married, a father? I wondered how long he'd survived in Vietnam.

And I thought it strange being accorded the privilege of knowing of his death days before his loved ones would. They may continue receiving letters from a young man who would never write again.

After viewing him for just seconds, I tried to re-wrap his body with the poncho but in the dark, with dim lights and air turbulence, it was impossible. My efforts were further thwarted by not wanting to touch his body. I'm not sure if I didn't want to disturb his peacefulness or if I was too scared to touch someone who had just died. After a minute or two, I gave up and returned to my gun position.

Shortly afterwards we landed at the Naval Support Activity station hospital (NSA) in Da Nang. Corpsmen and nurses were waiting and helped us off-load the wounded. Two corpsmen grabbed the stretcher with the emergency case and ran it towards the hospital. The remaining wounded were helped as necessary, and finally it came to the dead Marines.

The day after qualifying as a gunner, I moved from 1st Marine Wing Headquarters to the MAG-16 (Marine Air Group) on Marble Mountain. The change in locations was startling. I'd been at Headquarters for about five months and enjoyed amenities not often found elsewhere. Work hours there had been reasonable, with time off for athletic activities like running or handball. The mess hall had provided hot chow three times a day. Our sleeping quarters had been in old, comfortable, concrete buildings long ago erected by the French. We'd had individual racks (beds) with mattresses and mosquito nets. We'd also had commodes with an overhead roof-type structure and inside showers, albeit with a dirt floor. And our work area had been air conditioned, plus we had a Jeep that I could use for work projects.

The MAG-16 offered quite a difference in accommodations. My new assignment as an aerial gunner required long, tiring work hours, little to no free time, poor food (C rations), and vermin-dominated nights. I still remember quite vividly many instances of being too tired to eat or care about my sleeping arrangements, letting the roaches and rats move freely across my body. One time a roach crawled into my mouth and I remember to this day the sensation of waking up just enough to spit him out.

I grabbed the Hispanic Marine's legs while a corpsman lifted his upper body. We placed him on a medical trolley and they whisked it away. Another corpsman indicated he wanted my help with the second Marine. This Marine's upper body was at my end and although covered by a poncho, there seemed to be no outline where his head was supposed to be. I was uncertain how to handle this, and hand-signaled the corpsmen that I was not going to lift him. Another corpsman quickly came to my end of the body, took my place and tried to lift the Marine on the trolley. As he lifted him the Marine's shoulders came together oddly, confirming my suspicion that he was headless. It required a lot of maneuvering to get him on the medical trolley.

I still wonder today what type of weapon would have carved his head and upper chest from his body. I have thought that a rocket propelled grenade (RPG) probably did it but really don't know. I also wondered, when the body arrived home, if his family ever had a chance to view it.

We were on the ground only for a few minutes before returning to our "waiting" area, preparing for the next medical evacuation. The rest of the night passed quietly, with no more calls, and we returned to the helicopter facility at Marble Mountain early the next morning.

3

A Boy's Life in the Berkshires

I was raised to be a Marine. My parents didn't intentionally do this, but as I think about my upbringing, it certainly points in that direction. From hiking and camping with the Boy Scouts to target-shooting tin cans with Dad, I spent a lot of my youth outdoors. Coupled with a serious vein of patriotism and a desire to challenge myself, for me, ultimately the Marines were the only answer.

Few people have heard of the towns of Adams and North Adams located in the northern Berkshires. They sit adjacent to each other in northwestern Massachusetts, three hours by car from Boston and minutes away from the New York and Vermont state lines. This is where I grew up, and departed from Adams at 17 to join the Marine Corps.

Adams, a town of 8500 people at last census, and North Adams, with 13,000, are nestled on either side of Mount Greylock, which at 3491 feet above sea level boasts the highest point in Massachusetts. The area is heavily wooded and known for its abundant fall foliage. People come from miles around to traverse the area and discuss the woodland color. The mountainous Mohawk Trail, an official "Scenic Byway," provides memorable views year-round as it winds its way across the mountaintops and descends in to North Adams. Halfway down the mountain, at the hairpin turn, the view is particularly majestic, especially in fall and midwinter when huge icicles clothe the escarpment.

For most of the twentieth century, the Berkshires were home to textile, shoe, and electronic component mills, many of which closed in the 1970s and 80s, resulting in the loss of thousands of jobs. The area continues to remain picturesque, yet isolated and "job-challenged."

Living in this area during the 1950s and 60s, residents were socially isolated from the rest of Massachusetts. Mostly white Catholics or Protestants, we had limited exposure to minorities.

From my birth until I turned eight years old, my family rented a house in North Adams in a housing development on the outskirts of town. The small community was comprised of two- and three-bedroom houses, intended for use by returning World War II veterans. Our house was on Meade Avenue, and my earliest memories revolve around this close-knit neighborhood, riding bikes, attending Greylock grammar school, serving as an altar boy at Holy Family Church, and going on weekend visits to my mom's family.

My maternal grandmother, Agnes Dooley, was of Irish descent, and lived most of her life in North Adams. She was a stay-at-home mom while her husband, Claude Trottier,

My grandfather's barber shop in North Adams was on the same side of the street as Sears and the Paramount Theater (North Adams Historical Society, Inc.).

my maternal grandfather of French extraction, worked his whole life in downtown North Adams as a barber.

My mother, Alice, was the youngest and only girl in a family of six children. She attended local Drury high school and graduated from Saint Luke's nursing program in 1947. My father, Dennis, for whom I am named, was born in Montreal, Canada, served in the United States Army Air Corps, and was discharged in 1946. They dated during high school and were married on June 1, 1946, in Montreal. There is some mystery surrounding their marriage since there was no wedding party; few, if any, wedding pictures; and no publication of the marriage banns. As the story goes, there was a rule at Mom's nursing school prohibiting students from marrying before graduation.

Mom's five brothers lived nearby and we would often visit them on Sundays or holidays. I fondly remember the summer picnics at Grandmother's house playing with my cousins. The adults would gather around the picnic table in the backyard and share stories about World War II to which I listened, spellbound. Four of my uncles had served, as well as my dad. The day would end with the adults playing poker while their mesmerizing war stories rolled around in my young mind.

My father's parents, Thomas and Aurora, both French Canadians, worked in the shoe industry. They moved about Massachusetts and Vermont always seeking better-paying jobs. Eventually, although not permanently, they moved to North Adams and that's where Dad met Mom.

Dad worked as a design engineer at General Electric, in Pittsfield, Massachusetts, for 43 years. Mom worked part time at the Plunkett Memorial Hospital in Adams while we were growing up. Mom spent considerable effort ensuring we ate meals together,

Plunkett Memorial Hospital, Adams, Mass.

66090

My mother and Joe Daigneault's mother both worked at Plunkett Memorial Hospital in Adams (Tichnor Bros., Inc., Boston Public Library).

monitoring our school efforts ("you are capable of As and Bs"), and managing us as we completed her projects, both inside and outside the house.

Every weekday night, Dad arrived home from GE at 5:15 p.m., and supper was at 5:30. We usually ate spaghetti, Salisbury steak, stew, or some variation of a meat-and-potatoes meal. Suppers weren't elegant, but filling. Mom and Dad sat at the ends of the table with two boys on each side. Conversations varied from our daily transgressions to items Mom had worked on—but, most often, to Dad's work. He was a member of GE's Ordnance Division, so there was always a lot of discussion on ballistic missiles, helicopters, and guidance systems. Dad enjoyed and was very proud of his work. More often than not, Mom would ask us what we "wanted to be" when we grew up and emphasized the need to obtain a "sheepskin" (college degree).

Dad was a tinkerer and kept busy with house remodeling such as knocking down walls that Mom decided we no longer needed, replacing windows, building rock walls, and adding a front porch to the house. While a teenager I was drafted as his laborer.

Dad often spent summers building stone walls around the property. My brothers and I shoveled sand and mortar into the rusty, rickety cement mixer, then poured it into the wheelbarrow and hauled it across the property to Dad. Next, from the mountain of stones dumped in our driveway, we manhandled as many as possible and lugged them over. And so went the summer, night after night. I learned a lot about perseverance and endurance. Believe it or not, these are fond memories.

Many of my best times were spent with my cousin Bobby. Often on Friday nights I would sleep at his house. We would play toy soldiers, go fishing with his dad, and swim at a nearby lake called the Fish Pond. Bobby's mother, Irmalee, was especially kind towards me. One day while playing hide-and-seek, I fell on some glass and gashed open my right leg. My aunt carried me from the Fish Pond to her house, about a mile distant.

In 1955, we moved eight miles over to Adams, and my parents bought their first house, located on the outskirts of town. The town at the time had a population of 12,000, although shortly after our arrival the last textile mill closed, seriously affecting the town's employment and census.

Adams was a Norman Rockwell–type of town with a short Main Street that had every type of store and service a family needed: Adams Supermarket, Adams Diner, Adams Theater, Woolworth, town hall, police department, McKinley Square Apothecary, and—anchoring one end of Main Street—Notre Dame Church, School, Rectory, and Convent.

My parents enrolled us in the Notre Dame Grammar School, operated by the Sisters of Holy Cross. The complex of church, school, rectory, and convent formed another community within the small town of Adams. Both provided a sense of security and belonging for me.

As part of the congregation, I became a member of Notre Dame's altar boys and of Boy Scout Troop #38, together a sizable commitment. There was choir practice, training before I could serve Mass, and then mandatory attendance at the ten o'clock Mass on Sundays. Additionally, we served at weddings and funerals. We were also required to attend Benediction service every night for the month of May. There were more than forty

The four Pregent brothers (Dennis, center rear), looking quite pious in their cassocks and surplices at Notre Dame in Adams.

altar boys, and we were supervised by Sister Saint Claire, who occupied the first pew at church scanning for any unnecessary movement, sloppiness, jocularity, or inattention. Woe to the disobedient or rambunctious.

For exemplary service, we were permitted to go on the altar boy picnic, which was held at Look Park in Northampton. It was a great time with minimal adult supervision. We swam, jumped on and off the train, roamed about the park, and burned up energy on the paddle boats.

As Boy Scouts, we met every Thursday night in the school basement. It was cool on the lower level and the meeting was informal, although we did need to line up for roll call. In front of the room was a green felt-covered table displaying the various knots we needed to memorize, such as the clove hitch, bowline, square knot, etc. We usually wore our uniforms for special ceremonies and parades. Three or four adults supervised us and helped us qualify for different merit badges such as animal science, backpacking, camping, etc. Our troop was led by World War II veterans, some of whom were former drill instructors. They taught us close-order drills. Every meeting the instructors would devote some time to calling cadence and marching us around the school playground. The weekly practice culminated with our troop marching in the annual Memorial Day Parade. Our synchronicity was so precise that area communities would request our troop for their parades.

My most vivid memory of Scouts is weekend campouts at the foot of Mount Greylock and spending a week in the summer camping at Windsor Jambs, a local campground with a waterfall, swimming hole, and daily "dips" in the unbelievably icy river. Late one night, at the foot of Mount Greylock, our scoutmaster was signaling with his flashlight, and a passing plane thought his flashing light represented an SOS. Before long there were police vehicles at our camp looking to help with our emergency. It was a very exciting evening for a 12-year-old.

My three brothers and I would walk a mile across town to grammar school. The trek gave us a sense of independence. We were able to take shortcuts through railroad yards, throw rocks at pigeons, and buy candy from Blind Bill. We found Bill fascinating and scary. He was obese, bald-headed, had a round, pudgy face, and wore very thick dark glasses. We didn't think he ever changed his soiled, white-collared shirt and dark-colored pants, which were held up by thick black suspenders. Bill's store had glass cases filled with many varieties of candy. We had heard you could steal candy from him because of his poor eyesight, but I never thought so. He perched on a chair really close to the candy cases, and I just knew he saw my every move. After Bill's, our next stop was an old abandoned blacksmith shop near school. The two-story building already had many broken panes on the upper level, and that seemed to encourage us to join the ranks of other mischievous marksmen.

One day some boys caught me breaking windows and asked me my name and where I went to school. I gave them a fictitious Polish name and said I went to Saint Stanislaus across town. About an hour later, they were surprised to see me (and I them) at the French school in Sister Saint Luke's class. They reported me. Sister Luke invoked her punishment of rapping my knuckles with her ruler, had me clean all the classroom's blackboards, and then had Sister Superior call my parents. All in all, it was not a great day for me.

As I write about my early life, the good memories of growing up in Adams seem countless: riding bikes all over town with my friends Inky, Kenny, and Bobby; camping with Troop #38; riding to Russell Field to play a "pick up" baseball game; fishing with

Kenny at Cheshire Lake, hunting with my grandfather in the "Hopper" woods in Williamstown; going to the annual altar boy picnics at Look Park in Northampton; and hiking up our street to fish, hunt, and skinny dip in the Tophet Brook.

My father and grandfather were hunting and fishing enthusiasts, so these became our sports. They took my brothers and me fishing in the spring and hunting in the fall. They were accomplished outdoorsmen and helped us identify trees, animals, and bird calls as well as the tracks associated with game animals.

Fishing season always opened on the fifteenth of April, and the night before we would check our rods, reels, and other equipment to ensure we were ready for Opening Day. We fished for trout at the Green River in Williamstown or went to Cheshire Lake to fish for blue gill, perch, or pickerel. I especially remember wading in and out of trout streams using my homemade flies or an earthworm to try and fool local trout. Often our grandfather would accompany us, offering rewards for the largest or most fish caught.

As I got older, my parents would allow me to bike to Cheshire Lake with Kenny, rent a boat, and camp and fish on one of the lake's islands. We usually stayed there for a couple of days. At the time, I never thought how nice it was to be so independent, to be gone several days from home without any supervision or parental contact. Kenny and I would fish all day long and at night build a campfire and eat bologna sandwiches and marshmallows.

Family vacations were often at fishing sites like Spofford Lake, New Hampshire, and Perth, Ontario. The trips to Perth were strictly fishing vacations. Perth was a huge lake, we couldn't see the other side, and it harbored enormous fish: pike, walleye, perch, and bass. The accommodations were primitive: outdoor restrooms, no heat or air conditioning, no running water, and a muddy beach in front of our cabin unsuitable for swimming. When our grandparents came with us, Memère would cook the evening meal with the fish we had caught during the day. The rock bass or walleye suppers were delicious. Occasionally we did some local sightseeing, but fishing and more fishing were paramount. We would leave our dock early in the morning, return around 11:00 a.m., have a lunch usually comprised of peanut butter sandwiches and potato chips, take a nap, and return to fishing from the late afternoon till dark.

I can still remember how exciting it was to fish in Ontario. The cabin had several bedrooms and a main room with a kitchen. My parents and grandparents slept in the bedrooms and the four boys could choose sleeping spots on the floor. We boys hauled water for cooking, drank from a nearby pump, and used the outhouse about fifty feet from the cabin. We were cautioned about bears and told to take a flashlight with us at night. After the warning, I determined not to make any after-dark outhouse trips.

On one of our Perth trips when I was 10 years old, Dad and Mom allowed me to take out one of the rowboats, with a five-horsepower motor, with my brothers as passengers. I felt grown up and very trustworthy to be given this much responsibility, on such a gigantic lake.

While fishing was a nice pastime, nothing could beat hunting. I began accompanying Dad on his forays when I was eight years old, and at ten was given the honor of carrying his shotgun. This didn't occur until Dad was satisfied that I'd learned and exhibited the safety lessons he had taught me. My brothers and I hunted with both Dad and his father, often pursuing partridge and pheasants in the "Hopper." Occasionally we would hunt with our Uncle Vin, and he knew where there were stocked pheasants. At age 15, each of us participated in the hunter safety program and received a license. I will never forget

Proud Pregent boys (Dennis, third from left) showing off tonight's dinner, probably Green River trout from Williamstown.

purchasing my first shotgun, a Winchester Model 12 Pump, and getting a Remington .22-caliber rifle for Christmas from Uncle Vin.

While I hunted mostly with my father, grandfather, and brothers, I also spent many hours in the woods by myself and sometimes with my friend Kenny. I was fortunate that where we lived in Adams was about a quarter mile from open fields and woods. I would leave home in the morning and wander for miles looking for rabbits, squirrels, or ground-hogs and get back home in time for lunch or supper. When I hunted with Kenny, I would bike across town with my .22 rifle and meet him at his house and then hike to our hunting areas. Kenny lived about one half mile from where we could begin hunting.

I can remember preparing to deer hunt with Dad. The night before the season began, in early December, we would clean our weapons at the kitchen table, sharpen our knives, check our bullets, and lay out any clothes, boots, and bandoliers of ammo we would need for the hunt. The next day we would eat a hearty meal and leave the house at 5:00 a.m. We wanted to be in our favorite position before the deer started moving. Seldom did we bag a deer, although the memories of early morning dawns, big breakfasts, falling snow, tracking deer, the quietness of the woods, and sometimes the sound of shots being fired are indelible.

Hunting and fishing were great pastimes in our house but a priority was placed on chores which ranged from mowing our large lawn to mixing cement and assisting Dad in remodeling our old house. The yard was large where we lived on East Street, so (being the oldest) I had the front-tiered banks to mow, and my brothers had the side lawn and the back yard. Aside from mowing, we had to help Mom maintain her large flower and rock garden by hoeing, weeding, and raking. I was also Mom's partner on back-road excursions to collect unusually shaped rocks for her garden. We took them from farmers' stone fences. At the time, I never thought to ask Mom what she thought about filching these stones.

A big project we completed was lowering the cellar floor by two feet. Our house was very old and had a rock foundation and uncomfortably low cellar ceilings. It was Mom's idea to lower the floor so we could have room for a ping-pong table. The project required us to dig down two feet, move the loosened dirt by wheelbarrow across the room to the

Dad overseeing his work crew: A brief respite in the hard labor, before we started mixing cement (Dennis, second from left).

cellar window, empty the wheelbarrow under the window and then shovel the dirt outside. It was difficult work because the window was at least six feet over our heads. Then we needed to go outside, re-shovel the same dirt into the wheelbarrow and tote it away.

We also helped Dad install an in-ground pool. While he and friends erected a metal structure to hold the pool's liner, my brothers and I were tasked with making 720 large, brick patio blocks to go around the pool. The blocks were one foot by 18 inches and made of different colors. Dad made the forms for the blocks and we mixed cement, colored the concrete, and filled in the forms. When the blocks were dry, we removed them and started all over again. Dad taught us the right combination of cement, sand, and water to make the best patio blocks.

We also assisted in many inside projects such as stripping old wallpaper, tearing down walls, removing debris, and laying hardwood floors. We were responsible for shoveling the driveway in winter, a considerable chore. We had a shared driveway with some old crotchety neighbors and were restricted from throwing snow on their side. After a few snowstorms, the snow was piled six feet high on our side and we began surreptitiously shoveling snow onto the neighbors' lawn. It didn't take long for their ever-vigilant eyes to spot the travesty and start yelling at us, at which point we'd stop and begin throwing snow on our side. Once our driveway was shoveled, I would walk around the neighborhood shoveling other walkways and driveways for money. It was fun, and I often earned two or three dollars for a walkway and five to seven dollars for a driveway. After large snowstorms, I would be called into work at the local hospital to shovel their many outside walkways. When the shoveling was completed, my boss would have me use an electric buffer to strip, wax, and shine hospital floors.

In summer I worked for Mr. Millette, our across-the-street neighbor, who maintained a number of lawns in our area for the elderly. He was a small, quiet, slightly bent-over man with white hair who walked with a little shuffle. As he aged, I began to help with trimming and mowing yards. I used Mr. Millette's manual push mower, which he personally sharpened. Mr. Millette was exacting in his expectations, requiring me to cut lawns in precise straight or diagonal lines. I enjoyed the work and he paid me a dollar an hour.

After I graduated from Notre Dame grammar school in June of 1961, our high school choices were the local Adams public high school or the parochial high school located in North Adams. A certain portion of the eighth-grade graduating class opted to remain in town and attend the local public school, but the rest of us were headed for St. Joseph's.

I don't remember having any discussion with my parents on where I would attend school. I think it was presumed we all would continue to attend a parochial school. At that time, the cost of attending a Catholic school was subsidized by parishes and was a minimal burden to my parents. Therefore, I went to Saint Joseph's High School and was bused to school for my freshman and sophomore years until I could obtain my driver's license. I was a little anxious about what the environment would be like attending high school. The school, located on Eagle Street in North Adams, was an imposing three-and-a-half story structure occupying most of a city block. I remember on my first day of school thinking how huge the building was, and being anxious about not knowing many people. While I had nuns as teachers in grammar school, the high school nuns seemed bigger and stricter. Almost all of my classes were taught by the Sisters of Saint Joseph, who were accomplished in their different fields of study. I still recall all of their names:

A view of Main Street in North Adams with the iconic Rice's Drug Store on the corner of Eagle and Main (North Adams Historical Society, Inc.).

Sr. Teresa Edward (English), Sr. Catherine Thomas (Sciences), Sr. Maura James (mathematics), Sr. Eleanor Maria (French) etc.

After a while, I made a few friends and quickly acclimated to high school. It helped that I knew the kids from Adams who transferred, and also began hanging around with my cousin Bobby who was quiet and very bright and Mike who was impish but a lot of fun. I don't think any of our group would have been considered studious or scholarly (probably more in the B-student category), and none of us would have been considered great athletes. Most of the time we enjoyed fooling around and getting into mischief.

During freshman year, I spent little time with my school friends since I was commuting about six miles to school and did not yet have a license. During my sophomore year, I earned my driver's license, and I began working at a supermarket near school. When I wasn't working, I was hunting or fishing and did very little studying.

At 16, I bought a 1952 two-door Chevy coupe for $25 and gave it to my dad for a Father's Day present. The Chevy ran all right, but its rear fenders and the floor were rusted out. Dad decided to give the car to me and help repair it. The body was in tough shape. With much angle iron, aluminum, and epoxy, we fixed the floor and the fenders. Mom helped by making and installing leopard-print seat covers—and then she and I painted the car in our neighbor's garage with paint brushes. It was scarlet, aptly named the "Red Hornet."

The car allowed me to drive to school and significantly extended my sphere of independence. Once I was reported to have been speeding on the main road between North Adams and Adams. After being grounded by my parents, I was escorted by Uncle Vin to the North Adams police chief, a friend of his, for a very serious conversation about obeying traffic laws.

Through the years, I have thought about my reasons for joining the Marines. As a child, I often read books about pioneers such as Davy Crockett, Daniel Boone, and Kit Carson as well as stories about Audie Murphy, a famous World War II Medal of Honor recipient. I would often daydream about being the hero who saves family, friends, and fellow soldiers from a treacherous enemy. Family picnic discussions in the early 1950s were also an influence, as conversations often revolved around my five uncles and their World War II experiences. Then there was my immediate family—grandfather, father, and brothers—who all hunted, were familiar with weapons, and enjoyed using them.

As it would occur, during my senior year my desire for independence clashed heavily with my parents' expectations. At one point, my mother decided the military would "straighten" me out and, knowing I preferred the Marines, brought me to the recruiter in Pittsfield. After testing, I started to waver on my commitment, and the recruiter, noticing my hesitancy, asked if I was sure I wanted to join.

My mother said, "He's sure."

I headed to Marine Boot Camp on February 1, 1965.

4

Boot Camp, Parris Island

The author, as a senior at St. Joe's; and at Parris Island, 1965.
Navy/Marine Corps Medal, Air Medals

I had left home with a nice "send off" from my girlfriend, Carol, and my parents. Then I joined a group of five local recruits, all strangers to me, bused to the Connecticut airport for a flight that arrived after midnight in Charleston, South Carolina, followed by another 90-minute bus ride before entering Marine Corps territory: Recruit Depot Parris Island.

At times during the long day, I'd felt anxious and unsure of what to expect. I was 17 years old, and my life experiences to date revolved around one small town in western Massachusetts. I had traveled several times outside of Massachusetts with my parents but never flown in a plane. I sat alone for most of the journey, silently observing the other recruits. Everyone was trying to deal with the uneasiness in various ways: Some were quiet like me, while others seemed boisterous, joking and laughing. We could not possibly realize what was ahead of us.

"Now, now, now!" As the drill instructor screamed his greeting, we hurriedly and clumsily scrambled off the bus. I was scared, and frantically thought, "what have I done, what is going to happen to me?"

"Now, Now, Now! Get off my bus, you maggots. Hurry, Hurry, Hurry. Get out and line up! NowNowNow."

We lined up very tightly as the receiving drill instructor began marching us to a building, all the while uttering incomprehensible guttural sounds. There we entered a classroom and were told to sit at attention at one-piece school desks, hands on our knees, facing forward, silent for what seemed like hours. The drill instructor continued to scream at us and hovered nearby just waiting to catch a fidgeter. It didn't take long before a nervous recruit, sitting right beside me, started talking. All of a sudden he hit the floor. I just knew the DI had knocked him down, so I checked to make sure I wasn't breathing too loudly.

Shortly afterwards the drill instructor packed 70 of us into a tight column, "forming up" so close that each touched the young man in front of him. Once assembled, we were marched in the dark, up and down ditches. We were so disorganized and disoriented that many fell over each other, slipping and sliding in the mud. Finally, we arrived at a two-story white wooden building and were driven like cattle into the lower level. We were given bunks and told to sleep.

It was 2:30 a.m., and I lay fully clothed atop a narrow metal bed with a thin mattress and no blanket, feeling lonely and homesick.

Two hours later, every recruit in the barracks was roused from a deep, insufficient sleep. So began our indoctrination to a culture that would hold us captive for 12 weeks—controlling every move, requiring all activities to be performed in extreme haste, with screamed directives and responses.

We marched to a warehouse and were issued Marine Corps clothing, including skivvies, t-shirts, socks, boots, and work uniforms. This, too, was performed rapid-fire, a Marine "eyeballing" us for the right size and throwing each piece across the counter to be placed in our seabags. I can remember changing into our work uniforms (known as "utilities") and placing our civilian clothes in boxes to be mailed home.

"Health and comfort" items such as soap powder, a bucket, shaving items, and boot polish were distributed. Orientation meant skin-tight haircuts that took about twenty-five seconds per head. It was amazing to see the pile of hair that accumulated on the barber's floor. Next were physical exams, audio tests, vision screening, and inoculations.

For some inoculations, we were required to face a wall and drop our skivvies to the floor while a Navy corpsman raced down the line of bodies throwing a needle into each man's buttocks (much like darts) and then returned to the head of the line to plunge the serum. We also received inoculations by running a gauntlet of corpsmen, who simultaneously grabbed our left and right arms and used compressed air to inject a shot in each arm. We were cautioned not to move during the process because the air pressure could cut your arm. Several failed to follow instructions and were rewarded with one-inch cuts that bled profusely.

Once orientation was completed, we marched to an old wooden structure and were herded to the second level. This would be our home for the next 12 weeks. We met our assigned drill instructors, all three of them. Sergeant Lankford, a solid and dangerous-looking senior instructor (identified by his wide black belt), had a face like a bull dog. He wore a slight scowl and looked as if he might kill you for trifling with him.

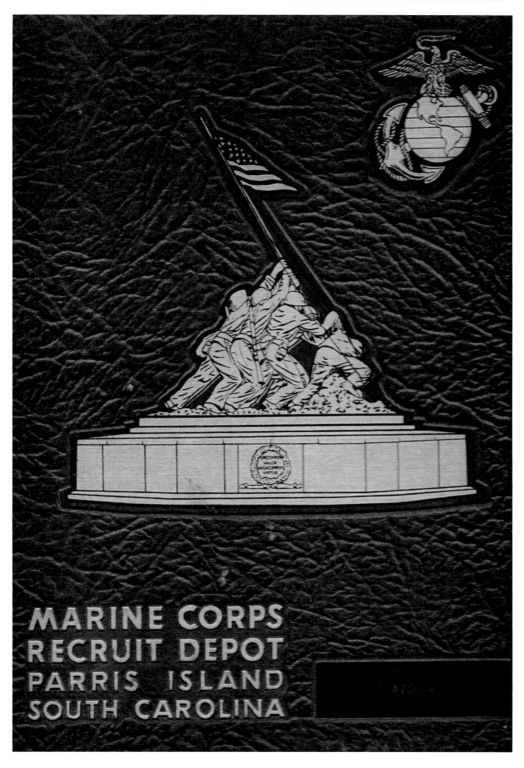

Platoon 211 boot camp yearbook: only 12 weeks, but transformative enough to fill a whole book.

Our junior D.I., Sergeant Clarke, was a tall, menacing instructor who seemed psychotic, irrational. Clarke had an evil aura about him and was always on alert for recruit transgressions. He would react forcefully to any perceived blunders. I was extremely fearful of incurring his wrath.

Our other junior D.I., Sergeant Johnson, was a short, wiry NCO who stood ramrod straight and was meticulous about his uniform. Initially, I thought he might be considerate of our "situation" and be the most humane, but this perception evaporated when I saw him descend in lightning fashion on another recruit. One of his signature moves was a quick jab to the solar plexus that took your breath away. In time, I drew his attention for whispering and received a mouthful of shaving cream; another time he bounced a tent pole off my forehead creating a good-sized bump. For whatever reason, I think he focused on me specifically. Looking back now, it's notable that not one of the drill instructors was a combat veteran; they wore only the good conduct and national defense ribbons on their uniforms. Within the next 12 to 24 months, most of us would have served in Vietnam and some of us would be dead.

It was a time of great uncertainty, knowing neither what might incense a drill instructor, nor what to expect of our daily schedule. I came to realize that being kept in the dark was part of the indoctrination: All commands were to be obeyed instantly and without question; all responses were to be shouted. It was very effective in conditioning us to react instantly to unforeseen situations. We had arrived a group of bewildered teenagers, accustomed to an environment of self-gratification, with lackadaisical responses, and we were entering a realm of self-denial, with unquestioned obedience. This was a warrior's arena, focusing on honor, courage, commitment, and selflessness.

Our platoon would rise at about 0500 hours (5:00 a.m.) to a drill instructor beating on a metal trash can (that he had first thrown down our main aisle), screaming, "Get up, get up, get up, ladies, get out of your fucking racks and count off!"

We were then required to stand at the foot of our racks with our sheets in our hands and begin roll call. Once this was finished, we made our racks, cleaned up the squad bay, showered and shaved in a matter of minutes, and then assembled on the parade deck for physical training. The training included jumping jacks, bends and thrusts, sit-ups, push-ups, and our morning run. This was accomplished all in the dark, holding flashlights.

After physical training (PT) we were marched to the chow hall. We had less than ten minutes allotted for breakfast. As we proceeded down the serving line, we held our trays at right angles. All food chosen must be eaten. Persons deemed "fat bodies" (overweight) had their food choices closely monitored by the drill instructor. After completing the meal, we rushed outside, stood at attention, and reviewed our little red books, memorizing Marine Corps information.

Next, we worked on marching as a unit (close-order drill) and spending considerable time executing the manual of arms with our weapons. Any misstep was punished by either running around the parade deck with rifle at port arms or performing bends and thrusts. I now realize that close-order drill was intended to get the platoon performing as a cohesive group. We were arranged tallest to shortest, and while marching maintained a 40-inch distance from the next Marine and an extended arm's length from the Marine on either side.

During one of our close-order drills, a fire hydrant split our column—and, not seeing it, I marched right up on it and found myself hung up by my crotch, ripping my utility trousers. It disrupted our march, and the drill instructor's wrath fell upon me. He bellowed with an angry red face, "Pregent, you numb nuts, what are you doing to my platoon? Get off that hydrant right now and get back in ranks. Get moving. NOW!" I quickly followed his orders, feeling like someone had kicked me in the groin.

Often when we returned from exercise or chow, we would discover our squad bay had become a disaster area: overturned bunks, sheets ripped from mattresses, and gear strewn everywhere. Though confused the first time it happened, we grew accustomed to a bellicose drill instructor screaming about a failed inspection and giving us minutes to straighten up the mess.

During the day, we attended classes on disassembling and reassembling our rifles and pistols, care of field equipment, Marine Corps history, the Eleven General Orders, customs and courtesies, chain of command, and preparation for uniform inspections.

Above: **The author in ranks, at port arms, drilling with Platoon 211 (Marine Corps Recruit Depot Parris Island platoon book).** *Left:* **Standing at the front of our racks, weapons by our sides, awaiting Regimental Commander's Inspection; the author, far left (Marine Corps Recruit Depot Parris Island platoon book).**

Evening meal was at 1700 or 1800 hours (5:00 or 6:00), followed by cleaning of the barracks, weapons, and equipment and preparing uniforms for the next day. We received one hour of personal time to shower, write letters, shine boots, or work on shellacking our M-14 rifle stocks to a high gloss. At the end of the day, we recited the chain of command (a line of authority organized by rank), sang the Marine Corps Hymn, and listened for the drill instructor to shout "prepare to mount," and then, "mount!" At these commands, we jumped into our racks and lay at attention not daring to move a muscle until he bellowed, "lights out!"

Throughout the night, Marines were assigned to one-hour "fire watches" that required them to walk up and down the squad bay. Each "fire watch" wore a silver helmet liner and carried a flashlight. Our drill instructor would occasionally disguise himself as a fire watch and catch us talking after hours, which drew punishment via innumerable push-ups or bends and thrusts.

Marine Corps culture brought with it a wealth of terminology. As the Marine Corps is part of the Naval Service, we had to learn a new vocabulary. The word "head" was used for bathroom, "deck" for floor, "hatch" for door, and "chow hall" in place of cafeteria. "Pogey bait" meant candy or sweets, "porthole" signified a window, a "bulkhead" was a wall, "Irish pennants" were loose threads, "trousers" said in place of pants, "fore" and "aft" instead of front and back. (Woe to the recruit who called his trousers pants. Only women wore pants.)

A very serious infraction was calling a rifle a gun. I can remember a chant meant to teach us: "This is my rifle and this is my gun (holding your penis); one is for fighting, one is for fun." We were known as "pukes," "ladies," "maggots," "pussies," "hogs," "girls," "queers," "shitbirds," "scum of the earth," and "lower than whale shit." None of this had existed in North Adams. One common threat was "I'm going to unscrew your head and shit down your throat if you screw up again." Several times when at attention, I was guilty of letting my eyes wander instead of staring directly in front of me. The D.I. would catch me and ask, "Are you looking at me?" to which I answered, "Yes, Sir!" And then: "Do you like me, Recruit?" and my answer would have to be, "Yes, Sir!" He would then say, "Liking leads to loving and loving leads to fucking, do you want to fuck me, Recruit?" I was caught in this mental quandary a number of times and just ended up doing many bends and thrusts.

Boot camp punishments from novels and movies can be legendary, and surely sometimes exaggerated, but the following I witnessed or suffered:

- As a "house mouse" I was one of two people who had access to the drill instructor's room. Our responsibility was to make his rack (bed), sweep the floor, and keep the room clean. We'd also shine his shoes as necessary. One day the other house mouse and I broke into the drill instructor's wall locker where he kept "illicit" candy and cookies. We ate the top level of cookies out of a large box to try and cover our tracks. The instructor found out and assembled the entire platoon to watch us finish eating the five-pound box of cookies in two minutes, then drink two quarts of warm water and start doing jumping jacks under our ponchos. It wasn't long before both of us vomited.

- The day after our platoon was formed, a recruit was talking and was required to do squat thrusts "forever" or until the drill instructor told him to stop. This recruit was agile and athletic but eventually fainted.

- For talking when I was supposed to be silent, my mouth was filled with shaving cream that had to be swallowed. Additional punishments for talking included holding the 12-pound M-14 rifle on the tips of our fingers with arms extended, or "watching TV," which required us to hang our feet over the lower rack at an angle while balancing on our elbows.

- One part of our morning exercise consisted of running half-mile loops, finishing at our barracks after six loops. One morning, when I was particularly tired, we ran past the barracks after six loops, then seven, then eight, and finally—psychologically defeated with no end in sight—I dropped out of the run, a major transgression. When we returned to the squad bay, the instructor suggested that "Miss Pregent rest" on a chair on the quarterdeck while he made everyone else exercise for my failure.

- For a slow response to a junior instructor's order, I was repeatedly hit on top of the head with a section of tent pole.

- Our wooden footlockers were placed on the floor at the ends of our racks. Inside of them, our gear was meticulously organized and marked with our last name. When full, they weighed about thirty pounds. Once, after a failed inspection, we performed the "manual of arms" with our footlockers, which must have been a ludicrous sight, whipping around thirty-pound wooden boxes like weapons. When this was completed, we were given just minutes to prepare the jumbled footlockers for inspection. Another time we had to dump our footlockers' contents in the middle of the squad bay, then retrieve and prepare for inspection.

- At times, when moving too slowly, our group was required to shower fully clothed. All the showerheads were turned on and we marched into and out of shower very close to the person in front of us. This routine was called "assholes to bellybuttons."

- One recruit ate some candy while we were cleaning the female Marines' hallways, and when the junior instructor found out, he hit the recruit in the mouth, caving in and breaking his lower teeth (which turned out to be a denture). He very casually told the recruit to get his ass to the dentist.

- On one occasion, my aunt sent me a letter with the stamp upside down. The instructor thought the letter was from my girlfriend and the upside-down stamp meant sealed with a kiss. This brought on 150 squat thrusts.

- Sand fleas were little bugs with a nasty bite. The drill instructors waited for one of us to swat at or brush off a flea (which they considered to be a protected species). If you hit one, you needed to get on your hands and knees, find the body and bury it. The fleas were so small you never found the body and ended up taking a physical punishment.

Some of the punishments were approaching sadistic, such as when the instructors had Joe, who was pigeon toed, wear a diaper with a red spot over his groin area signifying a women's menstrual cycle, run up and down the main street, and go over and hug a D.I. from another platoon. Joe graduated, but others withered and dropped out under this type of harassment. (One recruit from my hometown area was discharged for being too inept and clumsy.)

There was no way out. It was tempting to quit, but when others gave up, we noticed they were sent to the "Motivation Platoon" where the regimen was even more extreme. Motivation platoon members moved tons of sand with pails from one hill to another and back again. Once a man finished with the motivation platoon, he would be "recycled" into a new platoon just beginning boot camp. No one wanted to start the process all over with different people.

This type of treatment had its effect on us, and one time at the rifle range a recruit I'll call Robert was not qualifying with the rifle, so we gave him a "blanket party" late one night. This included pouring canteens of water into his mattress while he was sleeping and when he awoke covering him with a blanket and beating him. When later that day he qualified, we thought our "blanket party" was the main contributing factor. I later heard he earned a Bronze Star in Vietnam for taking out a machine gun crew with rifle fire, though I wouldn't dare connect our antics with that remarkable feat.

Each platoon spent three weeks at the rifle range. Our first week, we "pulled butts," which required us to work down range manning target pulleys for shooters. We would pull the targets down and mark them with white or black discs to show the shooter where he had hit. This allowed the shooter to adjust his rifle sights. The second week we learned marksmanship principles such as sight picture, alignment, and trigger pull. During this week, we practiced assuming different shooting positions, which was called snapping in. We were getting our bodies familiar with the main shooting positions, which were off-hand, kneeling, sitting, and prone. On qualification day, we would use these positions to shoot from 200, 300, and 500 yards.

Weapons assembly. The author, far right (Marine Corps Recruit Depot Parris Island platoon book).

The final range week was devoted to shooting almost every day, leading up to Friday, qualification day. Huge emphasis was spent on everyone qualifying, as we competed with other platoons for the shooting trophy. The pressure on individuals was extremely high. A recruit who failed to qualify, known as going "UNQ" (pronounced "unc"), would face a tirade from his drill instructor. The minimum qualification score was 190 points for a marksman badge, 210 for a sharpshooter badge, and 220 to qualify as an expert shooter. I shot sharpshooter with a score of 217. I was disappointed not to make Expert after working hard all week snapping in and target shooting, but I was very glad I had qualified.

Physical fitness was a significant part of our Parris Island life. Shortly after being formed into a platoon, we took a strength test that consisted of sit-ups, pull-ups, push-ups, and running. The test provided a benchmark of our physical abilities. Then several times every day we exercised in preparation for our final assessment at the end of boot camp. To help with our conditioning we ran obstacle and confidence courses and came to enjoy the challenge of climbing ropes, lifting logs, scaling walls, crawling along ropes high over water obstacles, and jumping over ditches.

A great emphasis was placed on the meticulous wearing of our uniform, personal hygiene, and the condition of our weapons, which resulted in daily scheduled and unscheduled inspections. Inspections could be held on the parade deck or in the barracks.

Our weapons were subject to inspection at any time and usually involved a precise execution of the manual of arms presenting our rifles to the inspector. At all times we must be perfectly attired and our possessions properly marked and stowed away. We also had "junk on the bunk" inspections, which required us to lay out clothes and equipment on our rack for inspection. A sloppy recruit might find his clothes and equipment strewn on the floor after an unsatisfactory inspection.

One morning we participated in combat swimming tests, which required treading water and swimming in our uniforms and boots with combat packs. We also were trained to remove and inflate our trousers so they could act as a life preserver. Towards the end of boot camp, we were force-marched to Elliot's Beach for field training. We assembled our shelter halves into tents, stayed in the field overnight, and were instructed and tested on how to live in the field and perform in various tactical situations.

Our 12 weeks of training culminated in a final physical readiness test (PRT), marching in front of the battalion commander, a regimental rifle inspection, and graduation. Shortly before graduation, based on an intelligence test and our backgrounds, we were given our Military Occupational Specialty (MOS) assignments. I was selected to go to Supply School and given the MOS of 3041.

After the completion of boot camp, our platoon was sent to the 2nd Infantry Training Battalion of the 1st Infantry Training Regiment located at Camp Geiger, North Carolina, for six weeks. We were transported by cattle car (picture a congested semi-trailer, filled with Marines, with some upright and overhead poles to grip). Based on the premise that "All Marines are Riflemen," we were taught the necessary skills needed in combat: patrolling, assaulting positions, live fire exercises, land navigation, map reading, and additional weapons instruction in the M-60 machine gun, Light Antitank Weapons (LAWs), and grenade use. I completed infantry training in mid–June 1965 and then had a two-week leave.

I spent the entire leave back home with my family and girlfriend. The freedom to come and go as I pleased felt great. I visited all my aunts, uncles, and friends and began realizing I had changed. I had matured, gotten more serious, and felt that hanging around with old high school chums seemed pointless, as we seemed to have little in common. I was proud of what I had accomplished and enjoyed answering everyone's questions about boot camp.

The two weeks passed quickly, and in early July of 1965 I reported in to Supply School at Montford Point located on Marine Base Camp Lejeune in North Carolina. The school lasted six weeks. I graduated third in my class and was promoted to private first class.

With all my training completed I reported in to my first duty station, Camp Elmore at Norfolk, Virginia. I was assigned to a supply section that managed inventories and ordering of goods for our

In dress blues, the author with wife Carol, at the Marine Corps Ball, Norfolk, 1966.

group. I was excited to be working with other Marines and enthusiastically assumed my role. Many of the senior NCOs in our group were Korean War veterans whose tales about overseas assignments sounded glamorous to me. Most of the people on base had just returned from Vietnam or were awaiting orders to go there.

With my orders to Vietnam almost assured, Carol came to Norfolk, stayed with friends, and we were married at Benmoreel Chapel on the Naval Base.

HEADQUARTERS AND SERVICE BATTALION
Fleet Marine Force, Atlantic
Norfolk, Virginia 23511

7:JRB:rcs
1320/3
2 Feb 1967

BATTALION SPECIAL ORDER)
NUMBER . . . . .9-67)

1. The following permanent changes of station are effected. TravChar appn 1771105.2753, MPMC-67, BCN 44690, AAA 27, -CC 74121.

Name	: Tr From :	DofD :	Report To	By
Cpl PREGENT G G ·	: ServCo :	0800	:CG MCB CamPen for TEMCON processing & furtrans o/s as Apr67 Repl:	2400
2117792	3041:	: 4Feb67	: for du w/FMFPAC WestPac GndFor (MCC 159) (Auth CMC Spdltr DFB1/:	5Mar67
QSN 901910	· :	:	: 2-nlm-16 16 of 39 of 19 Jan 67) Auth 20 das del in addition to ·:not before	
PEBD 2Feb65	:	:	: trav time provided "ByDate" is met Auth adv mil & 1 mo adv pay :	3Mar67 ·
	:	:	: (6 mos acdu remaining) (EAS 1Feb69) LvAdd 43 E St Adams Mass :	
	:	:	: 01220 LvBal 24 das adv	

WestPac Orders for Corporal Pregent, serial #2117792, to Camp Pendleton, received February 2, 1967: Arrive not before March 3, but not after 2400 hours March 5, 1967.

Months later, I was promoted to corporal and received WestPac (Western Pacific) orders, which meant a trip to Vietnam.

5

First Tour: Okinawa/Vietnam, 1967–1968

The time passed quickly between receiving orders and arriving in Vietnam.

After Norfolk, I enjoyed a short leave, then reported in to Staging Battalion at Las Pulgas, Camp Pendleton Marine Base, California. This was required training before going on a Western Pacific tour of duty. At the time, my rank was corporal, and I was assigned as the 3rd squad leader of the 3rd platoon. My squad consisted of twelve men who separated into three fire teams. Their ranks were private, private first class, or lance corporal. Their specialties ranged from administration to communications to artillery.

Initially, we were stationed in a two-story wooden barracks in the main part of Camp Pendleton. As our training progressed, we were sent to Las Pulgas (Spanish for *fleas*) for field training. Las Pulgas was located far from the main base and the conditions were Spartan. We lived in World War II Quonset huts and slept in old racks with soiled and thin mattresses. I distinctly remember the bathrooms (heads) because my squad was frequently assigned to clean them. There were twenty open toilets in a row and the same number of sinks and mirrors just across the aisle. When a man used the toilet, his thighs almost touched the person next to him, as there were no partitions. The lack of privacy and the closeness to others "doing their business" had me using the head in off-hours.

We trained arduously over the next 30 days. Much of the training was conditioning-based, such as running, calisthenics, and forced marches over mountainous terrain. This was our first introduction to C rations (individually canned and precooked meals), many of which were left over, and date-stamped, from the 1950s. The name *C ration* has been used generically for a long time. In 1958, new rations called MCI (Meal Combat Individual) were beginning to be produced, though the meals were still canned. The MCIs were comprised of three dark green tins with an accessory package (cigarettes, Chiclets, sugar, coffee, etc.). The green cans would contain a *heavy* (entree), crackers & peanut butter, and maybe a pound cake. Shelf life was 10 years.

The cans were heavy, considering all the additional weight the typical Marine or soldier carried into battle. (In the 1980s, MCI was replaced by MRE, Meal Ready to Eat, with new entrees and lighter, plastic packaging.)

Training included patrolling through a mock Vietnamese village, complete with the types of booby traps we might encounter in Vietnam, such as mines, punji stakes, and

35

grenade traps. We also received weapons familiarization with the M-14 rifle, .45 pistol, M-26 grenades, and M-79 grenade launcher.

Escape and evasion (E&E) taught us what actions to take if we were captured or became separated from our unit. In darkness, we practiced what we had learned by evading the "enemy" (Marine trainers) over miles of hilly terrain. Our E&E night was particularly cold for California, and the temperature hovered around freezing when we were captured. I vividly remember trying to keep warm around a fire with just a field jacket and a blanket. It was so cold that the water in my canteen froze.

In one of our survival classes, an instructor demonstrated the usefulness of animals caught in the wild. The instructor would begin by petting a tame rabbit. Then he would suddenly hold it up by its back feet and break its neck, eviscerate it, and calmly note the utility of its skin, organs, bones, and flesh for food, clothing, and bait.

While assigned to the Staging Battalion we received overseas inoculations, were given the opportunity to create a will, and learned about Vietnamese customs, first aid, patrolling, small unit tactics, and the Geneva Convention rules concerning wartime treatment of prisoners and civilians.

After our daily training regimen, there was time for recreation, but we were tired, needed to clean our weapons and gear, and usually had no money. On weekends we would go to the nearest town (Oceanside, California) and visit the USO or tattoo shops, or head to Disneyland in Anaheim. Several times we went to Tijuana, but it was pricey, in more ways than one. Marines were often detained by the Tijuana police for fighting, public drunkenness, or other minor violations. If jailed, getting released on bond was usually expensive. Detained Marines also ran the risk of being considered absent without leave (AWOL) by their units.

After training was completed in April 1967, we were bused to the Marine Corps Air Station in El Toro, California, and boarded a plane bound for Okinawa, Japan, a transient point for Marines on their way to Vietnam. We boarded a cavernous C-130 cargo plane, named "the workhorse" because it was used frequently to transport large groups of Marines, deliver bulky materials, and drop the occasional large bomb.

Suspended inside the C-130 were red cargo straps on both sides of the aisle that formed seating. Our plane was carrying a large number of pallets, and seating was scarce, so we sat and slept on the cold floor nestled against sea bags. The trip was long, more than 6,000 miles, and took about 13 hours' flight time. We landed at Marine Corps Air Station Futenma and were transported by cattle car (a converted cargo trailer with bus doors added to the right side and bench seating inside) to Camp Hansen in the northern part of Okinawa.

At Camp Hansen, we were routed to our next assignment. I was surprised to find myself and several others assigned to billets in Okinawa while the rest of the cohort proceeded to Vietnam. I was disappointed to be remaining while the others went ahead, and resolved to get myself over there. I was assigned to the Provisional Service Battalion at Camp Hansen. At the time my MOS was 3041, a supply man, although I was assigned miscellaneous jobs unrelated to supply. As a corporal, I reported to the 1st sergeant and was in charge of barracks cleaning, which involved supervising other Marines cleaning heads, buffing squad bay decks, and cleaning wall lockers. I also acted as runner delivering messages for the 1st sergeant.

One day shortly after I reported in, I went to the head and found a private leaning against the urinal having just slashed his wrists. Alarmed and almost panicky, I ran to tell the 1st sergeant who said to bring the Marine to him. I responded immediately and brought the man, who was bleeding profusely, to the 1st sergeant. The 1st sergeant looked at the private and said, "You stupid shit, Do you realize the amount of paperwork you have created for me? Get your dumb ass over to sick bay."

Another time I was used as a "chaser" with the responsibility of escorting a prisoner to the brig. The prisoner had been court-martialed and convicted of deadly assault; he was handcuffed and in an angry mood. As a chaser, I was armed with a loaded .45-caliber pistol and took my duties very seriously. This particular Marine asked me to let him go so he could escape into town and hide out at his girlfriend's house. When I refused, he said he was going to run for it anyway and that I wouldn't dare shoot him. I told him if he got out of the Jeep I would shoot him down "like a dog" and that my pistol had eight bullets in it so I wouldn't miss. That discouraged him, and shortly afterwards I delivered him to the brig. The often-repeated rumor was that if you lost a prisoner you would have to complete his prison sentence. I believed this rumor and was always cautious about how I handled prisoners.

I was disappointed to be left behind in Okinawa and "requested mast" (a Marine's right to talk to his commanding officer) to speak to our battalion commander. When the meeting was arranged, I presented myself at attention and asked for a transfer to Vietnam. He was angry that I was wasting his time and told me, "We all want to be in Vietnam but need to perform the duties we are given."

Not long after this meeting I was transferred to Camp Schwab, a small base located in the northern part of Okinawa. I was now in a supply unit called Tactical Organizational Supply Support (TOSS), and we outfitted units headed to Vietnam.

At Camp Schwab, processing materiel orders for units in Vietnam, with another supply man, John O'Mallory, left.

Quick-reaction firing drills in the Northern Training Area of Okinawa (photograph taken by author's instructor).

While at Schwab we trained in the nearby jungle known as the Northern Training Area (NTA). The heat and humidity were drenching and especially sapped our strength during long forced marches or when rappelling down cliffs and participating in live fire exercises.

I was surprised at the lack of discipline at Camp Schwab. When we fell out for morning roll call and our daily run, many of the Marines were disheveled and partially drunk from carousing the night before. Being Marines, they were still able to run, although as our pace increased, many vomited along the road.

Some Marines lived in town with local Ryukyuan women. This practice was prohibited by the Corps, but some ignored the rule and cohabitated nonetheless. They had to maintain a bunk and clothes in the barracks, and help with clean up, but as soon as liberty call was sounded they left for town. Some of these liaisons resulted in marriages. Most did not.

We were required to have liberty ID cards when we left the base. The cards authorized us to be off-base and must be produced when stopped by the military police. My card was stamped "Minor" because I was under 21 years old.

We were always short of money, and in order to stretch our pay we would begin drinking on base where alcohol was cheap, and finish our partying off-base where liquor was more expensive. Loneliness and idleness tended to encourage drinking as a misguided way to handle emotions. On weekends, the base enlisted club would hire twenty or thirty local women to dance with Marines, many of whom were drunk. It wasn't a pretty sight, and I thought it was degrading. Yet the women tolerated it because they desperately needed the money.

Other events on Okinawa still stand out in my memory. They pass through like a slideshow:

- Just after my arrival, I went to the enlisted club and walked right into a razor fight between two Marines. I jumped between slot machines to get out of the way, and someone called the military police who subdued the participants.
- One time, a Ryukyuan base employee invited me to his home to meet his family and eat dinner. The home was small and primitive, with cinder block sides, a dirt floor, a tiled roof, and two or three rooms. Outside was a small garden and several goats. While I was eating with the employee, his wife, and several of their children, a heavily tattooed hand reached out from behind a curtain and touched my back. I was startled, then found it attached to an elderly grandmother who long ago had been "adorned" with tattoos as a sign of beauty and adulthood. I was told the practice no longer exists.
- I remember when we went to sick bay there was a large chart on the entrance door showing deformed penises, intended to discourage Marines from consorting with prostitutes. We had all heard the rumors that if servicemen contracted the incurable black syphilis, they would be automatically transferred to a secret island to die, and their parents would be notified they had died in Vietnam. The rumor sounds ludicrous now but held some gravitas for us in the 1960s.
- When first arriving in Okinawa I hoped to search for Japanese World War II souvenirs such as helmets and pistols but found out the areas were off limits due to unexploded ordnance; local farmers continued to be killed or injured while plowing their land. I did get to explore some concrete pillboxes: Our barracks at Camp Hansen had been built in front of three of them. These dug-in bunkers were constructed by the Japanese Imperial Army with walls at least a foot thick and loopholes on each side for firing weapons. The structures were difficult to detect until almost upon them. I tried to imagine a Marine in the Battle of Okinawa stumbling across the cleverly concealed bunkers.
- At Camp Schwab, another Marine and I resided in the barracks in a cubicle with two bunk beds. The other Marine had the lower bunk on one side and I had the lower bunk across from him. He lived in town with his girlfriend, had a large supply of vodka in his wall locker, and was being treated for crabs (a sexually transmitted disease). He used to pluck crabs off himself and place them on a wall locker for races, always killing the victor and the loser. He was quite unusual, but we got along well.

- I qualified for scuba certification while on Okinawa, and between diving with a tank and snorkeling, I spent a lot of time spearfishing about a mile offshore. Mostly I hunted on a pristine reef that attracted a myriad of beautiful fish, with underwater grottoes that sheltered moray eels, sharks, water snakes, and octopi. We never ate the prey ourselves; there wasn't any place in the mess hall for us, and I'm not sure we'd have wanted to cook it anyway. We gave it all to our Ryukyuan base employee to bring home to his family.

- When I was re-qualifying at the rifle range, and we were practicing our firing positions of kneeling, sitting, and prone (*snapping-in*), another Marine near me was chewing on something. He said that they were VC ears. He handed me four sets of human ears on a loop. They felt like dried leather and were slightly shriveled. I gave them back to him, and he never said another word.

- Pawn shops and bars were abundant in every small town. A corporal's pay was $200 per month, given in cash. When the money wouldn't stretch the entire month, I would hock my speargun and wristwatch for extra cash until the next payday and then retrieve them. This was a continuous cycle for a number of Marines.

- When we had the money, we would travel to the plush enlisted club at Kadena Air Force Base, even though Marines weren't overly welcomed since fights almost always broke out shortly after our arrival. When funds got low I would travel by "skosh" cab to Moon Beach on the other side of the island to swim and lie in the sun. ("Skosh" was the shortened Japanese word for *sukoshi*, meaning little.) These tiny means of transportation were driven at fierce speeds and were cheap enough when two or three Marines shared the fare.

Finally, sometime in June 1967, I received orders for Vietnam. Early one morning a group of us was taken by cattle car to Futenma Air Station for transport to Vietnam. Although Okinawa had been a good experience, I had always felt I was waiting in a queue for my final destination. We boarded the C-130 carrying our rifles and sea bags. It was a five-hour flight, and while I felt enthusiastic about finally going down "South," I had some anxiety about the unknown.

Upon disembarking in Da Nang, my senses were assaulted by the oppressive heat, the roar of fighter jets landing and taking off on missions, the artillery volleys, and the sewer odor. Many commented that Vietnam smelled like a "benjo ditch," which is an oriental open ditch used as a toilet. I had not given much thought to the conditions we would face upon arriving.

We were herded into a cattle car with barred windows to prevent kids from tossing in grenades. I noticed a group of Marines getting ready to board a plane for home. They looked exhausted, shabby, and worn out as they mechanically boarded a commercial flight, what we called a "Freedom Bird"—a plane headed for the United States.

All-in-all, it was a disheartening start as we headed to Red Beach at Camp Books, my new home for ten months. Our trip was uneventful. I spent time observing this new land: Many people rode bicycles and motorbikes; ladies wore conical hats and form-fitting ankle-length tunics known as *ao dai* that were slit up to the waist with trousers underneath. Trash was strewn all about the villages, especially in each backyard. The houses were open in the front and had wooden wall supports with thin bamboo walls and metal roofs. Sometimes the roofs or walls were made out of flattened beer cans or sheets of tin.

Our ride took us past small, roadside Buddhist shrines and altars where incense sticks burned. The Buddhist temples were ornate, built of concrete, and colorfully painted. The temples prominently displayed swastika signs which confused me until I found out that Hitler had appropriated a centuries-old symbol of good fortune that also represents Buddha's footprints and heart. We also passed a number of large defensive concrete pillboxes left over from when the French occupied the country in the 1950s.

The people were of dark complexion, small in stature, and generally seemed to ignore our presence while going about their life. Mini-bikes held families of three, four, and five traveling about town. Older women wore wooden shoulder yokes carrying loads of wood, food, or even small stoves. These women often had black teeth stained permanently from chewing betel nuts. Whenever we slowed down, small barefoot children swarmed our bus begging for cigarettes or food. They were shirtless and wore threadbare shorts.

Once at Camp Books, we grouped into formation for our introduction brief-

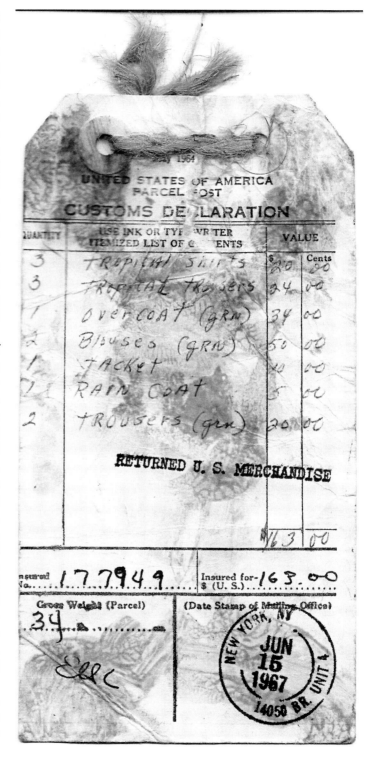

Before leaving Okinawa, I sent home all my uniforms: In the war zone, all I'd need was jungle utilities.

Top: Waiting to board the C-130 to Vietnam (the author in foreground). *Bottom:* Just arriving in Vietnam. That's our plane in the background.

Top: French pillbox as seen from inside a Jeep on Route 1 in Vietnam. *Bottom:* Exploring Da Nang City: off limits to Marines but that didn't stop me.

ing. A captain greeted us, announcing that our duty was to supply Marines who were fighting out in the field. He emphatically warned us about getting into trouble and the ramifications of brig time and extra-duty assignments. The city of Da Nang was unsafe and off-limits, by the way. The captain also stated that he intended to get two- and-a-half years of work out of us in the next 13 months. I remember his calculation: there were 168 hours in a week; he wanted only 105 hours of our time; we could do what we wanted to with the remaining 63 hours. His words translated to 15 hours a day, 7 days a week.

Next, we were assigned to hootches (living quarters) fashioned from plywood, with tin corrugated roofs and mesh screens over the doors and sides to allow air flow yet block mosquitoes. The huts were painted blue, and usually several huts shared an outside spigot for brushing teeth. The showers were 100 yards away. The huts were 16 feet wide and 20 feet long and housed six Marines. Once settled, I hired a Vietnamese worker to build a footlocker with some shelves to store my gear.

Daily routine at Camp Books in Da Nang, better known as Red Beach: I'm brushing my teeth at the outside spigot.

Most huts had a person that owned a large sound system. The sounds of the Supremes, the Temptations, the Four Seasons, and Simon & Garfunkel were played continuously. The chow hall was close by and we brought our own metal food trays in lieu of mess kits. The chow was good, especially considering that not far away the grunts were eating C rations. There were four or five metal trashcans filled with greasy hot water to dip the food tray, scrub it, and cleanse it.

During my work shift from 6:00 p.m. to 9:00 a.m., I pulled stock from bins to fill supply requests from infantry units for uniforms, boots, and other equipment.

I would get off work around 9:15 a.m. and thumb a ride to the Freedom Hill PX to browse items available for purchase. We either walked or thumbed to get anywhere off-base. We always traveled with an M-14 rifle and ammunition. Once I went by myself to Da Nang City for the day, taking pictures, being careful to avoid the military police. I normally returned to base around 3:00 p.m. and slept a few hours until my shift started.

Camp Books was supposedly a safe area, and yet in that first week, 122mm rockets had destroyed the hootch next to mine, wounding all the occupants; hit and demolished the side of a huge metal warehouse where I worked; destroyed the front part of the company office; and perforated our outside shower area and mess hall.

But that was war, and not entirely unexpected. What I wasn't ready for were dangers within.

I had been in Vietnam only two days. Prior to starting work on my third night, I was positioned in nightly formation waiting for announcements. As I stood at attention, I noticed my feet were in the middle of a large stain on the ground. Figuring it was an oil leak from the rough terrain forklift we used at the warehouse, I said as much to the Marine next to me, who corrected me: "A week ago, a black Marine shot a white Marine and killed him on that very spot."

Apparently, they were arguing, and the white Marine said to the black Marine, "You don't have the balls to shoot me." The black Marine leveled his loaded M-14 rifle and shot the other man through the heart, killing him instantly.

I found the story disturbing and was not sure if I believed it. Later that day, we did learn that a general court-martial was being convened for the trial of a black Marine. I still do not know whether the story was true, but at the time I believed it because word was out about similar incidents, including the recent fragging of the enlisted club (tossing a fragmentation grenade), resulting in one Marine's death.

When we picked up our mail at the company office, a bulletin board hung conveniently by the mail window. There we would read individual court-martial convictions for all sorts of serious crimes, ranging from drug use to murder. Usually convictions sent the guilty to Fort Leavenworth for some lengthy jail time. I was always surprised by the seriousness of the crimes, especially those Marines inflicted on each other.

Sometimes when grunts returned from the field and mixed with all levels of administrators living safely in the rear (disparagingly called REMFs, for rear-echelon motherfuckers), sparks could fly. After easily killing adversaries it didn't take too large of a step to fight a friendly who was aggravating you.

I heard that Da Nang alone had more than 500 accidental discharges and many deaths within a year's time. It made sense to me, with thousands of Marines carrying loaded rifles and pistols day and night. I think the combination of loaded weapons, drugs, and/or alcohol was a dangerous mixture. Consider also the close quarters of fellow Americans, black and white, when our own country's civil rights battles had barely cooled.

Add in hundreds of immature 18, 19, and 20 year olds often needing to settle perceived differences after drinking … and the gun was easily accessible and loaded.

I had flown to Vietnam convinced we were trying to save a nation, prevent the spread of Communism, perform heroic deeds, and win medals. I would do my part, as my dad and uncles had done twenty-plus years earlier. Now I stood in the apparent dried puddle of a Marine's blood, not killed by a VC but shot point blank by another man in the same uniform. Doubts began to form in my mind about the altruism of our mission. This was not what I expected when I'd left Norfolk.

While at Camp Books I had several odd assignments. I was told that the enemy rockets that hit our compound had a range of six to eight miles, and that there was a bright flash at the ignition source when they were lit. If a flash was observed and a warning yelled in time, it would allow Marines to seek shelter in a bunker. With this in mind, a sergeant put me on "rocket watch," scanning the horizon. After dark, I would climb 30 feet in the air atop our warehouse and sit in a roof vent with binoculars and a hammer. Once I saw an ignition flash, my responsibility was to bang on the roof of this huge warehouse, providing an early warning. I didn't think this made much sense, but it was an order, and I performed "rocket watch" a number of times. Nothing ever happened while I was on watch, but I often wondered how I would get down in time from this high perch once the attack began. One time I fell asleep and dropped the hammer, which caused a building evacuation and required me to concoct a story rather quickly.

Another temporary assignment was guarding a lumberyard some distance from our base with a Marine named Ernie. The yard was located at the entrance to an area known as Happy Valley, a VC stronghold. Every day we traveled by Jeep to the yard at dusk and stood watch prepared to shoot any VC we saw after dark. (Most locals would scurry home before dark to ensure they would not be shot.) The duty was boring, but Ernie and I were armed to the teeth with an M-60 machine gun, grenades, pop-up flares and our own M-14 rifles. Nevertheless I felt somewhat exposed, with just Ernie and me in the pitch dark some distance from friendly forces. Sometimes Ernie would leave me alone to visit his girlfriend in the "ville" after dark. I told him how dangerous this was, but he said he was "in love with her."

Once, a large Army convoy stopped at the yard overnight bringing with them huge quantities of beer and girls from the local village. It seemed strange, guarding this motley group of people. Our biggest accomplishment during these weeks was shooting a large German shepherd that appeared to have rabies.

Marines also took turns guarding the Camp Books perimeter. It was generally assumed the base was safe (excepting rocket attacks). One night on perimeter we received and returned small arms fire. The next day we were told we killed several water buffalo and an older woman. The same night, about 100 yards directly in front of us, four VC disguised as Americans, wearing GI helmets, threw a satchel charge into a bunker, killing all five Marines inside.

My time as a Red Beach supply man was short-lived. After three months, in August 1967, I was sent back to the Da Nang Airport for reassignment. A master sergeant told me my specialty was being changed from supply to infantry and that I was headed to the 1st MP Battalion. I told the sergeant there must be a mistake, since my specialty was supply. I still remember his response: "The Marine Corps doesn't make mistakes. You are now a fucking 0311" (an infantry designation). *Every Marine is a rifleman.*

I reported in to D Company, 1st MP Battalion, was given a hootch, and assigned squad leader duties. The company was located right next to Da Nang Air Base, which at the time was the busiest airfield in the world. The noise from planes and artillery was continuous and deafening. Red clay dust covered us, our equipment, weapons, and sleeping quarters.

The 1st MP Battalion was responsible for Da Nang Air Base security and had a three-day work cycle of patrolling and ambushes; sentry duty and bunker repair; and training and traffic control. As a squad leader, my role was to lead patrols and ambushes, direct and participate in bunker watch and rebuilding, and deal with traffic issues at the busy Dog Patch intersection (Dog Patch was a jam-packed area of ramshackle housing that harbored prostitutes, drug dealers, and VC sympathizers. It was strictly off-limits to U.S. personnel).

We slept in dusty, dark, and dank hootches marked by tin roofs and oil-soaked plywood flooring. Cold showers came from water collected in an elevated 55 gallon drum, and we had mess hall chow most of the time. Our personal areas had mosquito netting over our racks, with weapons slung underneath for easy access. Initially we all had M-14 rifles, which later were exchanged for new M-16s. As a patrol leader, I chose the option of carrying a shotgun on patrol. It was a Winchester Model 12, and I used double-aught buckshot for ammunition. The shells were heavy, but I still managed to carry forty rounds on patrol.

Initially my biggest concern was leading nighttime patrols and setting up ambushes. I had no experience, and I worried about getting someone killed due to my ineptitude. I decided that an experienced private in my squad, John, would run the show until I

All the comforts of home: mosquito nets, ammunition, and rifles stored in the rafters.

acquired the necessary savvy. He was a former infantryman, skilled in the bush, but had been caught visiting his "girlfriend" in Dog Patch and busted (demoted) from corporal to private. John was skilled at patrolling and quickly taught me the craft.

On the nights we were scheduled to patrol, I met with our platoon sergeant, was given a map overlay of our destination, and drew additional ammunition, grenades, and flares. The squad then located itself in a bunker on the periphery of the airfield and slept until departure around 11:00 p.m. We patrolled or lay in ambush until about 5:00 a.m. and then returned to the bunker and began day two of our three-day rotation. Often on ambushes, we would lie in rice paddies for concealment. This usually attracted leeches. We tried to remove them right away, but often needed to get back to the base where we had some light to work by. They were best detached with a lit cigarette butt, but often after they had grown fat from sucking blood.

During this time I led 15 night patrols. We never killed anyone in our ambushes, though we did detain a few people. One night we had been in our ambush site for an hour when a team member lit a cigarette. Our ambush was blown because of the light and the smell of the cigarette. I was irate and smashed him in the face. His actions had jeopardized the safety of the entire patrol; we had to return to base. He was a new guy but should have known better. I didn't report him, although I expect he appreciated the seriousness of his actions.

Chiều Hồi có nghĩa là được sum
họp lại với những người thân
và thoát khỏi cảnh cô-độc
ấm...

SP-1252 A

Another night after patrol, we were picked up by a cargo truck. I was the last to board the truck, counting off team members as they hopped on. The group was passing around several joints and offered me a smoke. I had to think fast and make a choice. Marijuana use was strictly prohibited by the Marine Corps; users could be court-martialed and spend time in the brig. Duty would require me to report the entire squad when we got back to base; my intentions would be obvious if I didn't share a smoke. So I accepted the joint, took several puffs, and passed the cigarette. I didn't report them, and fortunately, this type of incident did not occur again.

Sometimes our patrols would start at the Cam Le Bridge about two kilometers from the air base. We were charged with providing security for the bridge. Duties involved checking civilian identification cards and occasionally receiving Chieu Hoi passes, which loosely translates to "open arms." The leaflets, printed in Vietnamese, were dropped from the air and intended to be used as safe passage tickets by defecting Viet Cong.

Reportedly, up to 75,000 Viet Cong turned in Chieu Hoi passes. Those who surrendered were often used as Kit Carson scouts assigned to ground units in the areas from which they defected.

We also were responsible for keeping a look out for VC sappers (stealthy commandos) trying to blow up the bridge. Periodically we would drop grenades into the river to discourage sappers. I never knew if we killed any sappers, but we did blow up a lot of fish. Before patrols we would test-fire our M-16s into the river to ensure they were working properly. Shortly after I arrived at Delta Company, we traded in our M-14s for M-16s. This wasn't a popular switch: we experienced jamming issues with the M-16, while the M-14 had been tried and true dependable.

On day two of our cycle we stood watch and rebuilt two-story bunkers whose sandbags had deteriorated and were leaking. We would rip down old bunkers, refill new sandbags and re-build the bunkers. It was hard work done in the heat of the day, and seemed never-ending. I was told bunkers had about 15,000 sandbags. When we pulled down old sandbags we often found rats and would have a contest between us on how many rats we could kill. We used bayonets, heat tabs, and almost any method we could think of. One Marine used to punch the cornered rat in the face and then stomp on him. I didn't do this because I was concerned about getting bit. (Most of the rats were protecting litters and were quite aggressive.) I used my bayonet.

At night when on sentry duty we positioned ourselves in the second story of a bunker, watching our designated section of the airfield. Our shifts were two hours on, two hours off. Large and powerful conical lights shone right above us, attracting huge exotic bugs that would clang off the shield and then drop on our heads. When not on watch, the two other sentries slept in the lower part of the bunker. There, a man traded acrobatic insects for nocturnal rodents. It was difficult to sleep with them crawling over your body.

Sandbags: Haven for rats, hunting ground for Marines (courtesy William Buzzell).

One night I fell asleep on watch, leaning against one of the bunker supports. It had been a draining day, filling sandbags. Sleeping while on watch is a serious offense punishable by court-martial. This one evening about 2:00 a.m., the sergeant-of-the-guard stopped his Jeep next to my bunker. At least I was standing up. He knew we'd had a long day, so he generously (if emphatically) advised me to stay awake. I was lucky to escape with a caution.

Day three was our training day. We had classes on patrolling, small unit tactics, and weapon handling. My squad also directed traffic at Dog Patch. The intersection was chaotic with thousands of people and hundreds of mini-bikes and bicycles trying to weave through. I would stand in the center of the road on a 55 gallon drum that had been cut in half and painted white. It was exasperating. Few Vietnamese understood our hand signals. When we'd had enough, and needed to move traffic along, we would point our pistols at whoever we thought was the biggest contributor to the chaos, and traffic conditions would improve slightly. We also conducted sweeps of Dog Patch, looking for Marines sleeping with whores or conducting black market transactions. Both activities had proven dangerous.

While with the 1st MPs I saw the Bob Hope Show in late 1967. Bob was renowned for performing United Service Organizations (USO) shows for active-duty military. He and his troupe were flown in to Da Nang and performed at Freedom Hill in an

Nurses arrive to watch Bob Hope: For the men, it's the show before the show (courtesy William Buzzell).

Bob, his golf club, and the dancing troupe behind him known as The Golddiggers (courtesy William Buzzell).

amphitheater-like setting. Thousands of troops came to the show. Some were hanging off of light poles thirty feet in the air. Wounded troops were given the first three or four rows.

Bob had his traditional golf club and a red baseball cap with a capital M, standing for Marines. His jokes were rapid-fire and sometimes corny: "*Semper Fidelis* stands for Don't worry, Doc. Just nail it back on."

"Back home, everything is up! Prices, taxes, and mini-skirts." When the troops laughed, he followed up with, "If you guys were wearing mini-skirts, you wouldn't be sitting here."

Another favorite: "Marines are tough. When I asked one Marine who John Wayne was, the Marine said he didn't know her."

Every joke drew applause. His entourage included actress Raquel Welch; singer and actress Barbara McNair; that year's Miss World from Peru, Madeline Hartog-Bel; and Les Brown and his orchestra. The troops particularly enjoyed Raquel Welch and Miss World. Bob kept the jokes coming about women and Marines. The troops laughed uproariously.

There was a point in the show when Raquel Welch, who had been dancing by herself, asked the audience if anyone would come up and dance with her. The crowd went nuts, and it looked like the whole hill was going to try and climb onstage. As things calmed

The Armed Forces Vietnam Network broadcasted the show (courtesy William Buzzell).

down, the military police allowed six guys to dance with her. The crowd loved it and kept encouraging the dancers to get closer and grab her. This did not happen, but her mini-skirt with white boots was a tremendous hit. At the end of the show, Barbara McNair sang "Silent Night" and asked us to join in. It was a beautiful, albeit sobering, finale. The show lasted two hours, then the troupe was escorted back to Da Nang and flew on to their next show.

Shortly after Bob Hope's performance, I was scheduled to go on R&R and meet Carol in Hawaii. It had been nine months since we had seen each other, and during that time we had talked just once using the Military Auxiliary Radio Service (MARS), the only way to call home. Calls were connected using a "phone-patch" connection over shortwave radio and were limited to five minutes.

I was scheduled to leave Da Nang on December 20, 1967, returning on December 26, and I was getting very excited about seeing Carol. The day before my departure, I turned in my weapon and proceeded to the Freedom Hill R&R Center for processing. I checked in to the center and was prepared for a quiet evening.

But inside the processing center I ran into Steve; we had trained together in the Staging Battalion at Camp Pendleton. Steve, it turned out, had been on the Cambodian border most of his tour and had seen much action. He was also leaving the next morning on R&R, bringing with him an NVA helmet he had taken after killing its owner and a contraband .38 pistol that he kept for additional protection while on the border. Steve asked me to show him the local area, so we proceeded, after dark, to some seedy, off-limits marketplaces. It was about 9:00 p.m. when we were spotted by the MPs. Steve vowed he would not miss one day of R&R. He suggested we shoot it out with them. I was scared that we might go from missing R&R to murder charges. He seemed resolute that they weren't going to apprehend him. I calmed Steve down and acted compliant with the MPs, who ultimately released us with no charges, so we could make our R&R date. (We were fortunate; normally such infractions rescinded an R&R.)

I can remember landing in Hawaii wearing my summer uniform, fortunately without Steve. Upon deplaning, we were bused to Fort DeRussy, the Hawaiian R&R Center. I was so excited to see Carol. The bus dropped about 60 of us off at the center, and we were looking anxiously for our wives. I finally caught sight of Carol and as happy as I was to see her face, I was even more thrilled to hear her voice. We sat nestled together, half-heartedly listening to a one-hour orientation being presented by an officer.

Once the orientation was over, we rented a car and found our way to our motel, the Aloha Punawai, located near Waikiki Beach. We spontaneously decided to buy some colorful touristy clothes. Carol bought several pretty muumuus and I bought some wild Hawaiian shirts with accompanying shorts.

Our five days together went very quickly. We spent most of our time sunbathing on Waikiki Beach, shopping at various stores, visiting the International Market Place, watching some hula dances, and generally just relaxing and getting to know each other after a nine-month absence. We went to a club to listen to Don Ho, an accomplished singer and musician. He sang "Tiny Bubbles," the song he was known for. It was simplistic, but felt right for this momentary escape.

All too fast, R&R was over. I was leaving first, so Carol brought me back to the airport, and we said our goodbyes assuming it would be at least three more months before we would see each other again. It was a wrenching goodbye and so difficult to separate again. I won't say the thought didn't cross my mind that I'd like to go home with her that second.

But I returned to the 1st MP Battalion and resumed the same duties. After several months I rotated home to the U.S. We called it being "back in the world."

6

Second Tour: Quantico/Vietnam, 1968–1971

"I'm going to shoot the motherfuckers, but first I'm going to shoot you," he said, pointing a rifle at me from a distance of about 25 feet.

It was a sultry July day, 1968. I had returned from Vietnam about five months earlier and was stationed at Marine Corps Base Quantico, Virginia. Carol and I lived at Triangle Town Apartments, a large apartment complex about three miles off-base, occupied mostly by Marines and their families.

In our four-family building (two apartments up and two down) we had a scout dog handler, a tanker, an artillery man, and me—all of us married and recently returned from Vietnam. Each apartment was comprised of two rooms: one larger area that included a living and kitchen, and one smaller space that had a bedroom with a small adjoining bathroom. The entire apartment was about 800 square feet.

Over the course of a few months it became obvious that one of the downstairs couples, the tanker, Wayne, and his wife, had serious domestic issues. We heard loud verbal assaults and what we took to be physical abuse. The wife began sporting bruises on her face and arms. She was a beautiful, tall, blond-haired woman.

Everything was compounded by the husband's infidelity. At one point when his wife went to visit her mother in New York, we saw him move another woman into their apartment. When the wife returned unexpectedly from her mom's, she found the woman's belongings in the apartment and began throwing them on the front lawn: a stuffed bear, a phonograph, items of clothing. Wayne and the girlfriend left. At some point, Wayne and his wife reconciled and returned to living together in the complex.

We never thought of reporting the abuse and really can't remember any mechanism for reporting. But one day he broke his wife's nose, and she called the local highway patrol. Realizing this, the Marine got into his car and screeched out of the parking lot. At the time, several couples, including Carol and me, were sitting outside enjoying the weather, not realizing the authorities were en route to our apartment building. Just moments after Wayne returned, both the state troopers and the military police arrived in their patrol cars. Since we lived in a cul-de-sac, he was trapped. Wayne became infuriated and rushed to the trunk of his car. He opened it, took out a rifle, then pointed it at the police vehicles that had now come to an abrupt halt.

The officers took defensive positions behind their doors and fenders, drew weapons, and prepared to shoot. Most of our group, sitting on the front stoop, scattered while the drama unfolded about 50 feet in front of us. It was midday, and there were many other people, including children, in the immediate area.

I instinctively approached Wayne, who was still pointing his rifle at the authorities, about 25 feet away from me. I talked to him while closing the distance between us.

"Wayne, put the rifle down, or these guys are going to be real pissed off at you."

His only response was, "I am going to shoot the motherfuckers."

When I was about 15 feet from him, he turned and pointed the rifle at me.

"But first I am going to shoot you."

The officers, realizing Wayne was distracted by me, began cautiously approaching him. At that point, he turned the rifle back toward them.

I lunged at him, knocking him to the ground, and we fell behind his car out of view of the authorities. We traded a few blows and I disarmed him. The police rushed to my side and handcuffed him. Wayne was turned over to the MPs, who confined him for several days, and I was asked to be prepared to testify in court some weeks later. He was released and returned home in the meantime and was well behaved.

When we arrived at the courthouse that day, I was surprised to find that his wife had removed her bandages and retracted her statements. Wayne was released without punishment, beyond court costs.

Days after the incident, Wayne approached me in front of our apartments. I was sitting in a patio chair and he was standing. I was unsure of his intentions, and wary. He had a .38-caliber revolver in his hand, said he wanted to show it to me. He handed me the gun. I examined it to confirm it was unloaded and said it was a nice purchase.

I don't know what ever happened to them. This incident was a high-water mark of my time spent at Quantico. I would remain stationed there for nearly two years, assigned to S-4 (Supply/Logistics), Headquarters Company, Headquarters Battalion.

Colonel Carlock was our battalion commander, Major Neal his executive officer, and Sergeant Major Black the battalion sergeant major. Our battalion had a casual company comprised mainly of Marines between assignments who were recovering from wounds received in Vietnam. Some Marines were returned to full duty, although many were waiting to heal before being evaluated by the medical board. The board determined their percentage of disability, and once this was established most of these men were medically discharged.

Initially I reported to a first lieutenant who was the officer-in-charge of supply. The lieutenant was short in stature, dressed meticulously, had a precision crew-cut, and was an energetic no-nonsense leader, dedicated to the Marine Corps. Lieutenant Pisacreta was a former enlisted Marine and a great role model. He very capably led our office of six to eight people. Our duties included the acquisition, storage, and distribution of materiel supplying the battalion.

In July, when I disarmed Wayne, my efforts were recorded by the military police, and my battalion was advised of my actions. When I returned to work that next Monday, Lieutenant Pisacreta lauded my efforts and said I would be eligible for a Navy Commendation Medal, but he thought my courage may warrant a Navy Marine Corps Medal, and if I was willing to wait, he thought it would be approved by higher authorities.

After hearing the story, Sergeant Major Black, a Silver Star and Bronze Star recipient for heroism in Korea and Vietnam and a local icon, asked me why I unhesitatingly rushed an armed man.

The author receiving congratulations from Colonel Carlock upon promotion to sergeant.

"It seemed to be the right thing to do at the time," I told him. I will never forget him nodding his head and saying that's what prompted his actions in Korea. I felt honored by his words. After a while I began exercising at noon with Sergeant Major Black, and whether he realized it or not, I tried to model myself after him. He ultimately became the 7th Sergeant Major of the Marine Corps.

Later that summer I was recommended by my battalion for the Enlisted Commissioning Program. I was excited about the possibility of becoming an officer and as part of the application process was required to take a two-year-college equivalency test. My scores were marginal, and that worried me.

In September of 1968, I was promoted to sergeant and decided shortly afterwards to reenlist in the Marine Corps. The timing seemed right: Carol and I had a strong attachment to the Corps; she was pregnant; I already served my tour of duty in Vietnam; and I had recently been promoted to sergeant. I had applied for the officer program and was being recommended for the highest non-combat heroism medal that the Corps could award. With all this in mind, we thought the Corps would be a great career. I reenlisted for three years and received an $870 reenlistment bonus.

In November, I was rejected by the Enlisted Commissioning Board. They cited my scores on the equivalency test—too low, they said, for me to participate in this prestigious program. It was a huge disappointment. While I believed I had the capability to

Left and above: **Photograph required for the Officer Candidate School application, with reverse showing timestamp (Haleman, photographer).** *Below:* **Now married, back stateside. In this photograph, we're on the way to Mass with Carol's parents.**

become a Marine Corps officer, my limited education was the final determinant.

In the spring of 1969, we moved from Triangle Town Apartments to on-base housing, at 2961A Thompson Park. The furnished apartment was considerably less expensive than our off-base quarters, and we became close to other Marine families.

Two big events occurred that April. Our daughter, Lisa, was born at the naval hospital in Quantico, and I was formally awarded the Navy/Marine Corps Medal for heroism by Lieutenant General Lewis Fields, the base commanding officer. The award ceremony earned a feature article in the local Marine newspaper.

In July of 1969, my military occupational specialty was changed from a 3041 (supply administrative man) to a 3471 (allotment accounting man). Also in July, I received a second rejection, this time for the Temporary Commissioning Program. It became clear that officer candidate programs would be out of my reach until I had more education.

About six months later, I received orders to report to the Fleet Marine Force Pacific (FMF WestPac) for my second tour of duty in Vietnam. I departed MCB Quantico in February 1970, took one month's leave, and Carol, Lisa, and I spent most of our time with family in western Massachusetts.

In March, I reported in to the 3rd Replacement Company, Staging Battalion, Marine Corps Base, Camp Pendleton. The replacement training was similar to what I had experienced three years earlier prior to debarking for Vietnam: physical readiness, Vietnamese customs, and small arms familiarization. As a sergeant, I was a squad leader. A gunnery sergeant and a staff sergeant, both infantrymen and both headed for their second Vietnam tour, led our replacement group. The staff sergeant, a martial arts expert, had been on a scout and sniper team during his first tour. Scout snipers were usually organized as two-man teams that worked independently from large groups. One was a spotter, the other a sniper. Their jobs were hazardous, since most times they operated in remote areas, at times beyond the range of fire support.

One day during training, the staff sergeant, a quiet and pensive man, demonstrated his martial arts skills by asking a number of us, in turn, to try and stab him with our bayonets. He quickly disarmed each one of the 15 or 20 Marines who tried to impale him.

After training, we departed for WestPac, again from Marine Corps Air Station El Toro. We traveled on a C-130 cargo plane, and the flight to Okinawa was about 14 hours. During my first tour, almost every Marine on my flight went to Vietnam while I stayed temporarily in Okinawa. With the war winding down and my MOS changed to 3471 finance chief, I expected to remain in Okinawa. I was mistaken. After a short wait, I flew an additional four or five hours and debarked at Da Nang Air Base, once again in the Republic of Vietnam.

My second Vietnam tour began in April of 1970 and was quite different from my first. Throughout my first tour, I was with the 1st Marine Division in Da Nang and held supply, warehouse, and MP positions. Now I found myself assigned to the 1st Marine Air Wing. I was working as a section chief for the assistant chief of staff in the comptroller's office and volunteered to serve as an aerial gunner with Squadron 263, Marine Air Group 16, located at Marble Mountain in Da Nang.

During my first tour (1967–68), the number of troops in-country was at its peak—and before the TET offensive, the war was supported by the folks back home. During my second tour (1970–71), troop levels were rapidly decreasing, responsibilities were being turned over to the Vietnamese, and support for the war had evaporated. "Vietnamization" was the new priority: We continued to carry out duties, but we were focused on expanding, equipping, and training the South Vietnamese so our troops could return home.

Another notable difference in being assigned to the air wing headquarters: ground and air transportation were readily available, and our billets and food were much better. We also had more free time.

Shortly after landing, I was picked up by a driver and brought to the headquarters area where the finance office was located. The compound, originally built by the French, consisted mostly of one-story buildings approximately 20 feet tall, made of concrete with beige stucco exteriors and red tiled roofs. Our office area had Plexiglas windows and, to my surprise, an air conditioner! The front half of a nearby building was the office of engineers and carpenters, and the rear portion provided sleeping quarters for eight Marines. My rack was just inside the door to the right, and each of us had mosquito netting. We also had individual wall lockers where I stored some clothing, my flak jacket and my M-16 rifle with a half dozen loaded magazines. I often worked at night and slept in the office because it was air-conditioned. Outside our hootch were a number of sandbagged all metal "Conex" boxes that would provide shelter for us during mortar or rocket attacks.

The shower room, ten feet square with about six fixtures, had a slimy, dirt-infused concrete floor. The heads consisted of six elevated toilets. You needed to walk up three stairs to reach the commode. Then you would be facing six other elevated toilets. Dingy partitions separated toilets but otherwise they were open to passersby and to the Marine using the toilet directly across from you. It was a noxious area that lacked privacy, and yet was far superior to a field latrine.

When I was promoted to staff sergeant in November 1970, I moved to the staff non-commissioned officer quarters, which were in the same type of building but much cleaner and housed only two men to a room. We had an older Vietnamese woman who did our laundry and shined our boots. She was a hard worker and kept to herself. I bunked with a gunnery sergeant who was a great guy with strong Christian values and who played guitar. He would often serenade us at night with country and western songs. We both missed our wives deeply and occasionally got misty-eyed. He was an excellent role model for me, both as a Marine and as a husband.

The smells were nothing like home. Dirt roads were coated with some type of oil that reduced the dustiness but emitted a strong stench. Just across our protective fences the odors from a nearby Vietnamese village wafted our way, often from a pungent fish sauce called "nuoc mam." It was particularly odious. On top of that, when patrolling near

The assistant chief of staff, far left, pinning on my staff sergeant chevrons, 1970. Two weeks earlier, the company commander on the right had fined me $35 for speeding.

the airfield we could catch a whiff of embalming fluid from the nearby military mortuary.

Our mess hall was located near the helicopter landing zone and served three hot meals a day. There were no frills, but the food was comparable to stateside fare. Occasionally we could get apples and oranges. The best thing was the "Foremost Brand" orange drink, lemonade, and fruit punch. We usually tried to abscond with extras when we left the mess hall.

With the colonel's permission, we could even borrow a Jeep from G-2 (Intelligence) or G-4 (Supply) for local trips. I exercised off-base, running around parts of the airfield, and we even played handball on some old French courts.

Overall, the office of the assistant chief of staff for finance contained between 10 and 12 Marines (both officer and enlisted). The group was led by a colonel and assisted at different times by several majors or captains. Most of the officers were Marine Corps pilots on their second tour of duty.

Our primary responsibilities included tracking expenditures of the various 1st Marine Wing groups, matching the expenses with invoices, and resolving unmatched expenses. We also prepared briefing charts for the commanding general and group commanders and transmitted financial information to the 3rd Force Service Regiment (FSR) on Okinawa.

During this tour, I was much more mobile, visiting outlying groups and auditing their expenditures. I visited Marine Air Control Squadron (MACS)-4 located on Monkey Mountain. It was a radar station that provided aerial surveillance and traffic control. I visited 1st LAAM (Light Antiaircraft Missile) Battalion, located on the same mountain. I will always remember my first trip up, passing a crashed F-8 Crusader Jet sticking out of the tall mountain. I wasn't sure how far it was embedded, but it stuck out twenty feet. Rumor was the pilot ejected safely.

Our staff occasionally traveled to Ubon, Thailand, to a Royal Thai Air Force base used by the U.S. Air Force during the Vietnam War. When there was concern that Da Nang was going to be hit by rockets or mortars, some of its unprotected planes were flown temporarily to Ubon. Trips to Ubon were considered mini–R&Rs and only lasted one or two days. The flight to get there was a little over an hour and involved flying over Laos. I can remember taking an antiquated C-47, a three-wheeled transport plane still in use from World War II. As we boarded the plane, the cargo master gave each of us a parachute and, to encourage us, said there were very few of these planes left but they had good flight records. He then showed us how to use the parachutes, adding that if the plane went down over Laos, we should head northeast and try and get back to Vietnam!

These brief jaunts were known as "skivvy trips," and the single guys were usually looking for obliging women and a place to drink. There was shopping available and the ability to mail your purchases home. I can remember sending Carol a set of black opal earrings.

On one trip, when I arrived in Ubon late one night, I hired a "cab," a driver pulling a two-wheeled cart, to take me to a local hotel. The driver pulled me for about a half an hour until we were traveling on a dirt road in the pitch black with nothing around. I started having some anxiety about where we were headed and asked him to turn around, back to town. He refused but relented when I put my loaded .45 pistol against his head. We returned to a well-lighted area, and I found a cheap hotel. The next day, after more shopping, I returned to Da Nang.

One time I was sent as a courier to Marine Air Group 13 located at the Chu Lai Air Base about 60 miles south of Da Nang. I was only there for the day, and it was particularly hot. I ate in their mess hall, which was primitive. I remember asking what the warm orange liquid was in the large rectangle pans. The mess man looked at me like I was nuts and said the liquid was Jell-O.

Typhoons were prevalent in this part of the Pacific. Once when I was on another courier trip from Vietnam to Okinawa, just before a typhoon hit the island our small group of transient Marines was locked in a Quonset hut for our own "protection." We were sequestered for two days without electricity or running water. Men began urinating in the corners of the building once the commodes overflowed. We ate old C rations that had been tossed into the building before the doors were locked. After the typhoon subsided, a senior NCO let us out. He wasn't someone to argue with. We were released, relieved to smell the fresh ocean air and see the splendid sky.

For in-country relaxation our group would spend a Sunday afternoon at China Beach. The staff NCOs cooked steaks, and we drank beer and swam. We also played tackle football. I can remember being tasked with filling a trailer the size of a small pickup truck with Pabst Blue Ribbon, Black Label, and Budweiser, and then icing it down with 100 pounds of ice from a local Vietnamese vendor. It made a first-rate cooler.

All of the enlisted men in our group were assigned to Zulu Reactionary Company. Our purpose was to be a supplemental force for defending the Da Nang Air Base. Sometimes we were positioned at the end of the airstrip, near the mortuary, providing additional ground protection. We also conducted "sweeps" in areas around the base looking for weapons caches and VC.

Typically, we would surround a small village and send Marines in to search individual hootches for VC equipment or signs they had been there. On one occasion, another Marine and I were assigned to sweep an area near "Dog Patch." We slogged through the rice paddies between Dog Patch and 1st Division Headquarters, finding absolutely nothing, but returning covered in mud from head to toe, providing amusement for our friends.

One evening around midnight, two armed squads of Zulu Company were called out and transported to the air base. We were uncertain what was going to happen. Expecting the worst, we soon learned that we were required to unload forty ceramic elephants, each two feet high, that had been flown in from Thailand as gifts for high-ranking Vietnamese and Americans.

The Marines working in the comptroller's office were a close-knit group and we looked out for each other. When a replacement arrived and started smoking marijuana in our hootch, several junior Marines reported him to me, and I notified the military police. The MPs came to our hootch, searched his wall locker, found some drugs, and arrested him. We never saw him again.

I enjoyed the group I worked with and was well regarded by both my superiors and those who reported to me, but gradually I began to feel guilty about my REMF (*rear echelon motherfucker*) status. The headquarters area was peaceful, almost like working in the States, while several miles away Marines were dying. Two Marines from my staging battalion group had already been hit. One was shot in the head and killed by a sniper, and the other had been shot in the ass by friendly fire just before going on an operation.

I heard that some air squadrons were accepting Marines for temporary aerial gunner positions, and in August of 1971 I applied and was assigned to temporary duty with

Marine Air Group 16. I got what I asked for: a startling change from solid sleeping quarters and food to vermin-infested huts and a menu of mostly C rations.

I was assigned to Squadron 263 and told to be down at the flight shack, on the runway, at 4:30 each morning to find out which helicopter I would be assigned to, as well as what type of mission we would be going on. Once this was determined, we went to the armory, checked out a .50-caliber machine gun, and mounted it in one of the open windows on either the right or left side of the helicopter. If necessary, we gassed up before departing from the airfield. As part of my initial training, I was taught the Marine Corps triage system: wounded were categorized as emergency, priority, or routine. If the Marine was dead he was considered *permanent routine* and did not require immediate evacuation especially when receiving hostile fire.

A number of missions stand out in my memory even after 50-plus years. Most of our missions were spent rescuing wounded Marines and civilians, inserting recon teams, resupplying the infantry, and transporting Marines to and from different areas. Most resupply items were ammunition, grenades, and C rations. We also carried sniper teams, mail, and scout dogs and their handlers. Several times we delivered warm beer and melted ice cream.

Usually our two CH-46s traveled with two Cobra gunships for protection. We wore one-piece flight suits and flight boots and had radio helmets to allow conversation between crew members. We were also issued .38 pistols and continued to bring on board our personal weapons, including the M-16.

On my first flight, we had just completed a number of resupply missions when we were tasked with inserting a Marine recon team on a hilltop. We picked up the seven Marines at 1st Recon Headquarters, Camp Reasoner, and proceeded to their drop-off.

I really scrutinized them. Recon has a special place in Marine Corps lore as "the best of the best." They wore face camouflage and soft-cover bush hats. They carried M-16s and had caps on their rifle muzzles to prevent dirt from getting in. Each had between two and four canteens, rope, and one had binoculars, while another had a radio. All of them carried multiple ammunition magazines. I definitely looked like a REMF, taking their pictures.

We traveled to the insertion site with another CH-46 and two gunships. As we drew close to the drop-off, one gunship dusted off (fired into) the landing zone with his 40mm cannon. I presumed it was to set off any booby traps on the 100-yard-square hilltop. When the Cobra finished firing, we quickly set down, and the team disappeared over the side of the mountain.

1st Recon's motto was "Swift, Silent, Deadly" and this was not a silent insertion. After the team moved off, we left the area, only to receive a call several minutes later that the team was requesting an emergency extraction. No sooner had they gone over the hill than they began receiving fire from VC located in the nearby tree line. As the firing became more intense, the team leader decided to abort the mission and request an extraction.

We turned around and approached the hilltop from a different direction. As we got close, we noticed two of the team members were guarding the LZ to ensure our safety. We lowered our ramp, and five Marines got on, then the two team guards scrambled aboard. We left the LZ from the opposite side, avoiding gunfire and the VC scurrying up the hill to engage us.

The recon leader reported to our pilot that the VC had been "all over them" and

Above: Recon team member takes a final smoke before landing. *Right:* It's just another day for these highly skilled Marines.

that they'd expended half their ammunition just keeping them at bay. I couldn't help but notice how calm the team was. Most of them lit up cigarettes and looked absolutely unflustered. We returned them to Camp Reasoner in about 15 minutes and offloaded the team. For me, this was quite an exciting start as an aerial gunner. That day, in support of the missions, we flew about eight and a half hours, which is a considerable amount of time to be in the air. I was exhausted when we returned to base.

The next day we were assigned to resupply missions, and at one point were diverted to pick up some wounded South Vietnamese women and children. We were told they were hit by Marine artillery fire. We flew a number of kilometers from Marble Mountain and set down near the outskirts of a small village. Navy corpsmen (medics) and some Marine infantry were already on site providing security and care for the wounded. I don't remember the exact number, but we filled up both CH-46s with at least twenty people. We loaded the wounded on our helicopters with orders to fly them to the USS *Sanctuary*, a Navy hospital ship located in Da Nang harbor.

Most of the villagers had shrapnel wounds, although there were four or five amputees. The first person I picked up was a two-year-old girl whose left leg had been traumatically amputated. She didn't weigh much as I carried her to our helicopter. Her wound was very fresh, and the gauze bandage over the stump was leaking onto the front of my flight suit. I kept thinking she looked to be my daughter's age, about two years old. A severely wounded elderly woman was swathed almost head to toe in bandages that seemed to do little to staunch her bleeding. She had been identified as a VC sympathizer and minimal further care was provided her. The corpsman was busy treating friendly civilians. We rapidly got everyone on board and took off for the USS *Sanctuary*. Once we landed on the ship's deck, the onboard medical personnel helped to offload our wounded passengers.

After just two days, I felt excited and satisfied that I now had a front-row seat in the war and was providing support and assistance.

Several days later we resupplied a number of grunt units. On returning from one mission, we received a radio call from a squad of Marines pinned down in an open field by approximately ten VC.

Our ship commander, who was the senior officer in our flight group, ordered one of the Cobra gunships to "take out" the VC. The endangered Marines popped a smoke

I'm dialed in on the group radio frequency to monitor situations on the ground and in the air.

grenade, identifying their position, and advised the gunship where the VC were in rela-tionship to the smoke. One of the gunships was deployed and swooped down using his high capacity mini-guns to "spray" the area—in a matter of seconds eliminating the threat to the Marine patrol. We received thanks from the Marines as they checked the bodies for intelligence information.

The next several days it rained constantly, and we were engaged in resupplying grunts and transporting people all over the 1st Marine Wing's area of operations. Another day we transported a South Korean general and his staff to Marine headquarters. They gave each crew member a ROK (Republic of Korea) pin. During this rainy period, we brought a lot of C rations and ammunition to Marine groups located all over the province who were often set up on hilltops. The groups were platoon-size and lived in foxholes with only ponchos to ward off the rain. When we landed, our rotor wash would blow away some of these improvised "roofs." Most Marines I saw were lying in shallow foxholes half-filled with water. Often, after the grunts offloaded the supplies, they would ask me to mail letters for them. It seemed like the least I could do. At times like this, I really began appreciating the rodent-infested hootch where I'd sleep that night.

Several days later we helped our sister ship evacuate a Marine patrol in the Que Son Mountains. The patrol leader had requested an emergency medevac. The squad had been out for several days, and the previous night after making camp, they put out Claymore mines (anti-personnel explosives) to protect their perimeter. Sometime during the night the VC had turned the Claymores around to face the Marines. Early the next morning, the VC made some noises very close to the perimeter, and the Marines, in an effort to protect themselves, discharged the mines, sending hundreds of pellets right into them-selves, wounding the entire seven-man patrol, two or three of them critically.

After being notified, we flew directly to the mountainous area and hovered while our sister ship provided assistance. The helicopter kept attempting to negotiate the slope, trying to position itself to pick up the Marines. The terrain, covered with trees, was too steep to allow the chopper to get close. Finally it was able to lower a jungle penetrator, a long tube with fold-out metal arms used as seats to extract people from densely covered areas. One of the helicopter crewmen was lowered to help strap on the wounded Marines. They could only extract two members at a time, so it took a while to bring out all seven Marines, some of whom were screaming from having to sit on the metal arms with broken bones and multiple bullet punctures. Our sister ship brought the Marines to Charlie Med, and later we met with the crewmen to get the entire story.

On another resupply, we transported some sniper teams and a scout dog handler to LZ Ross, or Baldy. During the resupply one of our passengers was the staging gunnery sergeant from Camp Pendleton that I had trained with before coming overseas. During the flight, talking over the noise, the gunny described how at night the "gooks came out of the woodwork" and posed a serious problem for his group located on the LZ's perime-ter. He was hoping the sniper teams, with their Starlight scopes (night vision), would kill a few and make the VC more cautious.

He also told me that our martial arts platoon sergeant from the Staging Battalion had led a seven-man patrol that ambushed an entire platoon of VC, killing them all, without any injuries to his group. This was a significant accomplishment and the man was being recommended for a medal.

As my time wound down, I decided to volunteer for night medevac missions, which I had heard were dangerous. With only three days left on my temporary duty, I was assigned to a night mission. I reported in to the assignment shed and then went to the armory and checked out a .50-caliber machine gun. I found my assigned ship and mounted the gun and met the other gunner and crew chief. I also met the Navy corpsman who would accompany us to treat the wounded.

The crew chief had finished his pre-flight check and I gassed up the helicopter from one of the huge rubberized bladders that were pre-positioned at different locations throughout our area of operations. The bladders were protected by sand berms that provided some shelter from shrapnel. Fueling took about 10 or 15 minutes and was usually done by a gunner.

We departed, and after about 15 minutes of flight time, we pre-positioned ourselves on a large LZ (landing zone) and waited for a medevac call. It didn't take long. A group of Marines had taken some casualties. We flew in to what appeared to be a secure area, although it was hard to tell since it was pitch black. As soon as we touched down, about five or six Marines walked or were carried to our ship. Most seemed to be routine or priority medevacs and were only slightly wounded. The group included several Marines bleeding from shrapnel wounds, others with gunshot wounds, and one had a peculiar wound that had completely broken his ankle. He appeared to be medicated, probably with morphine, and didn't seem to mind walking on the stump of his leg while his almost detached foot flopped about him. We calmed him down and quickly flew to Charlie Med, where we dropped off all passengers for medical treatment.

An example of a medical clinic. A stretcher is propped to the left of the door (courtesy Michael Chalifoux).

Usually medical personnel would retrieve the wounded from the back of our helicopter, but sometimes I helped carry a stretcher to just outside the operating room. The medical staff performed their triage with haste, determining which patient needed more immediate care. During one of these times, I walked into the bunker operating room and noticed sawhorses set up to put the stretchers on for quick action. I saw how the room was slanted towards the middle with a sump area for blood to collect. The room itself was in a bunker, sandbagged on the roof and three sides. Large upright lumbers supported the sand-bagged roof and walls. I noticed that someone had stapled unit emblems and rank insignias on the uprights, giving stark testimony to the number of people who had passed through this room. The emblems had been cut from the bloody uniforms of the wounded. I'd say there were at least 50.

Another time I was pressed into service to help load ambulances transporting Marines being evacuated to Japan for a higher level of treatment. We loaded six Marines into an ambulance, and I was disturbed by the amount of screaming and groaning coming from the double amputees.

Another time I stopped by the critical ward, searching for a friend, and noticed a comatose Marine wrapped in gauze from his waist to his head. The wounds on his chest were suppurating, either pus or blood. I could see only his nose, mouth, and closed eyes. He was lying nude in the bed and also had many shrapnel holes in his penis. It was a sight I have never forgotten.

After my last day and night of this temporary duty, I returned to 1st Marine Headquarters and my job as section chief. I was relieved to be back "in the rear," especially after the previous night's medevac. I continued to perform duties in the comptroller office for the rest of my tour.

Carol and I again met in Hawaii for a week's R&R in January of 1971. We had the same wonderful experience of reconnecting, reveling in each other's company. Carol brought two-year-old Lisa with her. When I had left home the previous March, Lisa was just one, so after a ten-month absence she didn't recognize me. It took several days of cajoling for us to become buddies. Although we knew I would be home soon, the return to Da Nang was even more wrenching this time. I wouldn't have done it, but some guys went all the way back to the States; it would have been tempting to not return.

Finally, I left Vietnam in February of 1971. Briefly I went on leave, and then in March reported into Marine Barracks, Charleston, South Carolina.

While overseas I had applied for an "early out" for education. The application was approved for a release date in August of 1971, so my last five months of service spent at Charleston were long, tedious, and laborious. I worked for an exacting captain, who was none too happy to have to train me just so I could be released in five months.

For the first time ever, I found myself with a short-timers attitude, giving short shrift to work projects, wanting nothing more than to be discharged and get home. Once I would return to North Adams, I would come to realize there were many other St. Joe's boys in the class of '65 that had served in Vietnam. Some would go after me, but many others had gone before.

7

Mike Gorman—Army Helicopter Crew Chief/Gunner

Recipient of Air Medals and Purple Heart
Wounded-in-Action 1-23-1969

The helicopter crew spotted and surprised 15 NVA running through the woods, and the co-pilot and two gunners began taking them, under fire. The enemy was only 50 or so yards away. Mike could easily make out small details on their uniforms, the equipment they carried, and the type of weapons they were using. At this close range, the helicopter's M-60 machine guns were killing the fleeing insurgents. The floor-mounted guns were capable of firing 600 rounds a minute and in a few more seconds would have neutralized the remaining enemy soldiers.

On their second pass over the enemy, Mike noticed one VC who wasn't running away. He was kneeling calmly, returning fire at their helicopter. Mike could even see the blue flame from the end of his AK-47. This particular NVA's fire pierced the helicopter's front bubble, raked the side of the helicopter, and hit Mike who was sitting behind the co-pilot. Mike, who had been returning fire and was about to kill this sharpshooter, felt his M-60 machine gun jam, and while feverishly trying to fix it was hit by one of the enemy's bullets, just one. It hit Mike under the left arm, passing through his body, nicking his spinal column, and exiting through his back. The projectile, 7.62mm in diameter, weighing .6 ounces, and traveling at 2,350 feet per second, had the velocity to smoothly penetrate walls and metal vehicles, as well as human flesh.

When hit, Mike immediately fell to the floor on his back. The other gunner, Walter, rushed to his side, saw that his eyes were rolled back in his head, and thought for a second he was dead. Walter tore off Mike's helmet, removed his body armor (known as chicken plate) and noticed he had a hole under his left arm, about one inch outside of his protective shell. Initially Walt thought that the wound did not look too serious. He rolled Mike over on his stomach and took off his shirt. Then blood began gushing out of the hole in his back. The inside of the helicopter became splattered. Walt applied a compression bandage

Without his usual M-60 and helmet, Mike takes a day off from being a gunner, and even grins a bit (courtesy Kimberly Gavagan).

to Mike's wound, trying to stem the flow. It looked as if Mike might bleed out before they could get him medical treatment.

Noting the seriousness of the situation, the pilot unstrapped himself, turned the helicopter over to the co-pilot, and climbed in back to try and help the gunner, who was applying dressings. Mike, conscious for a few moments, apologized for not being able to get his machine gun more rapidly unjammed, and then passed out. Afterwards, Mike credited the pilot's quick assistance with keeping him alive.

While the pilot and gunner continued to work on Mike, the helicopter's engine began smoking and oil pressure was dropping. Another bullet had hit the engine. Mike and the chopper had both sustained grave wounds. The co-pilot needed to find a landing place away from the NVA, now, and where friendly forces would get to them first. He requested a replacement craft to be waiting on them, and a medevac. Just before the machine shut down, the co-pilot landed in an open field. The crew transferred to the replacement helicopter and returned to battle. Mike was carried to the medevac chopper and flown to the 93rd Evacuation Hospital.

The crew had flown together for more than four months on countless combat assaults. They had always managed to avoid serious injury. On this day their luck ran out.

Growing Up

For the first few years of Mike's life, he grew up on what was called the "city farm," sometimes referred to by local residents as the "poor farm," located in the current

Southview Cemetery on the outskirts of North Adams, Massachusetts. Mike's grandparents, Michael and Delia, managed the facility, but the responsibility fell solely to Delia when her husband died onstage, performing with a minstrel group.

Mike's parents-to-be, Jim and Shirley, who were to be married within days, said they would postpone their wedding. Grandmother insisted the wedding date not be changed, then asked the young couple to help her manage the farm. Delia, Jim, and Shirley became caretakers of the farm, operating it for the city and providing shelter and food for people too poor to own or rent a home. Mike's dad ran the farm, his mom helped her mother-in-law inside working with the homeless men and women. A local Chinese cook prepared all the meals.

The sprawling residence was almost three stories tall, and had a worn white clapboard exterior. It had a long hallway in the middle of the building, with smaller rooms alongside for a barbershop, kitchen, and dining room. There were separate large dorm rooms for men and women. The residents had a special place in their hearts for the little boy with brown hair, bright hazel eyes, and an impish smile. Mike had the run of the place, and the residents enjoyed playing with and entertaining him.

Mike's father was a quiet, hardworking World War II veteran who served in North Africa under General Patton. As a sergeant, he was trained in mechanics and managed the maintenance of Army equipment.

Eventually, Mike's family moved into town, and his parents bought a three-story apartment house on Meadow Street. Being particularly handy, Jim began remodeling each apartment. The family lived in the basement-level apartment until work on it was completed, and then they moved to the second-floor apartment. When that was remodeled, they moved permanently to a third-floor, two-bedroom apartment. Mike's parents slept in one bedroom, and Mike and his brother slept in the other. When his sister Kathy was born later in his life, Mike's parents ended up sleeping in the living room on a rollaway couch, and the sister had her own bedroom. At one point Delia, Mike's grandmother, moved into the basement apartment.

As interesting background, Mike's ancestors were named O'Gorman and originated from Ireland. Mike's great-grandparents died in England at a young age, orphaning their five children. Mike's grandfather, Michael, and his four orphaned siblings were brought to North Adams from England by a distant relative. When sailing to the United States, the five siblings assumed their host's last name, Pellows, in order to simplify passage. Years later before his marriage to Delia, Michael petitioned the court to re-assume his last name, but dropping the O, and became a Gorman.

Mike's mother Shirley's maiden name was Willette, a descendent of French Canadians whose family had Americanized their name from Ouellette. She was born in North Pownal, Vermont, and moved to North Adams at a young age. Her parents worked at textile mills both in Pownal and in North Adams.

Shirley was friendly, outgoing, and doted on the kids. She was also a determined woman who wanted her house clean and everything in its rightful place. She loved to laugh and sing as she did her chores and was uplifting to those around her. She had a strong faith and was a devoted member of Saint Francis Church.

In addition to running the apartment building, Mike's parents both worked at a cable and wire manufacturing company in Williamstown, Massachusetts. His dad worked as a foreman, and his mom on the shop floor. They would return home around 4:00 p.m., and Mom would prepare one of their standard meals: shepherd's pie, Salisbury steak, spaghetti and meatballs, or stuffed peppers. Seldom did they eat out. A special treat would be eating at Pedrin's or A&W, two local drive-ins. Grandma would always join them for the in-home meals. Mike's dad had rigged up a bell that would let her know when supper was ready, and she would walk to the third floor from her basement apartment.

Mike was the eldest son, and he, his brother, and his sister Kathy attended Saint Joseph's for elementary school. Mike went on to attend Saint Joseph's High School. The Order of Saint Joseph Sisters were his teachers, and the family were parishioners of Saint Francis Church. Mike enjoyed school and did well; reading and history were his favorite subjects. He was quiet, observant, and always looking to learn something new. He and his friends liked to ride their bikes to nearby Kemp Park.

Mike caught in a quiet moment, reading (courtesy Kimberly Gavagan).

During high school, Mike spent a lot of time with his cousin Greg, and they had their regular haunts, like Little's Pool Hall, located over the downtown Newberry's Department Store, for a game of eight-ball; or they'd stand in front of the Apothecary Hall, a drugstore and soda fountain, on the main street watching girls, checking out cars, and meeting with friends. They also ate and played pinball at Jack's Hot Dog Stand, a long-established institution on Eagle Street. For a little additional freedom, Mike and Greg would camp out behind the cemetery in Adams so they could stay out all night. This allowed them to meet pretty girls at the local Adams diner, which had a great jukebox. On one of these trips Mike met his future wife.

During high school, Mike worked as a press operator for the North Adams Transcript newspaper. He saved his earnings to purchase a car and became the proud owner of a red MG in which he used to take his little sister for rides.

When Mike graduated from high school in 1965, he began studying at North Adams State College. But when his grades waned and the hunger of the draft board increased, Mike, at 20 years of age, enlisted in the Army. His enlistment surprised both parents, but his dad was proud of him. He joined the Army in March of 1968, went to Basic School, and then was sent to Fort Sam Houston in Texas for an 11-week course on helicopter

Opposite, top: Little sister Kathy sneaks up on her big brother. *Bottom:* Fort Dix graduation. Mike's family: from left, brother Jim, mom Shirley, father James, sister Kathy, fiancée Linda, and Mike (both photographs courtesy Kimberly Gavagan).

mechanics. Mike spent a short time period at Fort Dix and then left for Vietnam, arriving in October, about six months after his enlistment.

Mike was assigned to an air cavalry troop, part of the 11th Armored Cavalry Regiment known as the "Blackhorse" Squadron. He initially repaired Huey helicopters, but his knowledge and skill grew at the same rate as the need for crew chiefs. He became an active crew chief and an aerial gunner flying daily missions. The group became renowned for seeking out and hunting down the enemy.

Mike served as Major John "Doc" Bahnsen's crew chief, and Doc was known for his aggressive stance in pursuing the enemy and his policy of "piling on" (using all available resources to include armor, artillery and infantry) to destroy the enemy wherever he was found. Many of their flights involved close contact. On occasion, their helicopter would land, and Mike and the other gunner would pursue on foot and capture NVA suspects.

Doc would often occupy the co-pilot's seat on the assault helicopter, and with the doors removed would fire only M-16 tracers, helping identify targets for his M-60 machine gunners. Doc always had a pail of loaded magazines at his feet ready for quick engagements.

Doc was very well regarded by officers and enlisted men of his unit. He was a highly-decorated officer and eventually achieved the rank of general. Doc was flying as co-pilot

Flight crew in Air Cavalry troop, fall 1968: from left, Mike Gorman, Mike Bates, "Doc" Bahnsen, Jim Gray (courtesy Doc Bahnsen).

the day Mike was shot. Another helicopter was flown in to replace the damaged one, Doc returned to the fight, and Mike was medevaced. Doc said he was "madder than hell" about Mike being hurt (initially he thought Mike was dead) and also about having his helicopter being shot down, so he returned to the battle scene, personally shooting a few more NVA from his helicopter before landing and leading a direct assault into the woods. His group killed more NVA and captured two enemy soldiers, one of whom was hiding in the hollow of a tree. Doc was awarded the Distinguished Service Cross, the second highest military award, for his intrepid leadership.

Back at base, Doc heard Mike was alive but paralyzed from the neck down. Later he received information that Mike's paralysis was in fact from the waist down. Doc was unable to see Mike before he was medevaced to Japan, although he and Mike remained close for the rest of Mike's life. They attended a number of 11th Cavalry reunions and continued to remain in contact via phone.

Mike had been in Vietnam less than five months. He was taken to the 94th Evacuation Hospital for emergency surgery. The 94th specialized in serious wounds, especially those involving the spine or head. Mike's spine had been hit at what was called the thoracic-six level, about one-third of the way down his back, causing an unrecoverable injury resulting in total paralysis below his chest. It took ten days to stabilize Mike, and then he was moved to the 106th Hospital located in Yokohama, Japan, for a higher level of care. Mike remained in Japan for ten days and then was transported to the United States Naval Hospital in Chelsea, Massachusetts.

The Gorman family first found out about Mike being wounded via a Western Union Telegram dated January 24, the day after he was shot. The telegram reached North Adams on the weekend, and the postmaster called Jim to tell him he had information that the family would want to see. It was only a several-minute drive to the post office, but the ride seemed much longer as Jim anticipated receiving bad news. His fears were confirmed when the postmaster handed him the following telegram:

The Secretary of the Army has asked me to express his deep regret that your son Specialist Mike J. Gorman was placed on the seriously ill list in Vietnam on 23 Jan 69 as the result of a gunshot wound to the thoracic spine with paraplegia while door gunner on a military aircraft on visual reconnaissance mission when hit by hostile small arms fire. Aircraft did not crash or burn. In the judgement of the attending physician his condition is of such severity that there is cause for concern but no imminent danger to life. Please be assured that the best medical facilities and doctors have been made available to aid him. You will be kept informed of any significant changes in his medical condition. He is hospitalized in Vietnam....

Kenneth G. Wickham, Major General USA, The Adjutant General.

Mike's little sister remembers her dad picking her and a girlfriend up and without mincing words telling the nine-year-old what had happened to her brother. She also remembers her dad going to the local *Transcript* newspaper office to talk with someone about Mike's condition. She isn't sure why her dad stopped at the paper but figured since Mike had worked in the press room, he had a number of friends there.

The news devastated the family. An incredible sadness settled over Mike's parents and siblings, and the family's life was never quite the same. Immediately, the family, including Grandma, began kneeling and saying nightly prayers for Mike and his condition. It would be three weeks before Mike arrived in the United States and the family could see him at the naval hospital in Chelsea, located 150 miles from North Adams, about a three-hour drive. Mike's parents, siblings, and fiancée visited him the weekend following his admittance. When they arrived at his hospital ward, they were shocked to walk through a gauntlet of men with the severest of wounds before reaching Mike. The visit had a visceral impact on Kathy.

On the first visit, the family began to realize the seriousness of Mike's injury. It appeared he would be permanently paralyzed below the waist. This news was reinforced by the image of Mike, immobilized, in a circular bed that allowed the nursing staff to periodically change his position in an effort to avoid bedsores. There was also the unsightly presence of a urinary catheter. (Mike was destined to have bladder issues the rest of his life.) His parents and fiancée were advised during the visit that paraplegics usually lived only to 40 or 50 years old. It took some time before Kathy began to understand what had happened to him. She kept asking him why he couldn't walk. Was he just fooling around?

His answer was always "no."

Mike would remain at the hospital for 12 weeks, and his family visited him almost every weekend. Towards the end of his stay, before his release, he was allowed to come home on weekends. Jim would leave work on Friday afternoons, travel to Chelsea, and bring Mike home late Friday night. Family members would assist his dad in carrying Mike up to their third-floor apartment. This process would be reversed on Sunday afternoon when Mike returned to the hospital. The home visits were helpful and encouraging for Mike and his family, as everyone got adjusted to his condition. Mike enjoyed the attention of family and friends and home-cooked meals, although his dad's new responsibility of helping Mike with personal hygiene was a sobering chore.

Mike remained a rehabilitation patient for 18 months. He was medically retired and released from the military on

Michael J. Gorman, 21, Badly Wounded in Vietnam

JAN 2 5 1969

NORTH ADAMS

A 21-year-old North Adams soldier was seriously wounded in Vietnam, Thursday, while on a visual reconnaisance mission as a door gunner on a military aircraft.

He is Spec. Michael J. Gorman, son of Mr. and Mrs. James M. Gorman of 9 Meadow St., who received news of their son's injury in a telegram yesterday.

The parents were told that their son, who has been in Vietnam since Oct. 4, received a gunshot wound to the thoracic spine, with paraplegia, when he was hit by small arms fire. The aircraft did not crash or burn.

The telegram told the parents that the attending physician judged his condition of such severity that there is cause for concern, but no imminent danger to life, and assured them that the best medical facilities and doctors have been made available to him. Mr. and Mrs. Gorman will be kept informed of any significant changes in his condition. Mail to the young soldier may be addressed to the Hospital Mail Section, APO San Francisco, 96331.

Spec. Gorman enlisted in the Army, March 29, 1968, had taken his basic training at Fort Dix,

MICHAEL J. GORMAN

N. J. After a 14-week course in single-rotor turbine utility helecopter repair at Fort Estis, Va., he was home on a 15-day leave prior to reporting to Ft. Dix for overseas duty in Vietnam.

He was graduated from St. Joseph High School in 1965 and completed a year of study at St. Joseph Business College, Old Bennington, Vt.

January 25, 1969: the *Transcript* runs an article on Mike's paralyzing injury (*Transcript*).

May 8, 1969, his twenty-second birthday, and for a brief period stayed at his parents' apartment. The day after arriving home, against his mom's wishes, Mike married his 19-year-old fiancée, and a month later their daughter was born. Mike's mom thought his paraplegia and their young ages were enough reason to not go forward with the marriage. The young couple disagreed and were married in Linda's backyard. (In fact, when Mike was wounded, Mike's CO in Vietnam was in the process of arranging for an emergency leave so Mike could marry Linda in Hawaii). She'd sent him a letter giving him the good news of her pregnancy a few months earlier. He was within a week of getting that leave.)

Once married, the little family lived in an apartment, but after some months they moved into a ranch-style house that had been specially built to accommodate his disabilities. The local veterans' groups gave Mike a generous stipend toward construction of the house, and Mike also received financial assistance from local car dealerships in securing a handicapped-equipped car. Mike had the distinction of being the first, and ultimately the only, local veteran to have been paralyzed in the war. The house's wide hallways/doorways and the modified bathrooms greatly aided in Mike's independence in simple things like getting out of bed, going to the bathroom, and being mobile enough to drive to activities and places. Mike's father oversaw some of the construction but never got to see it finished. Jim had been a smoker and died from lung cancer at age 51.

Mike returned to college, resumed his studies, and continued to be a voracious reader, especially of history. He enjoyed painting, sketching, photography, and astronomy, but genealogy was a passion for him. He feverishly researched his family's history and sent out letters to people and institutions to find out information on his parents' families.

At one point, Mike traveled to Ireland to examine documents related to his family. He pieced together his grandfather's immigration story, how his last name had been O'Gorman, but it was ultimately Americanized to Gorman. Mike also cofounded the local Vietnam Veterans Chapter and was an instrumental part in their efforts to distribute food to the needy and work with veterans. He attended a number of his squadron's reunions, always spending time with Doc. On occasion, he would take his daughter, Kimberly, with him and she was always touched to see the camaraderie displayed towards her dad. Mike's most enjoyable and active days, when the pain was almost manageable, seemed to occur well into his forties.

Mike enjoyed socializing and often frequented Unis's Bar & Grill on State Street, near Modern Dairy, where locals and college

Photograph appearing in the *Transcript* when Mike co-founds the Hoosac Valley Chapter of the Vietnam Veterans of America (*Transcript*—Noyes).

students hung out. Stories were told, beer flowed readily, and many a pool game was played. Mike won plenty from his wheelchair, chin on the table, pool stick in his right hand wrapped around his ear, shots taken while supported by his left hand.

Mike and I renewed our acquaintance on campus in 1971 and found we both had been assigned to helicopters as gunners. We talked for long periods of time about our experiences. Mike explained to me then how when he was shot he was wearing torso armor but was hit just under his left arm with the bullet passing through his body.

His cousin Greg once said, "Mike's sparkle diminished early." In a matter of 14 months, this son of North Adams had been drafted, sent to Vietnam, catastrophically wounded, hospitalized, discharged from the military, returned home, married, and became a father.

For a number of reasons, not the least of which was his injury, Mike and his wife eventually separated after 10 years of marriage, and he moved to an apartment while she kept the house to raise their daughter. Mike relocated a number of times to other places and states but eventually settled in Pownal, Vermont, and bought a cottage on the lake, right next to his younger brother.

Mike was in Vietnam for less than five months, and many of his stories will go untold. He was proud of being with the "Blackhorse" Air Cavalry Squadron and pictures show him working on, cleaning, and carrying his M-60 machine gun.

A former infantry leader named Francis, who was a member of an attached Aero Rifle platoon, was once wounded and medevaced on Mike's helicopter. Mike, noticing all the blood and how critical Francis' condition looked to be, began immediate first aid and is credited with saving his life.

The author sitting outside of his hootch with his M-60 (courtesy Kimberly Gavagan).

One of Mike's more poignant memories was about being sent out to assess the effectiveness of a B-52 bombing mission on a NVA sanctuary. After landing in the midst of torn-up landscape, the crew was surprised by the carnage and began searching the large number of enemy corpses for anything that might be helpful to military intelligence. On one mutilated body, a person who looked to be about Mike's age, he found a Bible and pictures of the man's wife and children. This chance recovery clearly had a deep effect on Mike, as he retold the story a number of times.

Another time Mike was scheduled for a mission but wasn't feeling well, so John

Yano, a Hawaiian, took his place as crew chief and gunner on Doc Bahnsen's helicopter. During the mission, a white phosphorus grenade exploded prematurely inside the helicopter. Despite being burned and partially blinded, Yano threw and kicked the remaining ammunition off the helicopter, saving the crew. He was posthumously awarded the Medal of Honor.

Civilian Life

Over his lifetime, Mike had persistent and serious medical issues from his wound and from being wheelchair-bound for more than 40 years. At one point in time, Colonel George Patton III, Doc's superior, had called Mike and made an offer to get him into Massachusetts General for an advanced type of surgery that might help him. Doc encouraged Mike to accept the colonel's offer, but he declined, concerned about the risk of the procedure.

September 1999: A happy moment for Mike at his daughter's wedding (courtesy Kimberly Gavagan).

He continued to have kidney troubles, and long-lasting bedsore issues. He was permanently hunched over. Reading, drawing, or playing guitar soothed his soul but yielded neck and shoulder aches. In his late fifties and early sixties, the medical issues continued, causing never-ending pain even when in bed because his trunk was so twisted. In the last three years of his life, even with powerful medications, the agony never went away. He got considerably thinner and at times was impatient and irritable from the continuous pain. At one point a hospital bed was rented and moved to the living room where he could watch television.

His brother suggested that he move into a veterans' home for additional care. They would have heated discussions about this topic, yet Mike repeatedly vowed to die in his own home. Some days before his death, Mike called his daughter, sister, and Doc Bahnsen to let them know his body was shutting down, and he didn't think he would be around much longer.

He remained in his cottage until his death in 2010 at the age of 62.

Mike's brother Jimmy went to check on him one morning and found he had passed away in his bed. Jimmy notified his long-trusted caregiver, Tina, and together they straightened up his cabin and notified the police. The day before, Mike with Tina's help had signed and left a detailed last will that included his obituary, people to be notified and detailed funeral and financial arrangements. Mike's last letter to his sister, in recent years known as Kate, outlined his funeral arrangements and the wording for his obituary, itemized who would receive his personal property, and asked his sister to kiss his daughter, granddaughters, nieces, and nephews for him.

The last paragraph of his will said, "I am not afraid! And I'm ready. I welcome death. That will be the best pain killer of all! Yours Truly, Michael Gorman." Mike requested that upon his death he be cremated, his ashes placed in an ammunition box, and be buried next to his mom and dad in the Southview Cemetery where his life began many years ago.

At the lake, a decade or so earlier, Mike had created a concrete memorial and millennium time capsule. The memorial honored all the 11th Cavalry's killed-in-action troopers who died in Vietnam and Cambodia. The time capsule included many items relating to the 1960s, including newspapers, Vietnam photos, currency, and magazines, all sealed in .50-caliber ammunition boxes. The granite memorial marking the spot reads: "*Pilgrim, a prayer in memory of 767 troopers of the 11th US Calvary Blackhorse Regiment killed in action 1966–1972, Vietnam War. Erected 1999 Michael Gorman, Air Cavalry Troop 68–69.*"

Military awards bestowed upon Mike Gorman included the Vietnam Service and Campaign Medals, National Defense Medal, the Air Medal

In the air, at the ready (courtesy Kimberly Gavagan).

with two oak leaf clusters, the Air Medal with a "V" for Valor, and the Purple Heart Medal.

Mike had been one of the contributors to Doc's book *American Warrior*. In turn, Brigadier General Bahnsen wrote a eulogy that was published in the Blackhorse Association newsletter under the heading "Warrior Down," describing Mike as "a superb soldier, a caring, loyal friend, a loving father, and a true American patriot." Doc was moved by Mike's resolve that, despite what happened to him, he would do what he did all over again.

8

Russell Roulier—
Marine Infantryman

Recipient of Purple Heart and Combat Action Ribbon
Killed-in-Action 6–21–1967

The firing was horrific. After returning from an exhausting and frustrating three-day patrol, K company's 2nd platoon leader found what appeared to be an easily defensible ridge. It looked like a barren moonscape, all the brush having been defoliated from Agent Orange. With night fast approaching and little brush to clear, they were able to establish firing lanes, set up a perimeter watch and put their M-60 machine gun team on the lower part of the slope for flank protection. It was noted that there was more brush on the lower part of the slope near the machine gun, but not enough to worry about in their exhausted condition.

The platoon had been searching for the elusive Viet Cong without success. Their patrol had seemed futile, and walking through thick brush in hot muggy weather had sapped their last reserves of energy. Even without underwear, and with towels wrapped around their necks to catch sweat, their clothes still stuck to their bodies. Most canteens were empty, and they had eaten the choice C rations earlier, leaving the ham and lima beans not so affectionately known as "Ham and Mother Fuckers" until their last meal. The good news was they were just five or six klicks (6,000 meters) from the base with a more open terrain to navigate in the morning.

The night was like so many others, with high humidity, continual mosquito assaults, visits by other outlandish bugs, and strange noises coming from the nearby jungle. The moon was out, providing grayish lighting as the Marines spread out their ponchos and slept fully clothed, each man's M-16 rifle within arm's reach. Even using the ponchos, they always awoke wet from ground dew. They were about four meters apart from each other, hoping to get a few hours of sleep before moving out. There was some comfort in knowing that in the morning they would return to base, enjoy a little more security, get some rest, eat better chow, and just maybe receive a care package or mail from home. They lit no fires, nor used heat tabs to warm their C rations, and remained quiet, although several softly bantered about their recent R&R conquests in Bangkok.

About 4:00 a.m., the moon went behind a cloud and a deep darkness descended over the platoon, inky blackness eliminating all visibility. Right then, at the peak of darkness, the perimeter was raked by a crescendo of what sounded like carbine fire and many grenade explosions. The Marines were shocked awake, receiving fire from three sides. They were unsure of the size of the enemy force, but knew by the volume of fire, they were in a fight for their lives. They quickly returned fire.

The enemy immediately knocked out the machine gun team on the lower part of the slope, killing Russell Roulier, the team leader, and wounding several others. With the loss of the gun team, the platoon realized they were in a dire situation: the small arms fire so intense, and the enemy so close, that artillery and helicopter support couldn't help. Realizing their grave posture, the platoon concentrated their return fire on areas where the greatest volume of green tracers and muzzle flashes were coming from, gradually suppressing the incoming volleys as daylight approached. After an hour, the incoming fire started to slacken, and a medevac helicopter was summoned.

As squad leaders began treating their wounded, someone conducted a head count and found Roulier had not responded. The squad leader and several Marines rushed to Russell's position only to find him draped over his machine gun with a head wound. He had evidently been killed instantly by rifle fire or a grenade. Wayne, the squad leader, wasn't sure exactly of the type of projectile that killed Russell; he had made it a practice not to look directly at dead Marines, it was bad karma.

Other members of the "gun" crew had also been wounded by grenade fragments and bullets. One squad member put Russell on his back in a fireman's carry and brought him up the slope to the medevac area, then laid him face up on a poncho. When the helicopter arrived, Russell was lifted aboard, as were some critical casualties. The walking wounded boarded last.

During the firefight, another nearby Marine platoon, hearing the commotion and realizing the 2nd platoon was in trouble, began to sweep the nearby area. In the process, they captured ten fleeing Vietnamese, tied them together and waited for another helicopter to bring them to the rear for interrogation. Many were convinced that this bunch had been part of the group that ambushed them.

The previous night, when the platoon leader decided to place a machine-gun team on the lower slope for flank security, there had been a discussion between Russ and his best friend in-country, Timothy Jacobs ("Jake"), about which person would take this responsibility. Initially, Jake said he would, but Russ, out of kindness, told Jake he was the senior corporal by two weeks, and it would be his team on the knoll. Both understood the gun team would be the first group to come under fire, if attacked. The M-60 machine gun had a prodigious amount of firepower, capable of spewing out 600 rounds per minute; it was usually the first target for the enemy.

Russ and Jake, the newbies, arrived in Vietnam about two weeks apart in September 1966. They immediately liked each other and served the next nine months side-by-side in the same squad. Both were initially assigned to "rockets" (3.5 rocket launchers), which look very similar to a World War II bazooka, and were used to destroy enemy bunkers and machine-gun nests. Both hated their military occupational specialty (MOS 0351): The rockets weighed about 10 pounds each, and each Marine needed to carry three or four rounds, as well as the oblong launcher, plus the rest of their equipment. Adding to the discomfort, when fired under damp conditions, the electrical wire used to ignite the rockets would hit the gunner in the face, causing cuts. The only good thing about manning a rocket was that its operators did not have to walk point. (Over time, Russ and Jake got out of "rockets" and got assigned to "guns," which meant they were part of a two- or three-man team on the M-60 machine gun.)

When they arrived in Vietnam, Russ and Jake were sent to the Chu Lai combat base (40 miles south of Da Nang) and within weeks transported north to Quang Tri Province (close to the DMZ) and participated in Operation Prairie. Then their company moved to Quang Nam Province, just south of Da Nang, conducting daily patrols and ambushes.

In December 1966, their unit participated in Operation Sterling. At Christmas, they found themselves at the Dong Ha combat base, sleeping on cots in wooden hootches and having perimeter watch. For a unit that was never in the rear, it was a welcome break from relentless patrolling and constant exposure, day and night, to the weather. It seemed as though they were always walking over mountains or through streams and rice paddies. Most times, they were covered with mud and pulling off leeches. Often they would walk all day and never know where they were.

Before Russell's death, he and Jake had already experienced numerous close calls. One night they were radioed and dispatched to a village where the security troops had been overrun by the NVA. In the pitch dark, their squad walked towards the village. Each kept his distance from the man in front and in back of him; they walked on both sides of the road. As they approached the "ville," the firing started to subside. Upon arrival, they found six dead Marines and an equal number of dead South Vietnamese Popular Forces (PFs) who had been shot repeatedly. They were surprised and relieved to find a seriously wounded navy corpsman who survived by playing dead while the NVA rifled his pockets. The corpsman was medevaced with the dead at first light.

In another instance, their platoon was sent to assist a reconnaissance team under heavy attack and trapped in the mountains. Their platoon left mid-morning and began climbing the fog-shrouded mountain. As they approached the steepest part of their climb, both of their point men were shot in the head, killed by a rifle barrage. The platoon pressed on, carrying their dead, and finally connected with the besieged recon team. Upon arriving, they requested a medevac to remove the dead and wounded. Because of the wooded terrain, the helicopter couldn't land; it hovered to bring up the casualties in a wire basket. This worked fine for the first few people, but on the third person the basket got caught in the helicopter's downdraft, spun out of control and caused the helicopter to crash.

The platoon, after retrieving the two injured pilots, moved to an area where a helicopter could land and called in a final medevac. Once the dead and wounded were removed, the platoon continued up the hill and found a large NVA hospital concealed in a cave. The cave contained hospital beds, equipment, bandages, and extra black uniforms. The platoon destroyed the entire facility using C-4 explosives.

Another time, Russ and Jake had just left a village after dark and were walking on a dike when someone thought he heard a noise. Their squad jumped off the dike and lay in the paddy water while an estimated 100-plus NVA walked right by their position, less than 30 yards away. The NVA were heavily armed, carrying mortars, base plates, machine guns, and were easily distinguished by their silhouettes.

Once, near the DMZ, after spending a night in their foxholes, the lieutenant had the platoon fill in the holes so the enemy couldn't reuse them. The holes had just been filled when enemy mortars hit the group, killing two Marines and wounding others.

When Russell was killed, his unit had been participating in Operation Desoto, a search and destroy mission in the Doc Pho district of Quang Ngai province. It wasn't until after the firing had ceased, and the medevac chopper was loaded with the wounded, that Jake learned his best friend had been killed. While maintaining his cover, from about 40 yards, Jake saw Russell's body being placed on the helicopter.

Decades after returning to the States, Jake created a web page honoring his friend's sacrifice. It read:

> Russell Rene Roulier
> Corporal
>   K CO, 3rd BN, 7th Marines, 1st MARDIV
>   United States Marine Corps
> 16 December 1946–21 June 1967
> Adams, MA
> Panel 22E Line 033
>
> 28 Feb 2004
>
> "You made a decision in Vietnam that took your life. I will always remember you each day of my life, best friends forever. God Bless your soul, I know you're there with him."
>   —Timothy William Jacobs

The testimonial included a link to www.VirtualWall.org, which maintains personal, military, and casualty data on Russell.

I had known Russell from the fourth grade through high school. When I saw Jake's testimonial years after it was posted, I found the words so moving that I spent considerable time tracking him down in northern Ohio. This effort was important to me.

I reached Jake in late 2010, and we talked several times about Russell. Even these many years later, the conversations were difficult for Jake, who also suffers from a number of military-related illnesses and is 100 percent disabled. During one conversation, Jake said that he had thought about trying to reach Russell's relatives when he returned from Vietnam, but Russell's death was too painful for him to talk about.

I recalled a visit I had with Russell's parents when I returned from Vietnam about nine months after his death. While still in uniform, I went to see his mom and dad, at their Corner Lunch restaurant on the corner of Summer and Spring streets in Adams, to offer my condolences. Our conversation was brief and I could see how distraught his mom and dad still were. I will always remember what his mom said to me near the end of our conversation: "We are keeping Russell's bedroom exactly how he left it, with his fishing pole and gear all laid out...." After only a few minutes, not knowing what to say, I excused myself and left the store, just wanting to get away from their deep grief.

After my recent conversations with Jake, I contacted Russell's mom, Phyllis. (His dad had passed away.) She and I discussed Russell's death. In 2011, even after all these years, she was still extremely sensitive about the topic.

"I loved my boy so much.... I sent overseas a wonderful nineteen-year-old boy, and all I got back was a box, and they said I couldn't look inside of it. The undertaker said he wasn't viewable." She also admitted, "I walked around for ten years in a fog and cried for years after his death; I felt dead and lost."

I decided to see if Jake would be willing to talk to Phyllis. With a bit of encouragement and cajoling by his wife, Jake agreed. Phyllis called him in July 2011, and both were emotionally overwhelmed by their conversation. They talked about many things—what Russell meant to each of them, about the tribute Jake had created in Russell's honor.

Phyllis sent some pictures of Russell to Jake, and he began sending her cards. I checked in with her after the call, and she told me, "It was wonderful that you would do this for me."

I found my contacts with Jake and Phyllis personally rewarding and began a long-term effort to find out more about Russell. I was fortunate to talk with his sister, his aunt, and a number of his boyhood friends, all who remembered him fondly. It wasn't difficult to find people willing to share their memories. He was described as caring, shy, could always be counted on, and would never let you down. Fifty years later, one friend said, "It's an honor to speak about Russell.... He was such a kind boy, would help anyone out."

The following is the rest of his story:

Russell was born in Chicago, but grew up in Adams, Massachusetts, went to Notre Dame Elementary school, and then to Saint Joseph's High School in North Adams. He was the eldest child and the only boy in the Roulier family. Russell was close to his two younger sisters, Cynthia and Jacky. His parents lived in Adams all their lives and were descendants of French Canadians.

Russell's dad was a World War II veteran who served with the U.S. Army in Guam. He was also an entrepreneur, owning first a small candy and newspaper store and then a restaurant. He also worked for many years as a school custodian. Phyllis, Russell's mom, worked at the family stores, the local FW Woolworth Company, and Waverly Fabrics, all located in Adams. The family moved a number of times, but always within the confines of Adams.

It seemed as though Russ, the only boy, was mom's favorite; his sisters thought she doted on him. He was also close to his grandparents who lived nearby. This didn't stop him from occasionally getting into trouble, like hitting his sister in the head with a rock and starting a fire near where the family lived, summoning a fire truck. One time he was playing on a merry-go-round in the school yard, challenged to stay on it while his friends spun it as fast as they could. Russ was thrown for some distance before a cement wall stopped his momentum.

At home, both parents took turns preparing the evening meal, which could range from pot roast to stuffed peppers, beef stew to pot pies. Sunday dinners were special. Grandma always brought dessert.

As a kid, Russ was skinny and usually taller than his friends. He had an olive complexion and as he grew older he sported a crew cut. Early pictures of his "gang" show him wearing a trapper's hat and usually standing a head taller than his friends. Many referred to his "smirky" smile that they enjoyed so much and still remember to this day. His personality was warm, and although he might not have been as outgoing as some, he had a friendly, non-threatening way that encouraged others to engage him. When his family lived on Howland Avenue, Russell and his eight buddies had the freedom to ride their bikes—which they all painted black with purple stripes—and be gone from home for long periods of time. They all lived in the Zylonite area (so named after a material produced by a local company for heat-resistant stove windows). The company itself was located nearby and provided many areas to explore. They would play in deep "silt" ponds, using planks to create challenging and sometimes dangerous bike paths.

Other times they would scavenge cardboard, canvas, baby carriage wheels for soap boxes and other treasures from the nearby Adams dump and then use an old trolley path to haul their finds back to their camp. The boys had used the cardboard and canvas for the walls and roof of a clubhouse. The frame had been pre-built from trees they had chopped down and nailed and tied together.

In their wanderings, they once discovered a large buried tank in the middle of a field. Once they made an access ladder, it was easily converted to a secret clubhouse, big enough for all of the boys to fit in and stand up. They would usually build fires for their covert meetings. At one point, the boys bought a Bugle cigarette rolling machine, secured some cigarette papers, scrounged some tobacco, and rolled their own cigarettes. After awhile, they upgraded their manufacturing process using filters.

The boys also camped overnight in local fields, eating food they prepared over an open fire. They were usually out all night with no one checking up on them. During daylight hours, they played "war" in nearby swamps and gullies, using toy guns along with helmets and backpacks their dads brought home from World War II.

Sometimes the boys would help a local farmer take in hay bales and be paid with bottles of Orange Squeeze produced at a nearby bottling plant. One of the boys' grandest adventures was constructing a makeshift boat out of scrap wood and cardboard and launching it on the river in back of their hideout. The effort was disastrous. The boat sank almost immediately, and they almost lost a crew member to the rough current. As the boys got older they would hunt squirrels with shotguns along the Hoosic River and nearby East Road.

Russ belonged to Boy Scout Troop #3, sponsored by the Adams Lodge of Elks. He was a Daniel Boone patrol member and enjoyed the winter campouts at the foot of Greylock Mountain. While camped in the snow, the boys would learn outdoor cooking skills, stalking, trailing, and wood lore.

As Russ got older, he and his friend Jim bought 150cc blue Vespa scooters from Jim's dad and began traveling, helmet-less, throughout the Berkshires. The boys would range from their hometown of Adams to Savoy, Cheshire, and North Adams. One time in Adams, Russ hit a curb with the scooter and landed face-first on the cement, knocking out his two front teeth. He came home bruised and battered, and Mom was upset when he presented his teeth. Russ enjoyed bringing Jim to North Adams and introducing him to girls. Jim remembers Russell "always had a smile on his face that would lift you up." At Russell's funeral, seeing the profile of his dad, Jim was unable to approach the family, just not knowing what to say.

During high school, Russ worked for Al Paradise's Appliances, assisting the owner in repairing small appliances. Whenever he got paid, on his way home he would buy donuts for his mom and sisters.

Russ's best school friend was Joe Daigneault. If you saw Joe, Russ wasn't far away. The boys knew each other throughout grammar and high school. They were the additional "sons" to each other's family, loved by both. In the wintertime on weekends, they skated at Russell Field and went sliding on "eighth hill" at the local golf course. When the weather was nicer they played in Bellevue Cemetery, near Joe's house, target shooting with their rifles into the sandbank, shooting bows and arrows, and swimming in the nearby river. They would often travel to a quarry called the Pinnacle and swing from vines. Sometimes they played pick up football at the Valley Street field. Often they would attend St. Joe's Friday night dances held in the church's annex.

After high school graduation, Russ worked at a local company for awhile, and then he and Joe decided to join the Marines on "the buddy system." It was a natural culmination of the environment in which they were raised. They left for Parris Island in March 1967 and were able to train together in the same recruit platoon for the next 12 weeks. Russ was the Platoon Honor Man, getting promoted to Private First Class just before they departed for Advance Infantry Training (AIT) at Camp Lejeune.

After the completion of AIT they were given a 30-day leave and told to report to Camp Pendleton, California, for an additional four weeks of training before Vietnam. A Pan American flight brought them to Okinawa where they spent two or three weeks, just enough time for them to enjoy the off-base bars.

They arrived in Chu Lai, Vietnam, in the fall of 1966 and reported in to the 3rd Battalion of the 7th Marine Corps Regiment. At this point the friends were separated. Russ was sent to the 2nd platoon and Joe to the 3rd platoon, both in Kilo Company, 3rd Battalion. When the friends arrived, the battalion was participating in Operation Prairie; shortly after its completion they returned to Hill 37 to resume their routines of patrolling during the day and conducting ambushes, listening posts or perimeter watch at night.

In January 1967, the battalion was part of a force involved in Operation Desoto, a search and destroy mission in Quang Ngai province located south of Chu Lai. The operation lasted until April, and the battalion saw significant casualties. The friends, while in separate platoons, had occasional contact until Joe was seriously wounded on April 1, just before the end of Desoto.

Russ (right) enjoying some liberty with a buddy (courtesy Jacqueline Haddad).

Russell heard about Joe's serious injury and wrote to his best friend at the Chelsea Naval Hospital near Boston. He felt both sympathy and anger at what had happened to Joe, never suspecting that ten weeks later, on June 21, he would be killed in action defending his platoon.

On Thursday afternoon, June 22, 1967, his parents received a call at their restaurant that they were needed at home immediately. A Marine Corps officer and a chaplain greeted them there, informing them of Russell's death. The parents were devastated. In one family member's words, "It took the life right out of them. They never got over it; it was as though a piece of your body was injured and would not heal."

The family also received a Western Union telegram dated June 22, 1967. It read:

I deeply regret to confirm that your son Corporal Russell R Roulier USMC died 21 June 1967 in the vicinity of Quang Na[m], Republic of Vietnam. He sustained fragmentation wounds to the head from a grenade while in a defensive position. The following information is provided to assist in making funeral arrangements. His remains will be prepared, encased, and shipped at no expense to you.... I wish to assure you of every possible assistance and to extend the heartfelt condolences of the Marine Corps in your bereavement.

Wallace M Greene Jr General USMC Commandant of the Marine Corps.

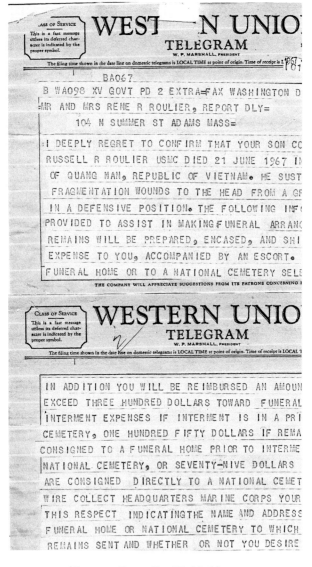

It took days for the coffin to arrive, and during this time period Russell's distraught parents numbly went through the motions of waiting and working at their tiny Corner Restaurant. They were finally called by Ed Pringle, the director of the Trottier Funeral home, with the news that Russell's remains would be arriving shortly.

The family gathered at the funeral home to support the parents. It was a heartrending moment when Russell's coffin was rolled into the room. The family knew he had died, but seeing the coffin made it real. A few minutes earlier, Russell's mom had said to her sister that she "hoped the coffin wasn't small since Russell was a tall boy." She somehow presumed his body would be intact if the coffin was standard. Seeing the normal-sized coffin gave his mom the littlest of relief. At one point,

(Courtesy Jacqueline Haddad.)

Caption from the North Adams *Transcript*: "Last March—Marine Corps detachment follows Edward Pringle of Trottier Funeral Home into Notre Dame Church with flag-draped casket bearing body of comrade Cpl. Russell Roulier, killed in action last week in Vietnam. Final rites took place here this morning" (*Transcript*, provided by Joe Daigneault).

Russell's mom wanted to see her son for the last time, but the casket's contents had been designated non-viewable and the funeral director strongly advised against opening it. It remained closed for eternity.

The funeral was held on June 30 at Notre Dame Church where Russell had gone to Mass while growing up. Five priests celebrated the Mass, with the main celebrant a priest from Haiti, being a relative of Russell's. The Marine honor guard carried the casket into a full church of mourners. Russell was the first and only Adams resident to be killed in Vietnam. His friend Joe, who was on medical leave from his wound, attended the funeral and sat with the family. He remembers feeling uncomfortable and deeply saddened over the loss of his friend. The funeral seemed surreal. Russ would be gone forever although there were times in the years that followed that Joe was sure he had seen Russell in different places.

At the Mass's conclusion, the body was conveyed to Bellevue Cemetery close to where Russ and Joe use to play. There, three volleys were fired by the honor guard, and Taps was sounded by a bugler from the detachment. The American flag that covered the casket was presented to Russell's mother by the Marine who had escorted his body home.

Russ had written home as frequently as possible, but usually conditions—weather, patrolling, and moving with his unit—greatly limited consistent correspondence. He wrote his mother, younger sister, and girlfriend Kathy most frequently. One mysterious detail was left unanswered. In letters, he wrote seriously about marrying his hometown girlfriend. Yet some of the last pictures of him are with a girl named Susan he met in Taipei while on R&R, and their relationship seemed momentous.

Above and right: **Russell on R&R, with reverse showing his note to Susan. She later gave it to his family (courtesy Jacqueline Haddad).**

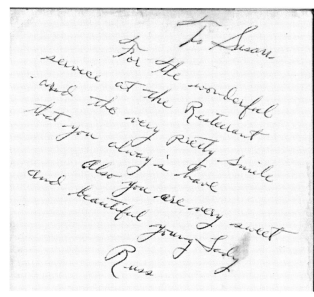

Pictures show a petite, Asian girl with dark shoulder-length hair, wearing a checkered dress, being held by Russell. It was no secret: Russ sent pictures of himself and Susan to his mom. Phyllis and Susan corresponded after Russ's death. In fact, it was Russell's mother who advised Susan of his death.

Susan's last letter to Mrs. Roulier in October 1967 described how sad she was upon hearing he'd been killed, how "when he was

around, it was as if the sun came out on a rainy day." She listed some of the places they visited during his R&R: The Central Theater, Ambassador Hotel Night Club, and the Twelfth Floor Club. Enclosed with the letter was a picture of Russell that he had previously given to Susan, but she wanted Mrs. Roulier to have it: The colored picture shows Russell wearing a yellow button-down shirt. His face is tanned and he has a fresh crew cut, the very image of life.

Because Russ cannot speak for himself, his sister Jacky shared some handwritten letters from this last year of his life. Like any teenager, he swings from topics like ice cream and cigarettes to casual commentary of the all-too-adult world he was thrust into.

Left: **The last known photograph of Russell, with girlfriend Susan in Taipei (courtesy Jacqueline Haddad).** *Below:* **Susan's kind letter, postmarked Taipei (courtesy Jacqueline Haddad).**

[Some excerpts from Russ's letters.
His original spelling and phrasing are left untouched.]

Parris Island, USMC Training Center, April 1966

Russ to Jacky:

For the past two days we've had Bayonet classes and tommorow we fight another platoon with what they call puggle sticks. We will where a protective mask, steel jock strap, and padding here and there. On the ends of the puggle sticks are padded balls. The object is to knock your opponent to the ground using basic bayonet formations. Man this is my big chance to let off a little steam and hope I can outdo the other guys as I'm going to be all full sore all over the next day....

All my love, Russ

P.S. Write soon and if [you see] Mom & Dad can tell them to write as often as they can. I getting kind of lonely.

Vietnam, November 1966

Russ to Jacky:

Boy I wish I was back home with you all. Viet Nam is sure a depressing place. And its real dirty too.... Thank you [for the goodies]. I wish you could send ice cream I'd tell you to send me a whole lot. It sure would be nice to taste some. In Viet Nam they have a few good things like bananas, pinnaples, coconuts, sugarcanes, etc. One thing that they have a lot of is rice, that all you see around here is rice paddies for miles upon miles of nothing but rice paddies.

I'm a three point five rocket launcher gunner. Yeh finally I've got a good job....

You asked if me and Kathy are still up tight.... It's all set me and Kathy are going to tie the knot and I think I'm getting cold feet about the whole thing.

All my love, Russ

Vietnam, December 1966

Russ to his parents:

The packages couldn't have come at a better time. I was all out of cigarettes and I had been bumming for the past few days now I have enough to last a while. Thank you for the fruit I know I'll sure enjoy that.

Well I got a package from Kathy too. She sent some books a deck of cards, some chew gum, a cross word puzzle book, cologne, and after shave lotion also. She's a real sweet kid and sometimes I think I don't deserve her....

Right now we're just running patrols around the area. But they expect that we'll be on another opperation soon. I hope not because that will mean I won't get mail and I won't be able to write any letters.... I'll try to keep them coming as often as possible. I don't want to let you down. Your both the most important people in the world to me.... You'll still and always be number 1. Always remember that, you know I'm a man now and I'm looking toward the future especially with Kathy and it might appear that she comes first but it's not true. Please try to understand me, I know it's difficult but I need you mom + dad and I'll always need you....

If I ever get a chance to go to Da Nang I'm going to buy one of those big Polaroids cameras and take all colored pictures of me, Viet Nam, the countryside, where I am, etc. I want you to have a few rememberances of me....

All my love, Russ xxx

Vietnam, December 1966

Russ to Jacky:

Well today is a pretty dull day. Nothing to do but hang around, write letters, read and maybe play cards. I'm really kind of bore because I'm used to doing something all the time. When I'm doing a whole mess of things I wish I had days like this. Do you think maybe I'm fickled. I sure don't know what I want. One thing I want very much and that's to go home. I wonder if that day will ever come...."

Lots of love, Russ

One of Russ's last letters to his sister. He called her Jack, or Jacky (courtesy Jacqueline Haddad).

Vietnam, April 1967

Russ to Jacky:

Dear Jack

How are you? How's school? Have you gotten yourself a job yet outside of the store?…

Well we've gotten out of that hell hole called Quang Ngai. We are now in Da Nang where there is no V.C. It's pretty Slack here so I'll be able to catch up on my mail. I guess Kathy's kind of P.O. because I haven't been writing.

I'm glad to hear she went down to see mom + dad and you. By the way Jack did she have much to say about me. You know girl to girl talk, you + her. Did she tell you that we're going to get married or anything like that. I'm just curious. I haven't heard from Kathy in about three weeks and I'm getting pissed off. Dammit I wish she'd start writting I'm kind of wondering what in the hell is going on.…

Well Jack its getting dark and I can't hardly see what I'm writing. So if you forgive me I'll end now. Until next time take care and be good. I miss you all very much. Thank you for writing.

    Lots of Love
    Your Big Brother

P.S. Write soon!

In slightly less than 15 months, from boot camp in March 1966, to his death in Vietnam on June 21, 1967, Russ was gone forever, the young, friendly, gentle man with an impish smile who died much too young.

9

Joe Daigneault— Marine Infantryman

Recipient of Purple Heart, Combat Action Ribbon
Wounded-in-Action 4-1-1967

They had been walking for days with little to show for their efforts. The platoon scoured an area just south of Chu Lai looking for the elusive Viet Cong. On this particular day, the platoon patrolled along a grassy flatland, with flankers out to prevent any surprise encounters.

Joe, who had been in-country about seven months, was in the middle of the platoon near his friend Tony, the radio operator and platoon leader. Joe was normally positioned near the front of the column, but today for some reason, he walked in the middle of the platoon. It was a little more relaxing being mid-column, although Tony's radio antenna served as a desirable target to the Viet Cong.

It was mid-morning, the sun shone brightly, and a faint breeze provided a little respite from the ever-present humidity. Joe's platoon had been sweating ever since they left their overnight site, but at least it wasn't raining. The relentless mosquitos had let up, and they weren't slashing their way through the jungle or climbing a mountain.

On patrol (courtesy Joe Daigneault).

Joe had adjusted to the interminable patrolling over the past seven months, losing about ten pounds and feeling as if he could walk forever. He had adapted well to the environment and even found some personal enjoyment in the challenging conditions. At five feet ten inches tall, Joe weighed about 165 and was wiry, tough, and possessed rock-hard determination.

That morning in the dark, they'd eaten only a C ration breakfast. But they had been walking since daylight, so the platoon leader signaled for the group to take a break. Every man dropped his knapsack where he stood, laying his rifle across his pack.

Suddenly enemy mortar rounds and sniper fire began hitting all around the platoon, someone yelled *Incoming!*, and the next thing Joe knew he was viciously spun around, taking in a 360-degree-view of his surroundings. Almost simultaneously he noticed his M-14 rifle on the ground, and in a well-trained reaction, he bent to grab his weapon with his right hand. His arm wasn't reacting to his thoughts. A glance at his chest revealed that the upper part of his jungle utilities, right at the top of his right shoulder, was torn and soaked in blood.

It dawned on him that he was bleeding badly, and his right arm was barely attached to his body.

Tony and others rushed to help, but he refused to be carried. He wanted to walk under his own power, which would allow him to hold his injured arm against his body. He worried that if manhandled by others, his arm would fall off. With some assistance, Joe staggered to the medevac pickup area. While waiting for the chopper, Joe gave his Puma knife to Tony, realizing if he didn't, someone back in the battalion aid station would probably get it. He was given an ampule of morphine, and at that point his memory begins to get foggy.

With some luck, a CH-34 helicopter was nearby and picked up Joe within minutes.

He was placed on a wire gurney, strapped down, and flown to the battalion aid station, which was filled with other seriously wounded Marines. This was Joe's second trip to the battalion aid station. Earlier in his tour, his leg had become infected and swelled up after a punji stake, covered with feces, lacerated his leg.

Upon arrival, his clothes and boots were cut off. He was triaged and waited for his turn to be operated on. While waiting, he noticed a fellow Marine right beside him, bleeding profusely from his neck. The young man's gurney was rapidly filling with blood. When the doctor came for Joe, he told them they should take the other Marine before him. The doctor retorted, "You are next."

Joe may have not realized how serious his wound was (or perhaps he simply stood a greater chance of recovery).

Joe was brought into the low-ceilinged, sandbagged, bunker-like operating room, anesthetized, placed on a stretcher which was then balanced on saw horses, an improvised operating table. Here's what most likely happened: The doctors tried to stanch his bleeding while the medics administered a blood transfusion. In a short period of time, the doctors had tied off his major arteries, slowed the loss of blood, and moved on to the next patient. It couldn't be determined at this point whether his shattered right arm could be saved, but it looked unlikely. It appeared as if Joe's wound was caused by sniper fire; the condition of his upper arm led most to believe it had been a high-velocity bullet.

Upon waking, Joe asked the doctor if his arm could be saved. The doctor answered

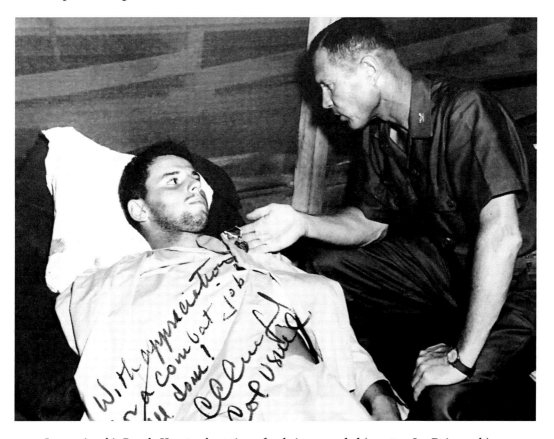

Joe receives his Purple Heart a short time after being wounded (courtesy Joe Daigneault).

in the affirmative, but Joe wasn't sure he could believe him. Was he just trying to make him feel better?

He spent two days at the battalion aid station, long enough to have the Purple Heart pinned to his pajama shirt by Colonel C.C. Crossfield, a member of 3rd Battalion's headquarters staff. A picture taken at the presentation shows the colonel, on an adjacent cot, placing the medal on Joe's hospital-issue pajamas. The colonel also autographed a picture of the presentation saying, "With appreciation for a combat job Well done! C.C. Crossfield, Col. USMC." Joe has a faint memory of the Colonel and the presentation.

During Joe's brief stay, Tony visited, updating him on the platoon's activities and informing Joe that they were the last two members of their group who'd arrived in-country together. Everyone else had been killed or wounded. Tony wished him well and returned to the company area. (Tony himself was wounded two times after visiting with Joe and rotated out of country in September 1967.)

Shortly afterwards, Joe was medevaced to Japan for further stabilizing care and finally to the Chelsea Naval Hospital. Up until and even after Joe's arrival, his memories remain vague. This was attributable to the significant amounts of pain medication he was taking. Chelsea would be where his medical evaluations concluded and his 13 surgeries began. At Chelsea, the Navy physician involved with his case was confident that Joe's arm could be saved. Fortunately, this conclusion meshed with Joe's strong determination that his arm would remain on his body—no matter the cost.

The day of his wounding, Joe's battalion was concluding Operation Desoto, tasked with finding and engaging elements of the 38th and 95th Viet Cong Battalions and assuming defense of the Doc Pho district from the South Vietnamese Army. The 3rd Battalion 7th Marine Regiment was also on notice that elements of the 1st, 2nd, and 22nd NVA regiments were operating in the mountains west of Doc Pho, the battalion's Tactical Area of Operational Responsibility (TAOR).

Joe (right) and a buddy with the 3.5 rocket launcher (courtesy Joe Daigneault).

Desoto had been going on for months and, while deemed successful, in March 1967, Joe's battalion had suffered 148 wounded and 10 killed in action; and in April, the month Joe was wounded, 44 were wounded and two killed in action. Replacements for the wounded and killed were continually brought aboard, but they never seemed to be able to replace people as swiftly as they lost them. A normal 12-person squad often operated with between six and eight people.

Joe had been in the Marine Corps just over a year when he was wounded. His initial military designation when he arrived in Vietnam was 0351, Anti-Tank Assault-man. This meant he would man the bazooka or "hump" the ammo for it. In some cases, he would do both. Most of the time, the bazooka was too unwieldy to carry, and the squad members would resort to slinging a LAW (light antitank weapon) over their shoulders. No matter his designation or what he carried, Joe was ultimately a ground-pounder, an infantryman, a Marine Corps grunt.

Early Life

Joe grew up in Adams, Massachusetts, and lived at 134 Commercial Street. The white, two-story house was located on the main road leaving Adams, about a mile from downtown, just over the hill from Aladco Laundry by the Hoosic River. He and his two sisters attended parochial elementary and high school.

His dad, also named Joe, was a Marine World War II veteran, and had served in the Pacific Theater in such places as Peleliu, Tarawa and Angaur. These islands were well recognized areas of engagement for Marines. Joe's mom, Jeanette, was born in Montreal. Orphaned at an early age, and raised by her aunt, she became a U.S. citizen in the 1960s.

Both parents were industrious and hardworking. Joe Senior almost always held two jobs. With his machinist skills, he found work at the local Berkshire Mills and Arnold Print Works, and after 25 years of service, retired from General Electric. On some evenings or weekends, he worked for a contractor building houses. Jeanette met her husband-to-be while working at the Berkshire Mills, a textile factory. Jeanette also worked at Plunkett Memorial and North Adams Regional Hospitals and enjoyed caring for people.

His mom was outgoing, generous, and hilarious. She and her close friend, who lived several houses apart, would imitate Lucy and Ethel's antics from the popular *I Love Lucy* show. Jeanette was very loving, at times the disciplinarian. She always made sure we "had what we needed," Joe said.

Joe's dad tended to be quieter when Mom was around. She had a talkative and fun personality, while Joe's dad could be funny with a dry sense of humor. He also liked to read. He didn't talk too much about his war years.

The household worked smoothly. By all accounts family members loved each other and lived in a tranquil environment, free from serious disagreements. They had birthday parties and enjoyed doing zany things on Halloween. His dad could even be encouraged to play the scary role of a dead person in the front hall closet.

Both parents enjoyed preparing

Home on leave before going to Vietnam, Joe and his father show off their Marine uniforms (courtesy Joe Daigneault).

family meals. On Sundays, you could find Joe cooking a pork or beef roast. Jeanette, with her daughter's assistance, would handle the weekly meals, usually from a pre-planned menu. She made a fantastic spaghetti sauce and cooked other household staples such as meatloaf, baked beans, and a special fried French pastry that the kids loved. Sometimes on Sunday nights, for a special occasion, Joe Senior would make hard boiled eggs, cut in half with butter, and allow the kids to eat in the den versus the kitchen. Meals on major holidays were eaten in the dining room using the fancy wine glasses. On these special occasions, the kids could get a small taste of wine.

Joe's mother had the biggest impact on his life, since she was more available than his dad. The family usually vacationed at Lake George, which had a frontier town and a North Pole. Sometimes Dad couldn't attend because he was working two jobs. Most every other year, the family vacationed in Canada with relatives from Jeanette's side of the family; on off-years, those same relatives would visit the Daigneaults at their Commercial Street home.

In his early years, Joe was a member of Notre Dame's Troop #38 Boy Scouts. He enjoyed the outside marching drills conducted by one of the leaders who had a great voice for cadence. Joe also served as a church altar boy under the ever-watchful eye of Sister Saint Claire. He walked to school with his sisters, though sometimes their dad would give them a ride or they would bicycle.

Joe remembers his earliest years of bicycling throughout Adams with two or three friends. They played in the nearby woods with bows and arrows and spent a lot of time at the Hoosic River in back of his house. The gang of boys used to bicycle several miles to the Tophet brook and enjoyed jumping off "Grey Rock" into the freezing cold water.

When alone, Joe spent considerable time sketching cartoon characters, and had a natural ability in this area.

As a child and into his adulthood, Joe was an independent thinker, self-confident, unafraid of giving his opinion, with a deep streak of self-assurance. He might be able to be persuaded that he was wrong, but this seldom occurred. Joe liked to lead. You could always find him by his hearty laugh, and he was especially loyal to his friends.

Very often in grammar school, the boys would have fights to settle differences in the Maple Street Cemetery. Classmates attended the fights, creating a circle around the contenders and letting them go at it. Fights were brief affairs, with the winner and loser shaking hands after the bout, and then everyone would head for home. Joe participated in a number of these encounters and never seemed to lose.

The "bouts" continued into high school, with the subterranean boys' bathroom serving as the boxing ring. Challenges would normally be settled there during lunch period with someone manning the doorway, in case an errant nun walked by, while the erstwhile pugilists went at it.

During high school, Joe had a close circle of friends. He would hang around with Gary, Ernie, and Russell Roulier. Russ was his closest Adams friend, and Gary and Ernie were his school friends. Russ ate dinner over all the time. He'd come in and say, "Hi, Mom!" to Joe's mom. It was like there was another kid in the family.

Joe named Ernie, Gary and himself the "unholy three," and when Russ asked what about himself, the name was changed to the "unholy three + one." The boys spent a lot of time together before and during classes, but after school each of them had a job.

Joe enjoyed music and was a guitarist for the Hi-Tones, a band composed of four school friends. They practiced in Joe's living room, and provided deafening entertainment for the rest of his family. While aspirations were high, engagements were not, and the Hi-Tones disbanded after a while.

Shortly after turning 16, Joe purchased a 1955 red-and-white Chevy Bel Air hard-top convertible and began driving himself and his sister to school. After a while, he traded in his car for a newer model, a 1957 blue Bel Air. This car was destroyed one night when a driver, going fast, swerved into Joe's front yard and pushed his car over the hill and into the river.

As he and his friends got older, on occasion they would go "over the line" to a tavern called Winarski's in New York State, where the drinking age was 18. Back then, their borrowed IDs had no pictures, and the young men certainly looked old enough to drink. Other times the "unholy three + one" would rent a rowboat at Cheshire Lake, buy some beer, and make an attempt at fishing.

Joe began working at the Adams Supermarket when he was 16 and continued to work there until the day he left town. He and Russ attended the local community college, and then one day they decided to join the Marines together.

One day before Joe's 19th birthday, on March 22, 1967, they left for Parris Island. Their route was much like my own. First they reported into the Springfield, Massachusetts, recruiting office; then flew to Charleston, South Carolina, and arrived via bus at Parris Island. After 12 weeks of boot camp, the young men proceeded to Advance Infantry Training at Camp Lejeune, North Carolina. After completion, they received a 30-day leave and then flew to Camp Pendleton, California, for four weeks of training with the Staging Battalion. As with most Marines, they had just enough time to visit Tijuana and nearby Disneyland.

They flew together to Okinawa, spent several days there, and proceeded to Da Nang, ultimately ending up in Chu Lai, a Marine Air Base about forty miles south. At Chu Lai they had two weeks of mess duty and then were assigned to Kilo Company, 3rd Battalion, 7th Marine Regiment. Joe went to the 3rd platoon, and Russ was placed in the 2nd.

Their company moved rapidly north to the DMZ and was welcomed that first day with incoming mortar fire—an ominous beginning to the tour of duty.

Vietnam Stories: Close Calls

Joe's grievous arm wound abruptly shortened his Vietnam tour. Normally he would have been in-country 13 months—the standard Marine tour—but inside seven months he'd absorbed a lifetime of experiences.

His platoon had been used as a reconnaissance group, always searching and probing for the enemy with very little time in the rear. They were almost always in the field and if ever a break occurred, they returned briefly to an obscure fire base, mostly to pick up C rations and more ammunition. Joe does not ever remember eating in a mess hall. On Thanksgiving and Christmas, lukewarm food was heli-lifted to the company in the field.

Their aggressive platoon leader, a youthful lieutenant, had been in-country for a while and knew his business. He sported a shaved head and carried a shotgun on missions. The men respected him for his willingness to lead in some of the toughest situations. They were further encouraged that he wouldn't ask them to do something he wouldn't do.

The platoon spent 90 percent of its time in the field, walking everywhere, seldom knowing their own location or the names of the villages they searched. It was a memorable instance when they were transported by cargo truck along Highway One. It was nice to be off their feet and have a chance to observe Vietnamese villages. Eventually they off-loaded and searched some houses in a small roadside village.

One of the only times Joe remembers being in the rear was when his platoon went to the Dong Ha PX. Joe's biggest treats purchased at the PX were a box of saltines, a jar of peanut butter, and two warm cans of 7-Up. Before leaving the PX they picked up some thick pieces of cardboard to construct temporary shelters and used candles to heat them.

They conducted ongoing patrols, numerous ambushes and search/destroy missions. Action almost always came during patrolling. Often their squad and platoon was at partial strength due to members being killed or wounded. In addition, the weather and elements sapped the platoon's strength, between immersion foot, insect bites, leeches, heat exhaustion, and malaria. Receiving and training replacement personnel was always a challenge, especially while in the field and in frequent combat situations.

Joe carried an M-14 rifle, 12 magazines on his cartridge belt plus two magazines in his rifle (taped together), a .45 pistol, four grenades, a bayonet, his Puma hunting knife, some C-4 plastic explosive, an entrenching tool, two canteens,

Joe, far right, with comrades Tony Choate, center, and David Block (courtesy Tony Choate).

C rations for three or four days, a medical pack, Halazone tablets for water purification, a flak jacket, helmet, poncho, and a green bath towel. Altogether, Joe estimates his "carries" weighed seventy to eighty pounds. One luxury that Joe allowed himself was a pipe and tobacco.

When they stopped in the evening they would dig a shallow foxhole, use heat tabs to warm their C rations, then eat and sleep under the stars if it wasn't raining. Flak jackets were kept on or folded into bulky pillows. Green towels or ponchos could be used for blankets. During monsoon season, when the nights seemed especially cold and wet, two Marines would configure their ponchos to provide the flimsiest of shelters and shiver through the night, sleeping side-by-side.

The need to be ever-ready required the Marines to sleep in their jungle utilities and keep their boots on for weeks on end. While in the field, an infantryman needed to be prepared and alert for immediate action. The practice of not removing boots required a certain amount of vigilance to avoid what was commonly called jungle rot: changing out socks was the easiest remedy. Some medics would be responsible and check feet now and then. Despite the conditions, Joe liked being out in the field. He enjoyed the extreme challenges provided by nature while they searched for the elusive quarry.

After several months in the field, Joe's squad was given an ambush mission. Viet Cong were using a nearby river to transport weapons and supplies, and the platoon leader charged Joe's squad with setting up an ambush near the river. For days, warning pamphlets had been distributed throughout local villages warning people about a dusk curfew. Those out after dusk would be presumed to be the enemy.

After lying in wait for several hours, the platoon detected a small flotilla of boats and challenged them to

In the jungle, looking a bit weary (courtesy Joe Daigneault).

stop. When the boats ignored the warning, the squad focused an intense barrage of bullets and grenades on the boats, sinking all of them and killing those on board. They requested some mortar illumination rounds to verify their success in interdicting a Viet Cong resupply group.

Much to their surprise and anguish, the light revealed that they'd ambushed a group of civilians used as decoys by the Viet Cong. The VC had remained upstream to avoid the ambush. The squad was disturbed about the lethality of their actions, but found some solace in intelligence reports that the VC often used civilians in this way. There was no enemy contact that particular night.

In another instance, the squad was called to help a reconnaissance team under attack in the nearby mountains. The squad departed from its overnight resting area late at night and was tasked to climb a sizable mountain in pitch-black darkness. It was so dark that, contrary to good patrolling, each man had to hold on to the man in front of him. Hours later, when they arrived in the early morning, the Viet Cong had slipped away and two recon Marines had been wounded. The squad set about the task of calling in a helicopter to medevac. After the wounded Marines were loaded on the helicopter, something went drastically wrong, and the helicopter began to spin out of control. It crashed on its side, killing its crew and the two wounded Marines.

Joe's squad spent the rest of the morning extracting the six dead from the mangled helicopter and placing them in body bags. It took the rest of the day to carry the dead Marines down the mountain to an area accessible by helicopters.

In another instance, Joe's platoon came upon an abandoned VC stronghold containing many bunkers. The VC were gone but had left a number of dead behind. This was memorable because the platoon sat and ate lunch amidst a bunch of dead Viet Cong, and it seemed to bother no one.

Joe remembers quite clearly when his squad crossed a rice paddy in mid-morning, and as they stepped up onto a small island, they heard VC talking nearby. About the time they realized there were a lot of VC on this island, the squad received a radio message to pull back immediately because artillery fire had been called in. They ran as fast as they could, with full packs, back across the paddy just as the shells began to fall.

His platoon had orders to advance on a village early one morning. In order to do this, the preceding night they took hours to climb a mountain to be in position to assault this village, on the other side, at the base of the mountain. The climb was arduous, and the platoon went from greater than 100-degree temperature at the beginning of their climb to 60 degrees once they reached its pinnacle.

The Marines slept that night on top of the mountain covered by flimsy ponchos. They lit heat tabs under their ponchos in an attempt to dry their sweaty clothing and warm themselves. The next morning they approached the village only to find out it had been abandoned.

Searching villages could be complicated. Often Marines received sniper and mortar fire from a village, requiring the Marines to advance and search it. In some instances, huts were burned when weapons, ammunition, or the past presence of enemy combatants was found. As experienced as Joe was, he can remember abruptly kicking in a hootch door only to find it empty but causing him to think he should have been much more cautious.

Joe had conflicting feelings about burning huts. Usually villagers were caught in the middle between U.S. forces and the Viet Cong, and they suffered greatly during the war.

One of his closest calls was being pinned down by enemy fire outside of a village. He was lying on his back in a slight depression. He could hear the crack of AK-47 rounds and feel the bullets pass inches over his face. Joe presumed his death was imminent, although after a bit, the fire slackened. He knew the next step was to get up and assault the village with no assurances that the enemy wouldn't start shooting as soon as he arose. His platoon arose from their firing positions and scurried through the village. They were lucky; the enemy had fled.

The platoon had an odd experience when an overbearing fire team leader, who had serious conflicts with his group, was mysteriously wounded during one firefight. He was shot in the chest by a small-caliber weapon. The corporal walked back to their area, was promptly medevaced and not missed nor seen ever again.

Accidents kept coming. After Joe had been medevaced, his friend Tony was the only survivor of a small patrol whose leader sat on a booby-trapped 81mm mortar round, vaporizing himself and killing the three other squad members. Shortly afterwards, the platoon lost another member when their part-time barber triggered a tree-mounted Claymore mine, blowing his head off.

The platoon regularly patrolled the northernmost part of the DMZ. They may have even drifted into Laos. Individuals usually carried at least three days of rations, which was about all anyone wanted to pack due to its weight. No one enjoyed the rations, but they provided enough nutrition to continue the work. Most found the jelly sickening, likewise the hardtack biscuits; even the non-smokers used the four-pack of cigarettes. Because the group saw almost continual action there was little use of marijuana, reportedly prevalent at the fire bases.

It's interesting the details combatants remember. Once when under fire, Joe jumped into a ditch only to find himself covered with duck shit. Another time Joe remembers climbing a path in the middle of the night and seeing luminescent neon green plants all over the side of the mountain. When a man stepped on one, it would generate a neon footprint.

Periodically, Joe received care packages from his folks or girlfriend. They usually contained socks, Kool-Aid, candy, cigarettes, and on one occasion a Puma hunting knife. The Kool-Aid helped to mask the chlorination of their purified water, making it nearly drinkable. Once the family recorded a Christmas message on cassette to Joe, but he doesn't remember being able to play it out in the field, with no recorder available.

Medical Operations

Upon Joe's return to Chelsea Naval Hospital in April 1967, his family and friends visited him right away. They were shocked and sobered by his condition and by the long orthopedic ward filled with other seriously wounded men, crammed on both sides of the aisle. The second most noticeable thing was the number of mechanical devices supporting broken and shattered limbs.

Joe, out of the fray for a few minutes (courtesy Ronald C. Darhower).

Joe's metal bed was at the far end of the ward, requiring family and friends to walk through a gallery of broken servicemen. Initially, Joe had a medical device on his right arm that looked to his little sister like "a large screw." She also remembers the broken man beside Joe in a large circular contraption that seemed to rotate his heavily bandaged body.

The ward was in the older part of the hospital, which had been constructed during pre–Civil War days. The walls were painted a sickening green, and the staff, while supportive, seemed overwhelmed by the volume of wounded. Joe remained in this ward during the early part of his treatments. For some reason, he was moved to the burn ward towards the end of his hospitalization and rested among severely disfigured and suffering burn patients.

Joe remained in the hospital for six months and 13 operations. After medical consultations, the doctors agreed that though his shattered arm was stripped of a tricep, it could be saved, although not without significant loss of function. The high-velocity bullet had disrupted tendons, blood vessels, and nerve endings.

One of Joe's earliest operations was to reset the humerus, which had been broken in numerous places. Once the arm was set and casted, they needed to wait for the mending process to begin before the next procedure. After some time, the doctors realized that

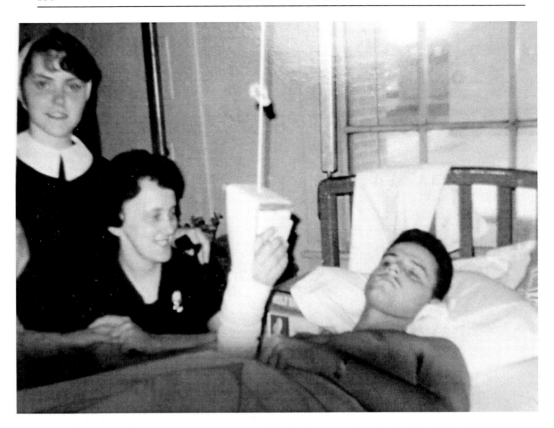

Joe's sister and mother visiting him several weeks after his arrival at Chelsea Naval Hospital in Massachusetts (courtesy Tony Choate).

the arm was not mending according to plan. The arm was re-broken and set again. Eventually it began to heal and the next operation was scheduled.

In this operation, the doctor (somewhat experimentally for the time) pulled Joe's right arm across his body, made a deep incision in his lower torso and wrapped a large flap of torso skin around his right arm. The hope was that this living skin graft, still attached to his torso, would be accepted by his body. The doctors told Joe it was the deepest skin graft ever attempted at Chelsea. If the graft was accepted by his arm, it would be cut loose from his chest.

After several months, and upon close inspection, the graft had worked, and the nerves began regenerating. The next operation would cut his arm loose from his torso, allowing him a minimal amount of freedom.

Next, since the donor skin area on his right side was so deep, the doctors decided to take a skin graft from Joe's upper thigh and replace some of the skin taken from his torso. After that graft was accepted, Joe told a corpsman he wanted to see his arm without all the bandages. It had been months since he was wounded, and it became important to Joe to see for himself how his arm was progressing. The corpsman initially discouraged him from looking at it, but Joe prevailed. When he looked in the mirror, the graft area was a deep purple and his arm looked like a hunk of meat. As strong and determined as Joe was, the amount of damage and the condition of his arm made him almost lose his breath. It looked like raw discolored meat.

Successful grafting of the skin around his arm was just the beginning. With the arm lacking muscle, tendons, and nerves, if nothing else was done, his right hand would hang limply by his side. The next operation removed the tendon on the inside of his right hand and moved it to the thumb area, allowing his hand to move up and down. The operation also allowed him to move his hand inward. Once the tendon was in place, in addition to an extended rehabilitation effort, Joe needed to begin training his brain on how to use these new connections.

While all these efforts were going on, Joe wore an elevated brace around his body immobilizing his right arm at face level. To add some levity to everything he was going through, Joe painted a face on his cast. At one point, he also wore a device on his hand that pulled back his fingers so his hand would not grow claw-like. Joe painted a face and hat on that device to resemble Santa Claus.

After several months, Joe was able to take weekend liberty, and his dad would drive from Adams to Chelsea in Joe's 1964 Chevy Super Sport Convertible, bought with the money he saved while in Vietnam, to pick him up and bring him home for the weekend. They would use a small cord tied to the roof to support his plastered arm for the car ride.

During Joe's convalescence, he received many visitors and hundreds of cards and letters from former classmates and military friends. Most admired how Joe had a positive outlook and was adamant about avoiding any pity parties. During his convalescence, he received a letter from Russell, his best friend and enlistment buddy. Russ worried about Joe and expressed anger that the Viet Cong had seriously wounded his best friend.

Russ ensured Joe that he would exact a punishment from the VC and would see Joe in four months. Ten weeks later, Russ would be dead, and Joe recovered enough to attend his funeral. It was extremely sobering. A heavy atmosphere filled the nearly packed church, and the playing of Taps and the rifle volleys at the cemetery left few dry eyes. Rumor has it that Russ was offered the opportunity to come home when Joe was shot, but refused to leave, wanting to continue the fight against those who hurt his buddy.

Joe received a letter from Tony updating him on the platoon's movements, listing those who had been recently wounded or killed, and a caution about not harassing the hospital nurses. Tony did not know that "all the nurses" were corpsmen.

Tony and Harry (another Marine Corps buddy) corresponded with Joe's mom Jeanette, admitting they were crestfallen about Joe's injury—"we didn't take very good care of him"—but, on a positive note, "he is now going to beat us home." Tony recalled how he had walked Joe to the medevac helicopter and helped load him on it. Both Marines thanked Jeanette for recently received care packages.

Tony continued to write while Joe was convalescing, letting him know that he was now the senior radio operator and that the unit had moved back closer to Da Nang. His job had become easier. He even had access to ice cream and milk! In May 1967, Tony let Joe know that he had just come off a Philippine R&R trip, was moving closer to the safer environs of Da Nang, and had three months left in Vietnam.

Recently, Tony and Joe reconnected by phone after almost 50 years. The Puma knife Joe gave to Tony is now carried by Tony's son, an active duty Marine Corps staff sergeant.

Once the extensive surgeries were completed, Joe's right arm was about one inch shorter than his left, and his mobility limited. The arm could be moved, holding it at a right angle, up and down, between six and 12 inches. Joe was permanently and medically retired from the Marine Corps on October 31, 1967. After his release from active duty, the medical authorities asked Joe if they could perform one last operation, which he agreed to undergo because it was the final effort in connecting his muscles and tendons.

Later on, Joe refused further requests for operations because he felt they would provide minimal results. Also, he needed to remain on antibiotics for months after his release from the military because of the possibility of infection. He was on them so long that he would begin to vomit when taking the medication. Joe eventually weaned himself off the drugs.

Once released from the Marine Corps, Joe needed to relearn many rudimentary movements, such as using his left hand to get dressed, tie his shoes, for writing, cutting his food, and playing musical instruments. He retrained himself to become an avid bird hunter. Joe learned to shoot left-handed.

Joe approached each challenge as he did with other events in his life—head on, no excuses, and overcoming perceived limitations. Several of his closest friends referred to him as their hero, praising Joe's attitude about getting on with life, having a great sense of humor, and not using his wound as an excuse for anything.

Career and Family

Once released from the military, Joe returned to the supermarket he had worked at from the time he was 16 years old. Even though he was at a disadvantage being able to use only one arm, he was successful in his initial positions of stockperson and cashier. One time, early in his career, when Joe overheard that baggers were opting to bag for him because he was slow, making their jobs easier, Joe re-doubled his efforts and in a short time became one of the company's nimbler cashiers. He never again heard from the baggers.

Joe's tenets of a strong work ethic, common sense, initiative, and loyalty would serve him well as he found himself being repeatedly promoted, ultimately to the position of store manager, which he held for 35 years. During that time, the company placed Joe at a number of different stores; they were always managed well and gave him the opportunity to mentor a number of young men and women who went on to successful careers. In Joe's final position, he supervised more than 100 people, and he doesn't believe any of the employees ever knew of his debilitating arm injury. That's the way he liked it.

Joe married his best friend Ellie well over four decades ago, and they live in their hometown of Adams. They have two sons who live nearby and four grandchildren. They both enjoy traveling and have been to Europe, Ireland, Costa Rica, and across the United States.

Joe was in the Marine Corps one year and seven months, including his seven months in Vietnam. Little did he realize at the time of his enlistment the effects this brief period would have on his entire life. As Joe reflects on his service, he acknowledges that he thought at the time we were fighting for South Vietnam's freedom, only to realize later in life that our government and its military leaders lied—or, worse, had no idea what they were doing. Joe's principal focus while in Vietnam was surviving and coming home. Initially when Joe returned home, he was angry with the anti-war protesters but not long after came to realize it was their right to do so. He was also disturbed by the TV show *M*A*S*H*, which although set during the Korean War seemed to mock front-line surgical units ... all too familiar to him.

When Joe enlisted, he explains, "[I] did what I thought was right." Today he often wears a Marine Corps baseball cap and displays a Purple Heart license tag on his truck. Joe's story is truly an amazing outcome: a young man, catastrophically wounded, who through sheer determination overcame adversity and adapted to civilian life as a successful businessman, husband, and father.

10

Ron Racine—Army Mortarman

Recipient of Combat Infantryman Badge, Bronze Star

It was so dark that Ron did not see the dead soldier. The incoming mortar bursts had initially affected his night vision, but after a few minutes, as he settled in, it adjusted, and he saw a man's body lying nearby. He was so close that Ron could touch him, but didn't.

After watching the soldier remain motionless, even with the deafening noise of supporting and incoming fire, Ron concluded that he was, indeed, dead. It looked like he had been recently hit. The dark stain on the ground underneath him seemed fresh, and although Ron couldn't see precisely where the man was hit, the size of the blotch was stark evidence that the soldier had bled out. He had fallen in an awkward position. His helmet was nearby and his flak jacket crunched underneath him.

Ron didn't know the soldier. He had been in Vietnam less than thirty days and knew few people.

The corpse gave Ron pause as he shifted into the same defensive position the dead soldier had almost certainly occupied. He spent a few seconds calculating how safe this spot would be before he began returning fire. There were no foxholes to crawl into, just a large log to hide behind. The log was eighteen inches tall and a foot thick, providing enough protection for Ron's body. But his personal safety zone became meaningless when he had to shoot over the log, exposing his face and upper body.

The night was inky dark, and the clouds blotted out the moon, although illumination rounds overhead provided enough light for him to spot any ghostlike figures trying to break through his area. He had a bandolier of M-16 ammunition plus his loaded magazines; he hoped it would be enough. The sergeant major stopped by, distributing the last of the hand grenades.

For the next several hours the soldiers exchanged fire with a VC sapper platoon attempting to breach the perimeter. Enemy mortar fire also continued and was particularly accurate this night.

Ron had arrived at LZ (landing zone) Bowman just three days before. Earlier this evening, the LZ was put on 100 percent alert, anticipating an attack at any moment. The company's sergeant major rushed all available soldiers to the perimeter, which pulled Ron away from his mortar-gun team. The base needed everyone's firepower. As a mortar team member, Ron had not expected to be manning the perimeter, serving as a rifleman, and waiting for an attack by a VC sapper platoon.

The LZ was heavily fortified. The brush surrounding it had been cut back to provide open fields of fire. The engineers surrounded the base with razor wire and "tanglefoot," an ankle-high level of barbed wire that crisscrossed the perimeter in a diamond-shaped manner. Also employed within the protective wire were Claymore mines and numerous trip flares.

What Ron didn't know at the time was that the VC were extremely agile and would often disable the Claymores and, in some cases, turn them around. The VC also tied off trip-flare spoons with elephant grass, eliminating their usefulness.

On this night, the sappers never breached the perimeter and were savagely cut down with barrages of gunfire. In the morning, they were found draped, lifeless, over the concertina wire. Around 6:00 a.m., the platoon commander ordered Echo Company to clear the enemy dead from their firing lanes and pile them in an open space near the command center.

There was one dead VC in front of Ron's position, and Ron wondered how to retrieve the dead enemy body entangled in the barbed wire. After a short time, a soldier came by and gave Ron a grappling hook tied to a rope to snag the dead body. He threw the hook a number of times, finally piercing the corpse and flipping it over. Ron then needed to wait a few minutes to ensure the body had not been booby trapped.

Once sufficient time had elapsed, they dragged the body forward to a safe place behind the firing position and placed it on plastic sheeting. Ron with three other soldiers carried him to the central gathering place. Bodies were being retrieved all around the perimeter. As they were transporting the dead VC, Ron noted that most of the man's leg had been torn off by a 50-caliber round and that he had a severe chest wound. He'd likely been killed instantly. Ron caught a faint yet pungent odor emitting from the corpse.

Once all the bodies and parts of bodies were gathered in one spot, a bulldozer dug a hole just outside the perimeter, and with help from others pushed, pulled, threw, and scraped the remains of the dead into the hole. They then saturated the bodies with diesel oil and set them afire. After just a short time, the bulldozer filled in the hole, covering the dead with tons of dirt.

Sometime during or after the assault, someone had retrieved the American soldier's body that had been elbow-to-elbow with Ron for most of the night. He never knew who retrieved it, nor did he find out the young man's name who had kept him company on that long vigil.

Early Life

Ron was born in January 1947 at Plunkett Memorial Hospital in Adams. He was an only child, and his parents were of French Canadian and Irish descent.

Ron's father, Albert, was a World War II veteran who served in the China/Burma/India theater of operations. He was in the Signal Corps and one of his responsibilities was to intercept Japanese messages. After his discharge from the Army, Albert worked as a machinist for many years at the local Sprague and General Electric companies. Albert also owned a bicycle and knife-sharpening shop where he worked evenings and weekends.

Anna, Ron's mother, first cooked for the Plunkett Memorial Hospital, then worked for 45 years at the Sprague Electric Company. She was jovial, thoughtful, fun to be around, and enjoyed cooking for her family. Some of her specialties were boiled corned beef and cabbage, roast lamb, chop suey, and delectable stews. Anna also was known for her extraordinary strawberry shortcakes. On occasion, the family enjoyed a new type of dining: Swanson TV dinners, served on innovative aluminum trays. Always the thrifty one, Anna canned many of the vegetables grown in their garden.

The family initially lived in Adams in a substantial home, built in the 1870s and owned by Ron's paternal grandparents who had a family of 12 children—seven boys and five girls. The white clapboard mansion was easily distinguishable from a distance by its size and a prominent white turret topped with a black ornate lightning rod. Its distinctive touches included latticework, carved wooden corners, and large fluted columns. The house was known as "Old Arcadia": rumor had it that at one time in the twenties or thirties, it had been a speakeasy. The space was divided into six apartments with three on the first floor and three on the second. Ron's parents were second-floor tenants.

The house sat on a large parcel of land that included a barn and at least five acres of planted vegetables. Ron spent considerable time with his grandfather cultivating tomatoes, corn, squash, strawberries, raspberries, and rhubarb—all intended for sale at their vegetable stand. By age 12, Ron was operating all the farm equipment, including the tractor. He readily acknowledges that his grandfather was one of the biggest influences on his life.

Ron's uncle also raised 3,000 chickens at a time, processing them through a three-story barn from incubation to slaughter. Ron vividly remembers the family working from 5:00 a.m. to 10:00 p.m. on processing day, turning poultry into meat to be sold from the back of his uncle's delivery truck.

Growing up, Ron's best friend was also named Ron, and his family the Szpilas also lived in the large white house. From an early age, the boys amused themselves outside. They hid in bushes and shook the limbs to simulate helicopters taking off or landing; played war games, hide-and-seek in the dark, and cowboys and Indians in the cavernous

Old Arcadia, ca. 2018. The home has always had an elegant presence, even with faded paint.

barn. One of their favorite pastimes was exploring the mountain right behind their house. They knew it as "Ragged Mountain," and it went for miles. They often scoured the hillsides for swinging vines, and after the briefest of "pull" tests decided which ones were safe. It seemed most were. They would swing from these vines over deep gullies and ravines, giving little consideration to potential dangers.

One time the two Rons climbed a huge sycamore tree in the front yard and after reaching the boast-worthy height of 50 to 60 feet became afraid to climb down. After many tense minutes, Mr. Szpila discovered their predicament and spent some time encouraging the boys' prolonged descent.

One of their favorite pastimes was playing baseball on the huge field in front of the barn. Ron, an only child, could be temperamental, and usually owned the baseballs, gloves, and bats. Since he controlled the equipment, the team needed to be sure not to anger him because if he got mad he would literally take his balls and go home.

In the winter in deep snow, hauling toboggans, sleds, or saucers, they would climb the mountain after school all the way to White Rock, one of their favorite haunts. Then they tobogganed back to the barn negotiating steep slopes and other natural barriers that added to their excitement. The downhill ride included zooming across a plateau, to become airborne for some distance. It was one of the greatest accomplishments if they could slide as far as the road and even better if they got to the other side without being hit by traffic! One successful slide begot another, and they would spend another 20 minutes trudging back up the mountain for their next. This occupied the boys until long after dark.

Ron lived in the big house until he was seven or eight years old. His dad then bought some acreage from his grandfather and built a home about 100 yards from the manor. The move kept the boys close, and as they got older led to some mischief. One time, as a Halloween prank, the boys covertly deflated the car tires of everyone living at the big house except for their own parents. They were promptly discovered, blamed, and punished. Come Christmas, dazzling decorative lights were too much of a temptation for two boys armed with a BB gun.

Early on, the boys wanted to communicate after dark and with some borrowed wire ran a line between the second story of the big house and Ron's new home. Cleverly, the walkie-talkie system included amp speakers with a toggle switch and individual microphones.

Ron's father wouldn't allow guns in the house, but the other Ron owned a .22 rifle and the boys used to meet high up on the mountain at "White Rock" and target shoot. Initially, they used cans or bottles, but gradually these shifted to sparrows, robins, chickadees, and trees. The chickadees would hop from branch to branch, oblivious to the deadly missiles until point of impact produced a puff of feathers. (It was at a brook near White Rock where they first experimented with cigarettes. Both got sick.)

The boys attended different high schools and would see each other after school, on weekends, or in the summer. Often they would watch TV—a phenomenon in the neighborhood, one of the first. They also entertained themselves with Ron's aquarium, played music on his record player, and listened to Ron playing his guitar.

Ron's father had built a milk box on the back porch so the milkman could place the quart bottles inside the box to keep them from freezing. It was a three-foot box with half of it sticking outside, half in. The milkman would push the bottles into the interior of the box, so they would get heat from the house. After school, if Ron Szpila arrived first, he would let himself into Ron's house by reaching through the milk box and unlocking the back door. He'd make himself at home, watch TV, or eat some cookies baked especially for him by Ron's mom.

Oftentimes Ron Szpila would find a place to hide in the house. He would hide in different closets or rooms and jump out and scare Ron. This became a routine between the boys, always scheming different ways to surprise each other. Once his friend put a tape recorder in a laundry basket, covered it with clothes, and was prepared to scare Ron with strange voices, but the plot was swiftly uncovered.

Ron Racine was bused to Saint Joseph's High School, in North Adams, about six miles' distance. He was the bus's last Adams pickup on the way out of town, and would normally stand in the crowded aisle talking with Al or Eddie, the alternating bus drivers, who lived in his neighborhood.

In high school, Ron was a guitarist for several bands. He played initially with the Hi-Tones, practicing weekly in band members' living rooms. When the Hi-Tones dissolved, the band re-formed as the Mustangs. The members purchased and wore black pants, sky-blue jackets with shiny black lapels and tiny roses embroidered into the fabric, along with heeled-and-pointed Beatle boots that hurt Ron's feet.

The band played three known times over several years of existence: once at the Polish Hall in Adams, and then two local Friday night teen dances. Their initial gig paid $25.00 for all five members. They had a limited repertoire of four songs with a special emphasis on "Wipe Out" by the Ventures. After a while, with little business and ongoing costs, the band happily dissolved. The group enjoyed its short lifespan, and the jackets.

Ron's car was an inexpensive 1959 two-tone blue Chevy Bel Air. It was his parents' car first, passed down to Ron in 1964. He only drove it on their property until he got his driver's license at 19.

His friends, Mike and Kenny, drove him to high school. When Ron graduated from St. Joe's in 1965, he began driving himself to McCann Technical School. After two years, he received a certification in machine technology. While at school, he supplemented his income working for Sprague Electric and at a local laundry company.

While attending McCann, Ron was exempt from the draft, but not for long; he knew his notice was imminent. Ron, now working at General Electric, knew he wanted to pick his branch of service rather than be drafted into the Army or Marine Corps and end up infantry. He took two different physicals for the Navy and flunked both because of a rash on his arms. Soon after that, the Army sent him a draft notice. He then took another physical and passed it. At this point he committed to a two-year enlistment.

When Army and Marine Corps recruiters were about to induct 30 local men including Ron, the Marine Corps recruiter had the men form a circle. Apparently short of recruits, he selected every other man to fill his quota. The men on both sides of Ron went into the Marine Corps, and Ron, on April 10, 1968, headed to Fort Dix, New Jersey, for nine weeks of Army basic training.

Ron's parents attended his graduation from basic training and were proud of what he had accomplished, yet became concerned when, on the same day, he was told of his new infantry-type MOS (military job specialty) and new assignment: He was headed for jungle training at Fort Polk. Mr. Racine wondered if he might be eligible for a deferment as an only son. It didn't matter: Ron was committed to serve his two years.

Ron's specific MOS was 11C (10), Indirect Firing Infantry—more simply put, a mortar man. At Fort Polk, Louisiana, in Advanced Infantry Training (AIT), the mortar men were trained on the 61mm and 81mm mortars, spending little time on the four deuce (107mm) heavy mortar. The group also received familiarization with the Light Antitank Weapon (LAW), the M-79 grenade launcher and other heavy weapons.

In escape and evasion training, Ron was the leader of a three-man POW group tasked with finding its way back to camp in the darkness without being captured. The group had a flashlight, compass, and map; the camp was five miles' distance. They successfully negotiated around the opposing force and all natural obstacles.

Once training was completed, Ron had a 30-day home leave and then started toward Vietnam, with stops in Washington State, Alaska, and Japan before arriving at the Cam Ranh Bay Naval Base in South Vietnam. His group, decked out in Army khakis, arrived in mid–September 1968. The stifling tropical heat yielded soddened, sweat-stained uniforms for all. Another week of processing found Ron flown to Chu Lai, a seaport city located in the Quang Nam province about 50 miles south of Da Nang, and then trucked to American Division Headquarters.

The replacements were then driven via a cargo truck to LZ Bayonet, headquarters of 198th Infantry Brigade. At this point, the group received individual assignments, and Ron was sent to LZ Bowman to join Echo company's four-deuce mortar platoon. He was now slightly inland from Chu Lai Air Base.

When Ron stepped off the Huey onto LZ Bowman, it was the beginning of his year-long exposure to a strange new world. From the air, he could see the base was denuded of foliage and heavily fortified. Ron was rapidly oriented, instructed that enemy attacks were always imminent, and warned death was never far away.

Almost as a confirmation, within 30 days Ron underwent his baptism by fire during the concerted all-night attack on the base. He would be awarded the Combat Infantryman's Badge for his actions that night.

LZ's and fire bases served a number of purposes. They acted as a center point from which to launch attacks on the enemy, provided heavy weapons support for nearby infantry troops, and in some cases were used as a lure or a nuisance to attract the enemy, hoping to annihilate them by superior firepower. The bases were located in strategic areas and often helped to interrupt VC and NVA troop movements. Usually an infantry company provided security.

LZ Bowman was an established fire base. There were hundreds of bases like this located throughout Vietnam. The base was in a remote area, cleared except for stumps, some grasses, foxholes, and bunkers. It resembled a barren moonscape with fine, red-clay dust swirling everywhere, kept in motion by volleys of cannon and mortar fire, strong cross winds, vehicle movements, and constant helicopter traffic.

July 1969: Ron (right) with a buddy from Hawaii, taking a quick break (courtesy Ron Racine).

The air was sticky, humid, ensuring that particles of dust penetrated clothing and invaded eyes, nose, and ears. Several areas of thick black smoke rose over the base, and early on Ron wondered if the base had been hit by enemy fire. As a new guy, it wouldn't be long before he was assigned to shit-burning detail, and discover that the smoke was a mixture of burning feces and diesel fuel after daily latrine duty.

A cacophony of noises came from vehicles, helicopters, artillery, and mortar barrages. It was a 24-hour, seven-days-a-week reality. Most bases had one or two helicopter landing zones, and while they could be resupplied by truck, helicopters were faster, generally safer, and provided additional firepower.

The base bristled with weaponry. Ron counted six 105mm howitzers, four 107mm mortars (4.2 inch, or "four deuce"), several 105 recoilless rifles, numerous M-60 machine guns, at times a quad .50-caliber machine gun, and individual arms like M-16 rifles and 40mm grenade launchers.

Ron and his squad manned a heavy mortar that was a muzzle-loaded, rifled, high-angle weapon. Its long-range, high-trajectory rounds were considered safer than direct artillery fire and often preferred by infantry units. While infantry units had smaller mortars with them, they did not have the destructive force nor range of the 4.2. The gun weighed more than 600 pounds and could be fired at a rate of 18 rounds per minute, and over three miles in any direction.

Ron had been trained for weeks on smaller/lighter mortars but when he reached Vietnam he was immediately assigned to the heavy mortar platoon. Through the briefest

Ron (center) and his mortar team preparing for a fire mission (courtesy Ron Racine).

Called "mortar cheese" charges because they resemble slices of American cheese, their purpose is to increase the distance the round will travel: the more cheese, the farther the round is propelled (courtesy Ron Racine).

orientations and some immediate on-the-job training, he quickly learned the intricacies of the four deuce. Ron would remain with heavy mortars his entire tour.

LZ Bowman, the base Ron served on, was created like many other bases. Bulldozers scraped the undergrowth back 75 to 100 meters, providing early visual detection of the enemy and clear firing lanes to repel them. The dozers also created an earthen berm around the base for additional security and elevated firing positions.

This fire base was surrounded by side-by-side coils of concertina wire, with another coil attached to the top of them. Then tanglefoot crisscrossed throughout the concertina wire. Claymore mines strategically placed along the perimeter interlocked with other mines providing a broad swath of protection for the defenders. The claymores were capable of spewing out 700 metal balls over a kill zone six feet high and 50 yards wide.

The soldiers set the mines at dusk and retrieved them at dawn. Often they would find them tampered with or turned around, positioned to fire on them. The base also deployed trip flares amidst the concertina wire, which provided early warning of an enemy attack and the visibility to see the insurgents. The flares were in cans a little smaller than soup cans, about two inches in diameter, with a trip wire attached to the triggering spoon.

Ron's gun platoon was dug in on the side of a ridge line, and he was assigned to the second gun squad. Each mortar platoon had four heavy mortars with one squad assigned to each. The squads were comprised of a squad leader, assistant gunner, and three or four ammunition bearers.

The platoon's four guns were staggered 100 feet apart, rising up the slope. Ron, who was on the second gun, was far enough away that he could not see the fourth gun at the top of the hill. The mortar platoon was part of Echo Company, which also had a recon platoon and a ground surveillance section. The company also provided a forward observer to each one of the infantry companies it supported (A, B, C, and D companies) and staffed the fire direction center (FDC) with four soldiers.

When infantry companies needed mortar fire, the forward observers embedded with the company would call LZ Bowman's FDC requesting illumination or protective fire, and provided the center with the enemy coordinates, friendly troop locations, and the type and numbers of rounds requested. The center would relay the request, via phone, to the nearby mortar squads.

Ron's assignment to heavy mortars meant that he kept busy with daily gun maintenance and calibration to ensure accuracy. The guns themselves were comprised of the angled mortar cannon, three add-on assemblies, and a mortar baseplate, upon which the components rested.

The guns were set up carefully with the baseplate firmly ground, ensuring there were no stones underneath it. Once the gun was assembled, the squad used two six-foot, red-and-white striped iron stakes to align their gun sights. Once all four guns were assembled and aligned, the platoon sergeant would "register" all four guns to ensure himself of their calibration.

Guns and ammunition stockpiles were kept in sandbagged bunkers. Ron was fortunate that his gun's bunkers were already built, although with the adverse weather and the limited life span of sandbags, it wasn't long before he found himself rebuilding. It was hot, dirty, heavy work. First, the deteriorated sandbags had to be pulled down and emptied and replaced with new bags filled with dirt or sand. Most bunkers were made up of thousands of sandbags, and rebuilding took days by the entire squad. The squad also needed to deal with hundreds of aggressive rats who had nests throughout the bunkers. Some squads kept track of their daily "kills."

The squad would use green, plastic sandbags which had loose, broad threads and were slippery to stack. Often they would use ammunition boxes to build walls on each side of the sandbags to prevent them from falling. Each mortar usually had a circular sandbag bunker about four feet high with a radius that allowed the squad to maintain, load, adjust, and fire the gun. Adjacent to the mortar bunker, the squad created an ammunition bunker that housed the shells. Often this bunker was open-faced to allow immediate access to the rounds, and sometimes the bunker would be constructed with a pass-through opening for the ammo bearers.

For the next 11 months, Ron's personal quarters would be underground in a 12-by-12-foot bunker shared with his seven squad mates. Incoming mortar barrages inspired great effort and ingenuity: Most living quarter bunkers were started by digging a nine-foot hole in the ground, 12 feet square. Next the builders would use 12-foot creosoted timbers, usually filched from the helipad, for corner posts and overhead beams. The beams were placed in the nine-foot holes with three feet remaining above ground. Interior walls were created by using empty ammunition boxes filled with dirt and held in place by fence stakes. The exposed section above ground was walled with more ammo boxes and finished off with three layers of sandbags. Roofs were covered with steel planking

A tired Ron in front of the pass-through at the ammo bunker. The poster is of General Custer (courtesy Ron Racine).

and three layers of sandbags. The floors were dirt, although some creative soldiers had cumshawed enough plywood for the walls and flooring.

After all this, Ron preferred sleeping outside, never in his bunker, usually on a cot nearby. The enemy was known to throw satchel charges through bunker apertures, and he did not want to be trapped inside. If his squad had night duty, he would sleep inside during the daylight hours. He rapidly adjusted and could sleep through nearby firings.

Ron's initiation on LZ Bowman oriented him to the requirements of belonging to a mortar crew. In a constant state of readiness, the mortar squad would unseal, take the projectiles out of cardboard canisters and prepare and attach the 2×2 gunpowder packets to the base of the round. The number of explosive packets was correlated to the distance requested.

One squad was always prepared to respond to immediate requests and usually had between 60 and 80 illumination rounds ready for immediate use. Eighty percent of their fire missions were at night, supporting two infantry companies, operating in the surrounding jungle. Most often the rifle companies requested illumination flares, which had small parachutes attached to them, so the flare provided brightness as it slowly fell to the ground.

There was also a high demand for 25-pound high explosive (HE) rounds. This particular round provided a 50-meter killing radius and, when all four guns fired, would saturate an area 50 by 200 yards. This was done with accuracy from over three miles away. The infantry units preferred the mortar's high trajectory shelling versus cannon fire, finding its arc a safer choice of bombardment. Ron's team also used smoke rounds for targeting and occasionally white phosphorus shells (known as Willy Peter) for enemy targets in the open.

The mortar squads were often ordered to fire high explosive rounds on pre-registered areas of VC travel. The concept of H&I (harassing and interdicting fire) had been used in Vietnam for years. With U.S. units stationary in their night locations, the idea was to keep the enemy off balance, at least from moving around comfortably. The mortars would target paths, roads, and intersections where VC activity was known to occur.

Ron's platoon fired their mortars daily to ensure they were registered. The number 2 gun was the first to fire, and the others followed. After firing every round, the team would realign the guns' sights to ensure continued accuracy. During this process, if the base plate had shifted, the squad would re-sight the gun on the aiming stakes, and prepare for the next volley of fire.

During a live-fire mission, the forward observers who worked with the infantry companies would request, via the FDC, a smoke round to identify the exact area to be barraged. After observing the area impacted, the observer would make any necessary adjustments and then request all four mortars to "fire for effect." This barrage continued until the enemy threat was eliminated.

In January 1969, Ron's mortar platoon was moved to LZ Professional, a firebase built on a small hill about 200 feet wide and a quarter-mile long. This LZ brought them closer to Laos and the famed Ho Chi Minh Trail, a redoubt and resupply highway for the North Vietnamese Army.

The squad spent a lot of time building and reinforcing bunkers. The platoon's four mortars were set up in a square about 50 to 60 feet apart with interconnecting trenches. Ron could see the other squads but not necessarily the guns.

With two of the battalion's rifle companies scouring the nearby jungle for NVA, Ron's mortar platoon was kept busy with fire missions. The squad was often on 100 percent alert—answering requests for illumination flares, too many to count. During their two-plus-month assignment the crews repelled a VC sapper group, killing 15 enemy.

In March, Echo Company moved to LZ Baldy for 30 days. While the conditions were still Spartan, the large base provided more security, a break in combat, and almost an informal rest & relaxation: They weren't under fire for the entire month.

Ron and his unit moved to LZ Stinson in April and remained there until his departure in August 1969. During these four months, the LZ was hit numerous times. Sapper units continued to try and breach the perimeter and get at the command center as well as blow up the artillery. They usually hit the hill at the dark of the moon. Instinctively, the soldiers' anxiety heightened as the nights got darker.

Ron and a group of six other soldiers patrolled the perimeter and were charged with killing any enemy that got into the LZ. They fired a lot of illumination flares, and at one point called in "Puff the Magic Dragon," an AC-130 gunship with Gatling guns to "hose" down the perimeter and push back the enemy. It could lay down lethal barrages of thousands of rounds per minute. When the gunship arrived on-station, it was shooting so close to friendly troops that everyone was told to hug their foxhole walls until the barrage subsided. The enemy was repelled and fire base life went on.

Fire Base Living

Even in the midst of a deadly environment, fire bases provided humorous and distracting anecdotes on occasion. Potable water, a scarce commodity, was delivered to fire bases in large metal wheeled containers known as "water buffaloes." Bases received their "buffalo" deliveries slung under helicopters. With consistent deliveries, soldiers were allotted five gallons each per day for drinking, cooking and showers.

Showers were not taken in any regular pattern, and they often occurred during a rainstorm, during which troops lathered up in public and used the rain for their rinse cycle. Sometimes they would use a two-and-a-half-quart canvas shower bag suspended from a tree limb to cleanse themselves. The ultimate shower stall would be three-sided with a saloon-like door. A 55-gallon drum, suspended overhead, would capture rainwater and erratically dispense cold trickles. The shower heads were often punctured rubber gloves.

Personal needs such as showers, toilets and mess halls were Spartan, nonexistent, or improvised. Small, aboveground shacks housed four seated commodes (known as four-holers). Once a week, the commode receptacles (55-gallon drums cut in half) needed to be emptied. This was accomplished by two or three reluctant participants, some diesel fuel and matches. The waste, when soaked with fuel, burnt quite readily and created huge dark clouds.

Some fire bases had mess halls, but very few. Fire base meals were usually C rations or lukewarm chow flown in by helicopters in insulated aluminum Mermite containers.

Usually during the daylight hours, the fire base was fairly quiet. Most missions occurred at night. There was always the noise of resupply helicopters, although they had become part of the background.

Ron's 40-plus platoon members received frequent sundry packages that contained three boxes. The smoking box had ten cartons of cigarettes (Marlboro and Winston preferred), and pipe and chewing tobacco. The candy box contained Hershey's "tropical bars," distinguished by a tan wrapper. They were super dense and hard so they wouldn't melt. Ron liked them because they tasted like dark chocolate, but they were hard as hell to bite. Lastly, the hygiene box contained soap, toothbrushes and paste, razors, razor blades, and combs.

Jungle utilities (uniforms) were laundered in several different ways. At some fire bases the platoon would pile their dirty clothes in a central spot. Once collected, they were placed in a large bag and flown to the rear to be washed. The clothes would return in the same way, and since none were marked, the soldiers could grab clothes that looked like they fit. Most times Ron would wash his own clothes using a plastic-lined ammo box, pouring in water, using octagon soap as a detergent, and scrubbing the fabric over the ammo box lid. A change of water provided the rinse cycle. Drying in the hot climate occurred when you put the clothes back on.

For their dress code, most fire base occupants favored bare torsos or green t-shirts with jungle trousers and boots. Few ever wore underclothes due to the humidity. Helmets and flak jackets were worn during alerts or trips outside the wire. Usually all clothing, after a short while, took on a reddish hue from the clay dirt and blowing dust. Skin absorbed the reddish color too, which could only be purged by repeated warm showers on R&R or when a soldier returned home.

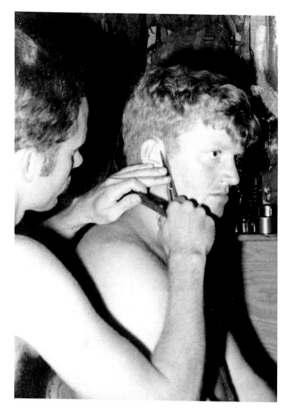

Ron was lucky to have a former barber in his squad (courtesy Ron Racine).

The most basic hygiene elements (showers, laundry, food) were available in primitive ways, vastly different from what Ron was used to, and yet he felt lucky compared to the infantrymen who lived outside the wire with none of these amenities.

During the day, once the guns were registered, sandbags filled, brush cleared, and shitters burnt, then crews could play cards, write letters, or play football. Sometimes the squads would engage in horseshoe contests using converted metal pieces retrieved from ammunition boxes for horseshoes. They'd set up pits about 15 feet apart.

Card games were most popular—poker, hearts, pinochle, spades and whist—to pass the time. Three card "guts" involved the most hopeful gamblers. Players anted, bet on cards turned over one by one, with the loser matching the pot.

Midway through Ron's tour, he purchased a 35-millimeter Minolta camera and began a photography hobby. The fire base was a rich resource for capturing landscape and everyday pictures of men at war. He particularly enjoyed capturing the many types of helicopters that resupplied his base. On a humorous note, he would take close-up pictures of playboy pinups and send the life-like pictures to his friends, suggesting a closer relationship than was possible on base.

The squad looked for ways to improve their food rations, and one time, out of kindness (or more likely necessity), invited a mess hall sergeant to the card game. The sergeant lost his money, but was grateful for the open invitation to play cards, and from then on, the squad feasted on the frozen chicken diverted from the mess hall to their bunker.

Ron's platoon was also at the center of obtaining and selling cases of beer. They would engage a Chinook helicopter from headquarters to deliver a pallet of beer plus 50 pounds of ice to their fire base. A pallet contained 80 cases, with 24 cans per case. Depending on the quality of the beer, the pallet would cost as high as $300. The squads would then sell the cases of beer at a significant markup, allowing them to schedule and prepay for their next delivery. Certain beers that were considered premium such as Budweiser and Schlitz would cost more per case. (Soft drinks were only $80 a pallet.)

On another occasion, Ron was bringing in a mortar to the rear, via helicopter, for calibration. After the gun was inspected and loaded on the helicopter to return to base, Ron and another trooper noticed a brand-new generator nearby and

At LZ Professional, enjoying a beer during a break (courtesy Ron Racine).

absconded with it to the helicopter. After returning to their base, they bought a TV, and through the Armed Forces Vietnam Network began watching *Star Trek*, *The Rowan and Martin Comedy Hour*, and *Friday Night Fights*.

When Ron was on LZ Stinson, the enemy noticed a lot of activity around a small plywood building. It didn't take long before the shack was targeted and destroyed by enemy mortars. The enemy may have presumed it was an active command center but in fact it was a four-hole latrine shack. There were no casualties.

Near the end of his tour, Ron was promoted to sergeant and became a squad leader. His quiet nature, attention to detail, and desire to do the right thing worked very well with most of his squad. There was one soldier, a drug user, who tested his good nature by defecating in the squad's bunker. Ron was irate, and his friend in the fourth squad recalls encountering Ron, armed with his M-16 rifle, searching for the miscreant. They stopped and talked for a while, and Ron calmed down. The soldier was sent to another LZ.

Ron's time in-country was down to 15 days, and as was the custom for "short timers," he was reassigned to LZ Bayonet and safer duties. Ron assumed mail distribution duties and flew daily to other LZs passing out the mail. He was relieved of mortar responsibilities and enjoyed his last few days in Vietnam cooking emancipated chickens, drinking beer, and watching movies. It was a distinct change from his prior eleven and a half months.

Ron remembers boarding the plane to begin the trip back to the United States. It was deathly quiet while the plane was taxiing, but once it became airborne the cheering was raucous. Ron flew home in August 1969 from Cam Ranh Bay to Fort Lewis, Washington, where his group arrived in jungle fatigues. As they passed through a long warehouse, they started to strip off their filthy clothes, and by midway through they were naked. As they continued with processing, they were given new clothing, and the end result was a clean-cut Army man dressed out in Class A uniform. Then he had breakfast, flew to Newark, New Jersey, and was bused to Hartford, Connecticut, where his mom and dad picked him up. Upon returning home, Ron discovered that he had been awarded the Bronze Star for meritorious Vietnam service.

After his leave, Ron was stationed at Fort Carson, Colorado, until April 1970, when he was released from active duty. For his last six months of duty, Ron was assigned to a mortar platoon as a squad leader on a mechanized armored personnel carrier (APC). This mobilization of mortars was quite different from his stationary duties in Vietnam. There was a lot to share with junior soldiers to acclimate them before heading off to war. He was proud of his contribution.

Coming Home

Ron was released from the Army eight months after returning from Vietnam. He found himself quieter, more in control of his temper, and focused on returning to work, getting married, and starting a family. His girlfriend had sent him a Dear John letter four months before he returned from Vietnam. Not troubled by this, when Ron returned home, his aunt recommended a nice young girl with whom she worked at a nursing home. Ron called the girl and asked her to go to a New Year's Eve party, and the blind date turned into something serious.

Ron and Anne were married in 1972 and celebrated their 47th wedding anniversary in 2019. They lived in Adams for a short while, moved to Clarksburg, and then settled in North Adams where they have lived in their current home for many years. Their two children and grandchildren live nearby.

Ron returned to his position at General Electric and worked there twenty-seven years as a machinist group leader at their Pittsfield and Albany facilities. Ron also worked evenings and weekends with his dad at their cycle and knife-sharpening shop. When the family shop closed in 1980, Ron, who enjoys keeping busy, worked two additional jobs in addition to his General Electric position: He helped out at a local furniture store and participated in National Guard meetings.

After his release from active duty he joined and rejoined the National Guard a number of times and ultimately was released in 1984. Then, in 1991, as part of the Individual Ready Reserve, Ron was recalled to serve in Desert Storm (at age 44) and had to report to Fort Benning, Georgia. After several weeks of processing, he was deployed to Germany for 21 days of additional mortar training. Part-way through the additional training, the Desert Storm mission ended, and he returned home about three months later.

In the 1990s he left GE to work for the Crane Company as an engraver, printer, and finally supervisor, a position he held until his retirement in 2010. Both Ron and Anne enjoy similar craft hobbies. They enjoy crocheting and knitting, and Anne also likes ceramics. At times, he works on a loom making scarfs for sale at the local artisans' shop. Over the years, Ron also acquired the art of working with stained glass. He continues to love music and has taken fiddle and violin lessons.

His close friends described him a "straight up" guy, reliable, not boisterous, and a solid friend. Some note that after his return from Vietnam he was quieter, less spontaneous, more likely to keep to himself and uninterested in talking about Vietnam.

As of late, he's been thinking of the parallels between the games he played growing up and his Vietnam service. The boys embraced the farm's acres to play war games, simulate helicopter landings, and set up mortars to repel encroaching enemies. He is proud of his service, but after reading more about Vietnam has concluded the politicians didn't know what they were doing, nor cared about the soldiers. Towards the end of the war, he felt, the South Vietnamese didn't even want us there.

Ron's life has been one of hard work and honesty, rewarded with a craftsman's natural ability, whether making stained glass, weaving scarves, or playing his violin. He has a quiet nature, is fun to be with, and readily admits to, occasionally, possessing an Irish stubbornness.

11

Pat Lupo—Army
Mechanized Infantryman

Recipient of Combat Infantryman Badge, Bronze Star, Purple Heart;
Wounded-in-Action 1-14-1967

Something hammered his right shoulder, spun him around, knocked him to the ground, and caused him to drop his M-16. It was a hard blow, like a severe open-handed slap. Initially he felt no pain, although was momentarily stunned.

As he struggled to his feet, Pat looked at his right arm, saw that his jungle fatigues were saturated, and felt a rush of fluid gushing down his arm. He realized he was bleeding but didn't want to look directly at the wound. A successful digit-test, touching each finger to his thumb, reassured him that it might not be too bad.

Then it dawned on him that he'd been shot on his right side, which meant by friendly troops. Pat started yelling, "Stop firing, Stop firing!" At first there was no response over the deafening firefight. Then came a lull. Nearby soldiers heard Pat shouting and slowed their rate of fire. Several soldiers saw Pat stumbling and rushed to help him.

The night had begun with the camp on 100 percent alert when Army intelligence indicated there would be an attempt to overrun the base. The officer-in-charge decided to bolster perimeter defenses by adding support soldiers—cooks, clerks—to the perimeter. They rushed in darkness to the edge of the camp with little instruction. Although marginally trained in the art of war, they provided the line with extra firepower and began returning fire almost immediately.

Unbeknownst to the leaders, several of the support personnel got confused in the pitch-black and settled into firing positions meters behind the actual perimeter. When the NCO heard a large volume of firing coming from the group of novices, he asked Pat, who had been in-country several months, to check on them. As Pat walked the line, several of the soldiers that were mis-positioned opened fire on him.

Pat was hit with a 7.62mm round just above and on the outside of his right elbow. The bullet passed through his arm without hitting the bone and did not hit his torso. Soldiers bandaged him, supported him to a nearby Jeep, and whisked him off to a collection area for the wounded. He was then airlifted to a nearby tent hospital and triaged.

Pat, still bleeding profusely, was not considered an emergency patient, yet it wasn't long before he was placed on a dried, bloody stretcher and brought in to a dimly lit, bustling operating room. The medics placed his stretcher on sawhorses. While they prepared to work on him, Pat noticed a soldier on an adjoining stretcher who had lost his leg. The young man was bleeding into his stretcher, and his blood overflowed onto the floor. The medical team worked feverishly to stabilize him. Pat also noticed eight VC being worked on, but remembers little after that because moments later he was IV'ed, anesthetized, and operated on.

Pat woke up late and groggy the next morning to find himself in pain, heavily bandaged, and lying in a tent with many other wounded soldiers. In a way, he felt fortunate that the wound was through-and-through (the bone was not hit) and did not involve any ancillary nerve or tendon damage. Two weeks later, he was released to his unit on light duty for two additional weeks. He was happy to be in the rear and off the line for almost a month. He never knew who shot him, and after he healed, felt sorry for the new guy and thought he probably should have thanked him for his extended trip off the front lines.

Pat was wounded in March 1967, early in his tour of duty. At the time, he didn't realize that his remaining nine months in Vietnam would be no less harrowing and provide the backdrop for many more close calls.

Early Years

Pasquale (Pat) Lupo was born in January 1947, right at the beginning of the Baby Boomer era. He was delivered at the North Adams Hospital to proud parents of Italian lineage. His paternal grandfather was born in Caggiano, Italy, a small thousand-year-old mountain town not far from Naples. His maternal grandparents both emigrated from Naples.

Angelo, Pat's father, served in the Army during World War II as a military policeman in London. Upon his discharge, he returned stateside and opened Lupo's Shoe Repair on Eagle Street in North Adams next door to the long-standing, beloved (and still existing) Jack's Hot Dogs. The shoe business was brisk, and Angelo ran the shop for 20 years. He also worked at Sprague Electric Company for ten years. Angelo died in 1991, and Pat credits him with being a major influence on his life in understanding the value of hard work and perseverance.

Olympia, Pat's mom, is alive, well, and 104 years old. She lived with her only son in Adams for many years and only recently moved to a rest home. Ever-resourceful, he was able to convert an old pair of his hearing aids for his mom to use.

Her other child, Angela, passed away from cancer some years ago. Olympia worked for many years at the Wall Streeter Shoe Company in North Adams as a vamper, on piecework, stitching together shoe parts. She was vibrant and untiring, often picking up groceries on her long walk home from work. Olympia was a great cook, and her Friday no-meat specialties were either "aglio e olio" with pasta or fried bread dough. At times, she would be frustrated with Pat's picky eating habits and his fondness for such banal foods as peanut butter and baloney. Pat's mom was frugal, and in the little spare time she had, Olympia made her own clothes. She was somewhat quiet and reserved, but Pat remembers her being very upset when the landlord wanted to increase their apartment rent from $22 a month to $24.

The Lupos lived on Furnace Street in North Adams, an Italian enclave ("Little Italy" they called it then), about a mile from Main Street. The hillside area had four corner markets that catered primarily to Italian families. Families had small gardens, and at dusk you would find most people outside socializing with their neighbors. Pat's grandfather owned a three-story apartment house made of brick and grey clapboard; the Lupo family lived in the third-floor apartment, with his grandparents on the second floor. Initially, the grandfather ran a soda-making business on the first floor, but converted it to an apartment just before Pat was born.

Their apartment was simple and did not have a shower or bathtub until Pat was eight or nine years old. He took weekly tub baths in the kitchen with water heated on the stove. His dad showered at the local YMCA on the way home from work, and Mom refreshed herself in the kitchen sink. It was memorable when the landlord installed a metal shower in the mid–1950s. In keeping with the times, his mom used a wringer/washer, and the family had a three-digit phone number.

With Mom and Dad working, Pat was free to roam with his friends after school and in the summers. His mom would tell him to be home when the street lights came on. Pat hung around with neighborhood kids—Bobby, Kenny, Joe, Dennis, and Eddie. In the summer, the boys spent a lot of time at Noel Field located at the bottom of their hill. Depending on the season, the boys would join pickup baseball or football games at the field. The field would also have crafts and other amusements supervised by local college kids. As they grew older, the boys would play "penny ante" poker in the grandstands, ride bikes up and down their hill, roam in the woods, and hop freight trains in the nearby rail yard. If they needed to get somewhere, aside from their bikes, they could easily "thumb" a ride. They played train tag, climbing idle train cars and jumping roof-to-roof. The only rule was that their feet could not touch the ground.

Most summer nights the boys headed to Prenguber's bakery to buy 25¢ grinder rolls and then devour them while sitting nearby on the long set of stairs between Aldo's Paint Shop and the barber shop. On occasion, some of the boys would conduct late night raids on neighbors' gardens, bringing their own salt, and taking only as many tomatoes as they could eat.

One time the boys snuck in to Modern Dairy, a local milk and ice cream plant, and liberated a large metal urn of ice cream. Even with seven spoons, it took a long time to finish it off.

During wintertime, the city would flood the baseball diamond at Noel Field for community skating, and the boys spent considerable time there on Friday nights and weekends. When it snowed, they would rally at the top of Furnace Street and slide between apartment houses all the way down to State Street. After the first snow was packed down, their speeds would increase, making downhill runs all the more thrilling. The boys would use sleds, single ski sit-down jumpers, and with his grandfather's help one boy even fashioned an early snowboard, two-and-a-half feet long.

As Pat grew older he became interested in hunting and would climb the hill behind his house for a short trek to the woods. The woods were called the "notch" and provided great bird and rabbit hunting for the young sportsman.

During high school, right after classes, Pat would work at his dad's shop shining shoes and waiting on customers. At the time, Pat was not a good speller and often misspelled customer names. Much to his dad's consternation, this made it hard to match receipts with customers picking up their repairs. He also caddied at the North Adams Country Club, worked at JJ Newberry's as stock clerk and janitor, and at the Four Acre Restaurant as a dishwasher.

The job he enjoyed most was working and skiing at Dutch Hill in Heartwellville, Vermont. This mid-sized ski area was 12 miles from North Adams—about a twenty-minute car ride. Pat taught skiing, was on the Ski Patrol, and at 18 became a professional ski instructor. One of his daydreams was for skiing to be his life's work. He was disappointed to realize that seasonal, part-time skiing work would not support him.

After high school Pat bought his first vehicle, a 1948 Jeep, for $400. He and his dad joked that they bought the Jeep at night, under a bridge, from a shady character; seen in daylight, the Jeep was in bad shape. Pat's dad gave it a quick brush-paint in a military-green and used his cobbler skills to fashion leather seats. They never did resolve why the vehicle shook when it hit 45 miles an hour. Pat was lucky in these years: One time, he and five friends were joyriding in Vermont after dark. Unable to negotiate a tight turn, and maybe traveling too fast, the car flipped several times with no injuries to its occupants.

After high school, Pat enrolled in some secondary courses at a local technical school, and when he stopped attending classes so he could ski, he almost immediately received his draft notice. Pat went to the second floor of the local post office, completed his paperwork, and entered the Army in July 1966. His basic training was at Fort Dix, followed by eight weeks of jungle training at Fort Polk. Within five months he would be in Vietnam assigned to the 1st Infantry Division also known as the "Big Red One." Pat's military designation would be 11B (Bravo) infantryman.

Vietnam: Too Many Close Calls

After training and home leave, Pat left for Vietnam. His trip was circuitous, starting in Albany, New York, then to JFK airport in New York City, on to San Francisco, then

Alaska and Japan, finally landing at the Tan Son Nhut Air base in Saigon. His group of soldiers was placed in a holding area while the Army determined permanent assignments. As casualties mounted, he didn't need to wait long before he was then helicoptered to the base camp of 1st Infantry Division's Headquarters in Lai Khe. He was assigned to the 2nd Brigade, 2nd Battalion, Echo Company, 3rd Platoon. One of his first memories as a replacement was receiving his military equipment and refusing to accept a helmet covered with blood. For a new guy, this was an inauspicious beginning. He recalls that his newly issued M-16 rifle continued to jam, and he was able to replace it with a Winchester 12-gauge shotgun. The shotgun used double-aught buckshot and provided him with a more secure feeling for close-in action.

Pat remembers a few stories from his first week in-country: two in particular demonstrate his resourcefulness. Once when he anticipated being placed on mess hall cleanup, he grabbed a mop and began swabbing for just a few minutes before, as expected, a non-commissioned officer entered the mess hall and said it was time for others to do their share of swabbing; Pat was relieved of duty. Another time, when Pat got to his tent he noticed that any man with night-guard duty had a sign hanging on his bunk allowing him to sleep during the day. Pat deftly "found" one of those signs and ensured himself of a late morning sleep-in.

In more peaceful times, Lai Khe had been an active rubber plantation managed by the French. The Army had converted the area into a small city with two long airstrips

Pat (left) enjoying a drink with two buddies at a fire base bar (courtesy Pat Lupo).

that could support the landing of cargo planes. (As a Vietnam oddity, many rubber trees still grew at their base camp on Lai Khe, and U.S. forces were obliged to compensate the French owners for damages caused to the trees during military operations.)

The base also contained two helicopter landing zones, a large ammunition dump, heavy mortar and artillery areas, and screened-in, tin-roofed hootches with cots or steel beds and maybe even mattresses, a luxury when troops returned from the field. The base mess hall prepared at least one hot meal a day. In the field, when it was safe, a hot meal might be flown out. Daily living was primitive but still immeasurably better than jungle conditions. Infrequently, cold showers were available that enabled most to take four or five showers over 12 months (not including the ad hoc ones, in rainstorms with a bar of soap).

Pat's unit operated in III Corps in an area northwest of Saigon up and into Cambodia. Most of their operations occurred around the towns of Ben Cat, Phuoc Vinh, An Loc, and Tay Ninh in the dangerous vicinity of the Black Virgin Mountains.

When in the field, Pat's unit often received one lukewarm meal flown-in daily. Laundry in the field involved stripping off rotted clothes and rummaging through a bag of jungle uniforms that had been airdropped. The men would look for a close-enough fit and the rotted uniforms were sent to the rear to be burnt or cleaned.

Pat was fortunate that most of the members within his squad had at least six months' combat experience. He came to realize that their combined expertise would save him from making serious, if not fatal, mistakes. Just after his arrival he heard that the former company commander and radio operator had been killed days before by a booby trap, reinforcing for him how dangerous the environment was.

Little time was spent at base camp. Pat's unit would normally spend 30 days in the field, returning to base camp for two days of resupply. Shortly after Pat's arrival, the division went "mechanized infantry" and received Armored Personnel Carriers (APC) to transport soldiers to battle. The APCs, known as M113s, were boxy, low silhouetted, oblong, tracked armored vehicles. They had excellent mobility, and were amphibious, although used almost exclusively on land. The M113s had a crew of two: driver and gunner. It was designed as a "battlefield taxi" to deliver 11 infantrymen safely to their area of operation.

The vehicle had one-inch aluminum armor thick enough to protect the crew and passengers from small arms fire, although susceptible to land and anti-tank mines. For this reason, contrary to its pur-

Back at the fire base, Pat and a friend who was later killed in action are preparing to go into the ville. Here, the APC looks roomy but the ramp folds up right by Pat's leg (courtesy Pat Lupo).

pose, most soldiers rode atop the vehicle. Often the APCs had several layers of sandbags around the top to provide protection and firing rests for the infantry passengers. Other modifications included metal shielding for the exposed driver and gunner. Its main armament was a .50-caliber machine manned by the gunner. Pat would act as a gunner for most of his remaining time in Vietnam. Although his unit would cover a lot of territory during those months, seldom did Pat or his squad know where they were or where they were going.

Over the course of the next ten months, Pat's unit would be involved in Operation Junction City and Operation Paul Bunyan and participate in the many battles in support of these massive operations, including the Battle of Prek Kloc. The company and its vehicles normally operated in open terrain, such as farming areas, rice paddies and areas covered with elephant grass. Seldom did they operate in hilly areas. Pat vividly remembers how the weather could transform from exceptionally high temperatures to continuous rain, coming down in sheets just twenty feet away, almost like a wall, before enveloping him.

One night while in the rear, when they had just finished hanging a large sheet between two rubber trees for a makeshift movie screen, explosions were heard nearby. Initially, Pat's squad presumed it was outgoing artillery rounds, until the explosions came closer and they realized the noises were incoming enemy mortars. Everyone scrambled to nearby bunkers. Pat inadvertently dove into a nearby bunker only to realize he had chosen an ammunition bunker for his sanctuary. Fearing the closing rounds were targeting the bunker and processing the risk of staying where he was, Pat sprinted to another bunker, some distance from his first choice.

Early in the Junction City operation, Pat's APC along with several others was sent to patrol a nearby roadway to keep it clear of Viet Cong trying to plant mines and to protect an airfield under construction by Army engineers. At the patrol's completion, and with the approach of dusk, they returned to their base and were met by enemy mortar fire. The sporadic fire quickly turned into a full assault. The commander pulled their APC on-line, in a stationary position, and Pat began providing .50-caliber machine gun fire support. Pat was sitting in the turret, legs drawn up, returning fire with the machine gun.

The driver, inside the vehicle, was getting more ammunition for Pat when a Viet Cong guerrilla, who had managed to sneak within forty feet of the vehicle and was hiding behind a fallen tree, fired a recoilless rifle, hitting the APC in the side.

The explosive round hit the driver in the right shoulder and blew up between Pat's legs and right in front of his face. Thinking the APC was about to explode from all the onboard munitions, Pat jumped off, scrambled to a nearby bunker, called for a medic, and continued to return fire with an M-79 grenade launcher. The seriously wounded driver was treated and medevaced. Unknown to Pat at the time, the recoilless rifle round had hit the vehicle's fire extinguisher lessening its explosive force, reducing the chance of a fire and saving Pat from a mortal wound.

The siege went on all night with helicopter gunships supporting the soldiers, and mortars providing a continuous barrage of flares. As morning arrived, the battlefield became quiet except for occasional sniper firing. The Viet Cong that had disabled Pat's APC was draped over the log from whence he had fired, with numerous bullet holes in his body. Pat observed that smoke was coming from some of the holes, those created by tracer rounds.

Pat in the gunner's position (courtesy Robert Fazio).

The troopers were ordered to gather the bodies, lay them in a row, and thoroughly search them for intelligence. They then loaded over 100 VC bodies into cargo trucks. Blood flowed out from underneath the truck's tailgate almost like water off a garbage truck as they were driven off a short distance to be buried. A bulldozer arrived, dug a large hole, pushed the bodies into it and covered them up.

Pat's company had lost three soldiers. Sadly, he knew one of them, a trooper named Joel whose young daughter and wife were waiting for him at home. They would get to see him much sooner than expected.

The platoon leader, recognizing Pat's skills, put him in charge of a squad, and when Pat was not acting as a machine gunner, he led day and night patrols. Pat was offered a promotion to sergeant after only 15 months in the Army and the chance to become a permanent patrol leader. He thought accepting the rank would only heighten his risk. Given his reluctance to assign others to dangerous missions, he knew he'd take on the jobs himself and increase the probability of his going home in a box. He declined the promotion and it was given to Westley, a friend of his. Westley was killed a short time later.

On a blistering hot afternoon, Pat's patrol uncovered an unexploded artillery round. The decision was made to explode the round, so it wouldn't provide the VC with any more explosive devices. As the engineers were placing the explosives, Pat, who was sitting on his APC behind the .50-caliber machine gun, decided to hop down for a drink of water. Someone yelled "fire in the hole" just before the huge explosion, and a large piece of jagged shrapnel, about 12 inches long, three inches wide, and a half inch thick, ricocheted off the turret where Pat had just been sitting. His thirst saved him from a deadly accident. On another occasion, Pat, while on foot patrol with his squad noticed an unexploded mortar round sticking out of the ground. They decided to move to another rest area.

On a search and destroy mission, Pat's APC triggered a grenade that had been booby-trapped at a height of three feet off the ground. Every man sitting near Pat on top of the vehicle, to his left and right, was wounded. The platoon leader was hit in the leg, the driver in the eye, and the medic, a friend of Pat's, was hit in the head. Pat put a field dressing on the medic's head, trying to stop the blood flowing down his face. All three men were checked out at a field hospital, stitched up, and returned to duty.

On one patrol, his squad won a duel with a sniper and decided to put the body on the front of their APC, on top of a roll of barbed wire. As they drove through villages, they thought it would act as a warning to other local guerrillas. In another instance, two South Vietnamese soldiers had been ambushed and killed just as Pat's unit was traveling the same road. The three assassins ran into a grove of trees, and Pat's group surrounded and killed them. They laid their bodies along the road and spent the next three days patrolling the area. The bodies were never moved or claimed during that time and became quite gruesome lying out in the sun for three days.

Late one evening after setting up in a defensive position, the lieutenant sent Pat's squad outside the perimeter to establish a listening post. The group would sound the

After hitting a booby trap grenade, the driver plus two others were wounded. Pat (left) was unhurt (courtesy Pat Lupo).

Minor grenade damage to the APC (courtesy Robert Fazio).

alarm should it detect an advancing enemy. It was a dangerous duty since an assault was said to be imminent. The group climbed on armored vehicles, drove outside the perimeter, and silently jumped off while the vehicles were in motion, hoping to remain undetected. The men ended up hiding in a rice paddy. The squad took turns on watch and one new member kept imagining he was seeing insurgents sneaking up on them. The group did not want to fire and give away its position, but when the apparitions got to within twenty feet, the new guy opened fire. There was no return fire. The group remained silent and was picked up the following morning.

Probably one of the scariest times for Pat was when he and five soldiers were out on a night patrol. Separated from their main force, they found themselves in a field of six-foot-high elephant grass. The grass was thick and provided a useful resting place for the night. Shortly after midnight, on Pat's turn for security watch, he began to hear Vietnamese voices within mere feet of his position. He knew it was the enemy, probably in search of his squad. They were so close Pat dared not move and found himself wondering if they could hear his heartbeat. He did not attempt to waken his squad since he thought the slightest noise would give away their position. Pat cautiously placed two grenades in front of him for easy access, pointed his shotgun at the oncoming voices and waited. The VC were talking loudly and seemed to be joking, not realizing how close Pat's squad was. Finally, after a few hours, the voices faded; Pat urgently woke the rest of the squad and everyone returned to base.

Occasionally there was humor in serious situations. Early one morning the platoon was receiving incoming small arms fire from a wooded area, when the new lieutenant yelled "charge!" No one moved, knowing it would be reckless to charge blindly into the woods. The lieutenant realized his mistake and, in the future, asked advice from some of the seasoned combat veterans.

Another time, Pat's group was told to take cover from an accidentally fired white phosphorous mortar round that was going to land nearby. Not knowing just where the round would land, everyone scattered in different directions: some seeking low spots in the ground, others running into the woods, no one knowing where safety would be. The round exploded seconds later deep into the wood line, and no one was injured.

In a curious coincidence, Pat met a medic named Joe Lupo, recently assigned to his company. Joe and Pat became friendly and enjoyed sharing jokes and Italian family stories. Just before Joe was scheduled for R&R, he was killed in action helping others. Friends of Pat read of Joe's demise in *Stars and Stripes* and presumed Pat had been killed. They were quite relieved to see Pat alive the next time they met.

The 20-ton APCs were powered by a large diesel engine that moved tracks on both sides of the vehicle around five wheels. Though durable, all-purpose, all-terrain vehicles, the tracks made them susceptible to land or tank mines. In an armored convoy, Pat's vehicle was right behind another APC that detonated a land mine, blowing the tracks off the vehicle and sending some of its 200-pound wheels flying off in the distance.

Another time, with an armored convoy deep in enemy territory, in rough jungle conditions, Pat's APC became mired in thick mud, threw one of its two tracks, and was immobilized. It was dusk, and the convoy leader wanted to find a safer place to camp, so the rest of the personnel carriers moved on and told Pat to catch up with them once the track was repaired. Not wanting to be left in deep jungle by themselves overnight, the crew and some soldiers fixed the track in record time and joined the convoy before total darkness.

After joining the convoy and heading out the next morning, Pat and another soldier were walking point about fifty feet ahead of the armored vehicles when suddenly there was an explosion to their rear. A Viet Cong guerrilla had let both soldiers pass by his hiding place before detonating a powerful land mine, blowing the tracks off the vehicle that was right behind them. Soldiers jumped out of the vehicle. Aside from some bumps and scrapes, no one was injured, but the enemy slipped away.

While on another patrol, the convoy approached a large, open area and sent a few soldiers ahead to see if the enemy was lying in ambush. The soldiers were immediately fired upon and retreated to the edge of the jungle where the convoy waited. Normally the group would aggressively advance, firing as it went, trying to break up the ambush. In this case, a new Company commander decided this action was too dangerous and called in artillery to saturate the area. After a few barrages, the convoy crossed the open meadow with no return fire. The group appreciated this commander's method of calling in artillery, versus the convoy fighting its way through the meadow and taking casualties.

Shortly afterwards, the armored patrol received sniper fire from a nearby village. Unable to determine its exact source, a commander ordered Pat to fire into a hut outside of which a young child was standing. Pat hesitated on firing, and at the same time someone pulled the young child into the hut. Still ordered to fire, Pat unleashed his .50-caliber machine gun at the hut's roof, ripping it apart. Upon advancing and entering the hut, the soldiers found five civilians huddled in a hole dug in the floor. No one was hurt. The sniper was never found.

After ten months in Vietnam, Pat applied for R&R but his request was denied because he was told he had too little time left to serve in Vietnam. Pat then went AWOL (Absent Without Leave) and spent four days in Saigon. One night, when he was celebrating his unauthorized leave the military police stopped him and asked for paperwork. Unable to produce it, he was arrested (Pat's concealed pistol didn't help matters). Pat's unit was contacted, they sent a Jeep to pick him up, and no action was taken. When he was released, his pistol was returned to him. (Pat, like many other troopers, carried extra protection when on patrol. Some possessed specialized hunting knifes and many carried an extra pistol for close-in, last-ditch protection.)

Pat's dad had mailed him a .25-caliber pistol hidden in a box lined with tin foil, then filled with popcorn. The pistol came in handy several times. One of his experiences was eerily similar to mine: when being taken to a local bar, Pat realized the rickshaw driver had begun transporting him instead to an isolated area. Pat surmised he was in a dangerous situation and encouraged the driver to turn around by placing the gun against his head. The driver complied.

On one final convoy as Pat's tour was coming to an end, he was ordered to dismount from his vehicle and, using a head set, operate a mine detector out in front of the convoy. It was particularly hot and he was nervous, never having operated a detector. He proceeded cautiously and became even more tentative as the detector began picking up numerous signals of metals in his path. He thought the signals were coming from cans or scrap metal, but each time the detector picked up a signal, Pat needed to dig up the object to verify its source. As he continued to be cautious, and the column crawled along, his lieutenant brusquely ordered him to go faster, and Pat replied that maybe they should get someone else to do this work. They did and Pat was delighted.

As was custom, weeks before Pat was due to come home he was sent to the rear. Just days afterwards, his unit was hit. His replacement and three others were killed in action.

Returning Home

Pat returned home in December 1967, just in time to celebrate Christmas with family. After his leave, and with only six months left on his enlistment, Pat reported into his next duty station: Fort Hood, Texas. Uncertain of the reason, his unit began training in riot control techniques, and in the summer of 1968 he was flown to Chicago. The unit was designated to assist in riot protection for the 1968 Democratic Convention. The troops were issued live ammunition and waited for three days in the Mayor Daley Gymnasium to be deployed. The orders were never issued and the unit returned to Texas.

The Army found itself with many returning or rotating veterans from Vietnam with little for them to do. Pat fell into this category. There was little work to do, even less direction. Consequently, he found himself idle most of the time (e.g., reading books in empty tanks, sleeping-in during morning reveille). Eventually, just before his discharge, failing to report in for roll call got him in trouble, and he was busted one rank from a Specialist Four to a Private First Class. He was released shortly afterwards, in July 1968, and after returning home he was surprised to receive a Bronze Star for his meritorious actions in Vietnam.

During Pat's 12 months in Vietnam, seven men in his squad were wounded and three died from their wounds.

Career and Family

Pat returned home right after his discharge in July 1968 and tested for a post office position. He passed the test and was offered a position by the local postmaster. After some consideration, he declined the job offer, thinking that after his time in the military he no longer wanted to wear a uniform, and that the everyday routine might not fit with the risk-taking he enjoyed. For the next two or three years, Pat searched for the type of work he would enjoy. He worked as a construction foreman, at a race track, and found a second job delivering groceries for a local food store.

In the early 1970s, Pat was accepted into the Pittsfield, Massachusetts, Laborer's Union and began his career in construction drilling. There was little official training and skills were obtained by listening to senior operators and working on the job.

His memories of Vietnam are vivid and, many times, early morning and rainy day smells bring him back there. He remembers feeling so "alive" when he was there. For a long time after returning home, he was hyper-vigilant and anxious. Pat describes it as "paranoid." Once, Pat was watching fireworks with his kids in Williamstown and needed to leave the field because the sounds mimicked mortars exploding. Another time, on a construction site, a huge tailgate on a truck fell down, making a loud clanging noise—and Pat dropped immediately to the ground. One habit Pat attributes to his Vietnam service is eating his meals rapidly. In Vietnam, with mortars coming in while soldiers stood in the chow line, Pat learned to gobble up his meals and get back to his vehicle.

Over the course of the next 30 years, Pat would work in many cities up and down the East Coast. The work, at times dangerous, would involve drilling from considerable heights to secure buildings, dams, and roadways. If possible, the drillers would perform their work from a crane bucket; otherwise, they (and their percussion hammers) would be harnessed and suspended from two ropes high over the work site. The rope work was exhausting and could be debilitating. Pat retired from the union when he was 54 years old with more than 25 years' service.

Pat married twice during this time period and has four daughters and eight grandchildren. Most live nearby, and they see each other weekly.

Always the entrepreneur, Pat and his second wife opened Lupo's Restaurant in the early 1980s. The restaurant offered breakfast and lunch menus and was a thriving business. Often there were lines of patrons waiting to be served. Open for three years and managed by Pat's wife, Carol, while he traveled during the week, the business needs became too demanding for a woman with two small children. They sold the business for a handsome profit.

Pat's next venture was buying apartment buildings in Adams. Over two decades, he bought, managed, and rehabilitated four apartment buildings with 20-plus apartments before selling the last of them several years ago.

Pat readily admits to being a risk-taker and has gambled most of his life. Playing cards at Noel Field led to betting on horses and other sports. He now enjoys spending time daily on the stock market, researching, buying various stocks, and opting in on "puts and buys." Pat enjoys making stained glass items and has a huge, colorful, stained glass window of a Harley Davidson motorcycle. He and his granddaughter worked on a vase and flower pane. Pat owns a camp in Stamford, Vermont, on 50 acres that he enjoys and escapes to periodically. He doesn't hunt anymore, but enjoys target shooting. Pat has two motorcycles: an Indian and a Russian-made one. He enjoys riding both and delights in the bemused looks he gets when driving the Russian bike that comes equipped with a sidecar and a removable, imitation machine gun.

Pat thinks a lot about Vietnam since he retired, and attributes the delay to the business of work and family. Pat is classified as 100 percent disabled by the Veterans Administration. This is attributable to his gunshot wound and the effects of PTSD. He also suffers from Meniere's Disease, an inner ear disorder that causes dizziness without warning, intermittent hearing loss, and ringing and ear pressure.

Pat indicates that he doesn't consider himself outgoing. He can be standoffish and doesn't smile. (People often ask, "What's the matter with you?") He repeated his high school freshman year, which further enhanced his aloofness. Pat's closest friends were his Italian neighbor buddies. He has tended to be a loner and remains so today. Pat does meet weekly on Sundays at the local Daily Grind with four cronies he worked with in construction.

At the time he was in Vietnam, Pat presumed we were fighting Communist aggression and that the politicians and military leaders knew what they were doing. He no longer believes this, and after much reading on the subject is disillusioned with their lack of understanding and honesty.

Pat made a great life for himself, enjoys doting on his mom, and still remembers Vietnam as the ultimate high—like climbing in construction work, he enjoyed the danger and the risk.

12

Leo Chaput—Army Infantryman, Medic

Recipient of Combat Infantryman Badge, Cross of Gallantry

The understaffed platoon had been patrolling in the Central Highlands for days. Their ongoing search had them trudging up and down slippery hills and across dense plateaus from dawn to dusk. They found scant sign of the 66th NVA regiment that was rumored to be operating in the area.

Early this particular morning, after arising from their rocky dirt beds, quietly eating a cold C ration breakfast, and burying the evidence, they resumed their search for the enemy. They had slept atop one of the many peaks and now found themselves cautiously patrolling down the side of a fog-shrouded mountain.

Assuming a 15-foot distance between each man, the platoon began traversing its way down the slope, little realizing the several things working against them. The point man was new and had just arrived in-country to replace a trooper that had been wounded.

Equally as important, the company commander continued to push the platoon's leader to go faster because they had a lot of ground to cover this day.

Partway down the mountain, the sun appeared from behind the clouds and burnt off the protective fog, dissipating it in just a few minutes and exposing the green line of troopers. At almost the same time, snipers, nested high in large banyan trees, spotted distinguishable targets and began firing. Soldiers fell as shots hit their mark.

Before Leo could drop to the ground, the soldiers in front of and behind him were hit. From his angle, it looked like both troopers had upper body or shoulder wounds that might not be fatal. Leo, who was carrying the M-60 machine gun, threw himself to the ground just as another volley of bullets hit all around him. They tore up the ground, kicking rocks and gravel into his sweaty face.

Then it happened. A bullet struck Leo's helmet, tearing apart its camouflaged cover, producing a fist-size indentation, and sending the helmet spinning twenty feet into tall grass. Dazed, he scrambled over, retrieved his helmet, knocked out as much of the dimple as he could, making it wearable, and returned to the line.

Leo had given his M-60 to the assistant gunner, and once he returned to the line began returning fire using one of the wounded soldiers' M-16s. Seconds later, as the snipers continue to "walk" fire in on the patrol, Leo's helmet was hit again. Another glancing blow. Again he retrieved it. Leo never again complained about wearing a helmet.

During the ensuing minutes, sniper fire lessened, and the M-79 grenadiers found the NVA's treetop hiding spots and began killing them. The troopers focused on killing three or four soldiers that were providing support fire from the base of each sniper's tree.

With the fog lifted, the soldiers in front of the platoon could now see another group of NVA collecting at the base of the hill and quickly, while the teams leapfrogged down the slope, brought that group under concentrated fire, killing all of them.

Between the snipers, their support groups, and the enemy at the bottom of the hill, the soldiers had killed 15 to 20 NVA, but not without a cost. Three troopers were killed and four or five wounded. The soldiers, using open ponchos for stretchers, began collecting their dead and injured. They brought them to the bottom of the hill to be medevaced by incoming helicopters. Tom, the platoon's medic and a friend of Leo's, feverishly cared for the most severely wounded, and lastly treated Leo's face and arms, which were bleeding from rock chips.

The troopers dragged all the dead, bullet-ridden NVA down the hill and, laying them side-by-side, began searching the bodies for important papers, maps, or battle plans. They also piled all the captured NVA weapons in the same area. Most were AK-47 assault rifles.

Once this was done, everyone broke out a C ration and ate lunch. Even though rigor mortis had not set in, the medic found it convenient to use one of the NVA bodies as a table. The platoon leader got upset when he saw this. "What the hell are you doing?"

Tom said the gooks were dead and wouldn't mind being used for a table. The lieutenant walked away angry and frustrated.

Early Years

Leo was born on January 22, 1947, at Saint Luke's hospital in Pittsfield, Massachusetts. While his parents lived in North Adams, a major flood that week had prevented them from using the local hospital. Leo was the first born of three, then along came Edward and Margaret.

Leo was named after his dad, a World War II veteran, who served in Europe. Shortly after being discharged from the Army, he met and married Catherine Robare. Leo's dad worked for many years as a laborer for the city of North Adams. He was a short man with broad shoulders and uncommon strength. He was also known for his harshness.

Leo's mom, Catherine, was a homemaker. She had a quiet, caring, and peaceful nature, cooked great meals and served as a buffer between her children and their father.

Leo's paternal grandparents, Medric and Louise Chaput, emigrated from Saint-Esprit, Quebec, a tiny town located on the banks of the Saint-Esprit River. Soon after arriving, they established a small grocery store. The French-speaking grandparents lived above the store, and early in Leo's life, his family resided in an apartment behind the store. One of Leo's earliest memories was being permitted to take one cookie from the store's bin each day after school.

Leo's maternal grandparents, Bill and Cecelia (Flaherty) Robare, lived on Fuller Street in North Adams. His grandfather had moved from upstate New York, and his great-grandfather had emigrated from Canada. Leo's great-grandmother was an O'Reilly and had made the trip from Ireland to the United States when she was five years old.

Both sets of grandparents were born at the end of the nineteenth century and passed away in the 1950s. The Robares left their Fuller Street house to their daughter, Catherine. After renting apartments on East Quincy and Union streets, Leo's family happily moved into their first house. Their one-and-a-half-story home, located on a dead-end street, had white clapboards and a slate roof and was built around 1900. A previous owner had added a kitchen and a utility room off the back of the house. The land it sat on had been part of the Fuller Farm. Leo and his brother Eddie shared one of the two upstairs bedrooms and Margaret occupied the other. Their parents shared a small bedroom off the kitchen. Leo would live here until he left for the military.

Tragedy struck the small family early on, when Leo's mom, Catherine, died of breast cancer. She was 39 years of age, and Leo only 10. Catherine suffered with the disease for two years before succumbing to its ravages. The children not only lost their mom, the center of their family, but their protector.

As the oldest child, he became responsible for his brother and sister. Leo ensured they got home safely from Notre Dame Grammar School, watched them after school, prepared supper and waited for his dad to get home.

Leo's dad was known as a harsh disciplinarian, but became more so after Catherine died. Leo seems to have taken the brunt of his dad's wrath. He recalls a number of sad, scary, or abusive incidents involving their father's temper. One time Eddie stole a pair of sneakers from a store. After the police questioned him and left, their father beat Eddie and then thrashed Leo because he should have known what was going on.

From 10 onward, Leo was on his own, working part-time jobs to cover clothes and spending money. He took care of a dozen elderly people's properties, painting, deep cleaning inside, mowing, shoveling snow, and also had a number of commercial customers. In wintertime, on snow days, Leo would get up at 3:00 a.m. to shovel at his house and then attend to his downtown business customers. His work pattern usually involved a stop at Dunkin' Donuts before heading to school. His work hours before and after school negated any possibility of participating in school activities.

As a youth, Leo had asthma, but he didn't let this interfere with being an outdoorsman. On weekends he would leave his backyard, cross several fields, and begin hiking the Appalachian Trail. Leo and his friends, brothers Jim and Tom Luczynski, spent most of their free time outside hiking, fishing, or hunting. The boys often spent all day hiking up Mount Greylock, the highest peak in Massachusetts, or riding their bikes to Cheshire Lake, fifteen miles away, to go fishing. When on foot, far from home, and tired, the boys could easily hitch a ride back home.

In the winter, they would snowshoe for hours, with .22 rifles on their backs, on the snow-covered mountains just north of their hometown. They would bring small mess kits, start a fire, and add snow and bouillon cubes for a satisfying broth. They often hiked up to the Mohawk Trail, crossing many rock walls created by farmers going back to the Revolutionary War. Leo usually took Rex, his German shepherd, on these outdoor forays.

Come springtime, Leo helped Jim and Tom collect dandelion leaves for their basement wine-making efforts. His friends universally described him as easygoing, busy, and quiet. He enjoyed the company of his friends and being away from home.

A sand bank located just above Petey Dinks' restaurant made a good spot for pickup baseball, but the sand bank had many uses—from skating at the bottom of its pit in the winter, to providing a backstop for their target practicing sessions. Leo and Jim, as soon as they had accumulated enough money, would buy several boxes of .22 shells and hone their marksmanship skills. Leo's prized possession was his .22 Mossburg, bolt-action rifle with the black hinged forearm.

Once, Leo and a friend named Mike got stuck in quicksand there, up to their waists. Out of earshot from any type of help, the boys struggled mightily to free themselves, only to become more mired in the muck. Finally, they lay on their backs, did a modified backstroke which helped loosen their legs, and they "floated" out. A lucky ending to another adventure.

The young comrades joined the local YMCA and enrolled in Judo lessons given by a leathery retired Army sergeant. The sergeant was knowledgeable in judo, karate, and jujitsu, forms of martial arts he had perfected in Okinawa and Japan. Leo took classes from him for eight years, until leaving for induction into the Army. When the boys weren't practicing judo, they wrestled, learning multiple "takedown" moves. In high school, Leo was given the nickname "Chops" for his judo prowess.

Leo befriended Mr. Wright, an elderly gentleman, who lived across the street several houses down from him. Mr. Wright was an artillery veteran of World War I. People would often see the old retired lineman and Leo smoking pipes together on his front porch. The man was nicknamed "Stubby" because of his height and stocky, powerful build. Mr. Wright had been an accomplished outdoorsman in his youth, and their conversation always involved forest lore, fishing, or hunting. He taught Leo woodland tips, including how to sharpen knives and axes. Stubby's wisdom was absorbed intently; his prowess was well illustrated by the huge mounted black bear head presiding over the living room.

As did many young boys of that era, Leo had a fascination with taxidermy. Over time, he saved his dimes from lunch money and purchased a correspondence taxidermy course. He began working diligently with small animals and birds, proudly mounting his first candidate, a tiny chipmunk. Leo worked in the back shed cleaning tiny skulls, preserving miniature skins, and mounting his trophies.

During his teenage years, Leo also hung around with two more brothers who lived nearby. He was sometimes invited to their camp in Vermont and remembers contrasting their family's interactions with his own. One time, Leo spilled a salt shaker, dumping a load of salt on his meal. Without thinking he put the lid back on and continued eating the over-salted macaroni. Surprising him, the mother said, "you don't have to eat that," and brought him another plate. Leo's father would have made him eat the salt and cuffed him for being careless. He came to realize that his family life differed from other families.

The spring of 1965 found Leo secretly completing his Army enlistment paperwork. The day after graduation, much to his father's chagrin, he left for Army basic training. Leo knew the military would provide steady employment, possibly a career, and decided it was time to get away from his mercurial father.

Joining the Army

Leo began his Army life at Fort Dix undergoing ten weeks of basic training and was assigned the military occupational specialty of 11B (Bravo)-infantryman. He became trained in the use of light weapons such as the M-16 and the M-60. His cadre was also familiarized with heavier weapons such as the .50-caliber machine gun, various mortars, and the 105mm recoilless rifle.

Next stop was the nine-week Advanced Infantry Training course and then the Army's three-week, rigorous Airborne Jump Training Camp. While at jump school, Leo had a hard landing when his parachute did not fully deploy. He believes the landing caused his lifelong back and knee problems, for which he receives medical disability. After the accident, Leo needed crutches to support his black-and-blue legs and speed his recovery. Shortly after the incident, while still on crutches, he received orders for Vietnam. Though not yet healed, he needed to surrender his crutches or Army regulations would not permit him to be sent to a combat area. Leo surrendered his crutches.

His turbulent family background made the harassment and discipline of basic training and jump school tolerable. Leo had heard that the jump school "black hats" (DIs) had a goal of washing out half the class through lack of sleep, exhaustion, or harassment. He reminded others that jump school was only three weeks, and they could easily tolerate any treatment for that long.

Vietnam

Five months after his enlistment, Leo arrived in Vietnam and was assigned to the 3rd Platoon, B Company, 2nd Battalion of the 502 Infantry Regiment, 1st Brigade, 101st Airborne Division. This became his overseas home for the next twelve months.

Leo's unit operated in II and III Corps areas in central Vietnam. The regions ranged from the unit's headquarters in Phan Rang, north to Tuy Hoa, and as far inland as Cambodia. Most of their time was spent in the Central Highlands.

Leo arrived in November 1965, not long after his unit had been stationed in Vietnam. They were deployed to search, contact, and destroy NVA and VC elements found within their areas of responsibility (AORs). They wasted no time, and Leo's company started spending three to four weeks in the field searching for and conducting air assaults on known enemy areas of activity. The units would come out of the field for two or three days to resupply and then resume another extended search.

During Leo's time in-country, his unit was involved in ten or more combat operations and more than forty air assaults and skirmishes in regions that included lofty plateaus, impenetrable bamboo jungles, rubber plantations, and triple-canopy jungle. Climate conditions ranged from extreme heat to very cold nights and arid landscape to torrential, mud-sucking rain. Often patrol movements were restricted to whatever their machetes could chop in the heat of the day.

Leo (left) and a friend just before moving out to Dak To in the Central Highlands, 1966 (courtesy Leo Chaput).

Personal hygiene was minimal. Troopers did not shower in the field, but reserved that luxury for their return to base every four or five weeks. They were reluctant to bathe in rivers because they were often under enemy surveillance and water holes made excellent ambush sites. One of their company's platoons had recently been ambushed by snipers hidden along a river bank. As Leo said, "after a week you stop itching, after a month you don't care." Troopers carried a toothbrush, but no toothpaste, and dry-brushed their teeth. They shaved sometimes, but the real cleanup occurred when they came out of the field.

Most people in his unit smoked, but usually not in the field. Lit cigarettes could be smelled for some distance, and either way the odor would permeate their clothes, a beacon for the enemy. They often formed little clay-like balls of C-4 explosive, about the size of Alley marbles, to heat their coffee or cocoa. C-4 burns white and fast, lit with Zippo lighters since matches were often wet. The smell of C-4 was minimal compared to the noxious fumes of the bluish heat tabs used more commonly back on fire base.

Leo initially served on a mortar crew, but due to his strength and conditioning, he was moved to the two-man M-60 machine gun crew. He and the assistant gunner would alternate carrying the machine gun, which weighed twenty-seven pounds. When Leo carried the gun, he would drape four 100-round ammunition belts around himself and carry an additional 600 rounds in a three-pouch canvas sack. While patrolling, he would keep a 20-round belt of ammunition in the machine gun for immediate action. He and the gunner would also farm out extra ammunition belts to the infantrymen.

The gunner carried a .45-caliber pistol, four hand grenades, one Claymore mine, trip flares and a Light Antitank Weapon (LAW). The assistant gunner would carry more ammunition belts, an extra M-60 barrel, cleaning supplies, and his own personal weapons. One of the team members would also carry a thermite grenade to destroy the M-60 if it got disabled or became unserviceable. One carried an M-16 rifle: once in battle, they could scavenge a rifle and magazines from the dead. Every soldier carried a bayonet, some C-4, and a small "jump" knife. Some soldiers would carry small pistols (.25- or .38-caliber) for personal protection.

In addition to the weaponry, Leo carried a poncho and poncho liner for sleeping. He also carried C rations for two to five days (depending on the mission), but they came in a small box which was too bulky. Most men would just choose two or three heavies (entrees) and leave the other contents behind. Some might take the toilet paper, or maybe a pound cake and some crackers. Leo took to slinging a sock of raw, hard rice around his neck or tied to his rucksack. The nibbled rice, while not very tasty, was a distraction from gnawing hunger and expanded in his stomach, plus it was easily accessible and didn't need to be heated. It started

Leo with his constant companion, the M-60, in Tuy Hoa (courtesy Leo Chaput).

out white, but turned greenish after a while. Even moldy, it was something.

Rucksacks weighed around 80 pounds: The best strategy was to strap on the pack while seated, and then be pulled to standing by two other team members. The troopers were very conscious of weight, and their focus was on firepower, ammunition and food. Since Leo arrived in Vietnam in the early stages of the war, this meant no flak jackets. This was okay with him because he could carry more ammo.

Life in the Field

Leo's unit never had racks in the rear since they were almost continuously in the field. After four or five weeks in the field they would return to Tuy Hoa and go straight to the supply tent for new jungle fatigues and boots. Patrolling, especially through elephant grass, tore into their uniforms, sometimes shredding their fatigues. If that didn't occur, the pant legs usually rotted out from dampness.

In the rear, they also received Red Cross packages containing Luckys, Camels, and Chesterfield cigarettes, chewing tobacco plugs, soap, toothpaste, a toothbrush, and shaving items such as razors and shaving cream. The items were revered but often left behind when returning to the field.

When in Tuy Hoa, the troopers dug holes about four feet square and deep, sandbagged the walls, and ran the sandbags a few rows above ground. Then they used ponchos or tent halves for a roof. This was luxury. The comforts disappeared when they returned to the field, used helmets for pillows, and slept rolled in a poncho liner flat on the ground. If it was raining, they would use their ponchos too, although the expectation was you were going to be wet eventually.

Mail was distributed to ever-moving troopers when they were in the rear area. Leo received some letters from friends and his sister. He wrote occasionally.

Leo's platoon was seldom at the recommended strength level of 50 soldiers. The average number of men present ranged from 18 to 22. Replacements for the killed and wounded were slow in coming. Leo was told that wounded troopers remained in the active headcount even if they were recovering from injuries for two or three months in Japan. These "active duty" soldiers needed no replacements.

When returning to the field, the troops might be informed the night before that they would be air assaulting another area, often involving the platoon or the entire company. The troops never knew their destination. They would proceed to a staging area, receive more rifle ammunition, grenades, LAWs, and sometimes be advised if active resistance was expected.

Air assault transportation was via UH-1 (Huey) helicopters that carried between five and eight fully armed soldiers into battle. Leo would sit on the edge of the floor with his feet hanging out the side door and his M-60 ready for action. Landings were always filled with anxiety, not knowing if you would come under fire, what the terrain would be like, and how high you might be from the ground when you were "dropped off." It was difficult for the pilot to gauge the height of the elephant grass with their skids skimming it. Disembarking soldiers might have a two-foot or a five-foot drop (with 80 pounds on their backs). When under fire, the Hueys might be coming in too fast and drop troops off while still in flight.

Once the squad hit the ground, they established perimeter security and then quickly left the area, presuming the enemy had heard the helicopters and were close by.

On one of Leo's first Huey rides, his squad was helping transport water cans to their unit. They had picked up full water cans in Tuy Hoa, and when they landed and started to unload the cans, Leo realized the can he was sitting on was empty. When he turned it upside down, investigating, he found that a bullet had pierced the floor of the Huey and the water can without anyone noticing.

Battle Actions

One day while on a company-size patrol, Leo's 3rd platoon was on point. At noon, after a rest and some chow, another platoon took the point position. They trudged through the jungle about an hour, then while rounding a bend they came under fire from a hidden bunker complex.

The NVA machine guns immediately killed or wounded six troopers. A lieutenant braved enemy fire and kept retrieving the bodies of the dead and wounded while the remaining platoons destroyed the bunkers with LAWs. Upon closer examination, the bunkers were well placed, blended in with the thick foliage, and strategically located to be mutually fire supportive.

Once the bunkers were destroyed, the patrol began hearing Vietnamese movements across the entire ridge line above them. They caught the clicking sounds of bayonets being fixed to weapons and the sounds of three different bugles indicating a large force of NVA.

The company commander told everyone to fix bayonets, and what initially seemed like a basic-training drill became deadly serious in an instant. The platoons spread out, organized themselves into a long line and began assaulting, by fire and maneuver, straight up the steep hillside. The jungle was thick and the enemy unseen. They passed the four destroyed bunkers at the base of the hill, and Leo designated someone to fire into the bunkers ensuring all threats were neutralized. The unit continued up the mountain, firing continuously. The enemy was returning fire, but their bullets were passing overhead and showered the soldiers with twigs and leaves.

As the soldiers reached a slight plateau, they found many NVA bodies, but continued aggressively firing and maneuvering up the hill. The enemy was forced off the ridge top and retreated down the backside of the hill, walking right into a pre-planned ambush by another platoon—killing yet more NVA.

On one dusk assault by Company B, the three platoons split up and searched an area with no signs of the enemy. The company commander decided to search another area and called in helicopters to transport the company to a new area. By now, darkness had set in and there was just a hint of moonlight.

The platoons began following a trail, usually a dangerous choice, but it was too dark to machete their way through the jungle. They stopped at the edge of a large clearing about three or four football fields across and not quite as wide. Leo's platoon was designated to follow the path straight through the center of the field, with the other platoons skirting the wood lines to the right and left. All of a sudden, they started spotting brief flickers of light throughout the field: small campfires. As the troopers approached, they found the ashes hot and saw bamboo tripods propping up cooking pots. The field was covered with these small flickering fires. The NVA had left hastily, within minutes.

Everyone wondered if the ambush would come from the nearby wood line. The moon grew brighter, making the threatening wood line visible, but not much else. For sure, each soldier was thinking, "Oh boy, here we go." It was tense, and yet the commander decided to proceed across. Leo's undersized platoon was designated to continue straight on the trail; they very cautiously moved across the clearing, meeting the other two platoons at the wood line.

On this night there would be no contact. The company would move to another area, rest and sleep for several hours, and then continue hunting the elusive quarry. Leo suspected the campfires belonged to the very regiment the company had been seeking, but it was never verified.

Another time Leo and his platoon were back in Tuy Hoa resupplying for their next patrol when they were ordered to search a nearby village for enemy troops. When they arrived at the village, it was empty, most of the concrete buildings severely damaged by bombs and strafing. There was no sign of life.

One soldier discovered an unexploded 250-pound bomb, and the accompanying engineers decided the safest disposal was to blow it in place. Leo's platoon moved about 100 yards away and sat down, waiting for the fireworks. A small field with waist-high cactus separated the platoon from the unexploded ordnance. Fortunately, an NCO happened by and told the platoon they'd better lie flat, now! When the explosion occurred, shrapnel trimmed all the cactus down to about two feet high. They'd have all had their heads cut off.

In another instance, Leo's platoon was coming in to be resupplied, somewhere in the Central Highlands, and the 1st Air Cavalry was providing perimeter security. The resupply was on the side of a mountain, on a notched-out road with a four-foot earthen wall on one side and a drop-off on the other. The platoon proceeded very cautiously to the rendezvous wanting to ensure no one would get "trigger happy" before the groups connected.

They met without incident, dropped their packs, got against the inside cut of the road, and sat in the dirt on the side of this steep hill. There were officers walking around, and the cavalry was waiting for a hot meal (noon chow) to be flown in by helicopters. They were also bringing supplies to Leo's platoon.

The troopers could see and hear the five resupply helicopters coming up the long valley, getting close, when the helicopters came under fire from the top of the mountain right above Leo's platoon. The VC had not seen the troopers and were focusing on shooting down the helicopters with small arms fire.

Leo and his platoon reacted fast. They started up the hill, firing as they walked. Leo used up a 12-inch ammo belt for the M-60, and his A-Gunner threw him a 100-round belt as they made their way up the hill. Leo sprayed from left to right and back again: long bursts of fire bit into the dirt line at the crest of the hill. He couldn't see anyone, and the hillside was very slippery. Leo began using the recoil of his M-60 to pull himself up as he continued to climb. Leo and Morales, the M-79 grenadier, made it to the top first and headed for the wood line about two hundred yards away. A medic who had been following the two-man team yelled at them to pull back because an artillery barrage was going to begin. About the same time, Leo noticed an artillery spotter round (that normally precedes a barrage) hit in the middle of the field. He and the grenadier ran back to the hilltop.

It appeared as though the VC had been hanging around all day. No one had bothered to check out the top of the hill. The quick reaction by Leo and the grenadier had produced ten enemy deaths and about the same number of recovered weapons.

In war, there are humorous or dark stories that troops never forget. Leo recalls one that he has labeled the "spontaneous hand grenade mutiny." The Army wanted platoons to use up all the old, serrated "pineapple" grenades date-stamped from the Korean War era before using any new grenades. Often the pineapple grenades failed to explode, and the platoon joked that the only VC likely to die from the grenades were those knocked in the head.

Headed out on patrol, his platoon stood in line picking up more ammo, but no one selected any old-style grenades. They'd be just a waste of weight. The platoon sergeant took note of what was happening and told the men to pick up four or five grenades. They refused. Then a lieutenant told the men to pick up some grenades. Again they refused. The lieutenant threatened the men with courts-martial and prison time at the Fort Leavenworth stockade. They still declined, said they'd prefer to go out without grenades. Someone located a supply of newer grenades, and the troopers never saw the old pineapples again.

Once after being in the bush for three weeks, his company was airlifted to an isolated resupply point. When landing, a colonel appeared with an entourage of officers and newsmen. The colonel, pointing to a map on the easel, began orating about how his understaffed companies would be flown into an area to trap and wipe out two VC regiments. The troopers were incredulous at the presentation and understood it to be a public relations effort by the colonel. But platoon commanders began passing out pencils and paper for any soldier wanting to write his last letter home, and platoon sergeants began telling people look to your right and left and some of these men will be dead before the day's over.

The colonel invited the press to send representatives on the imminent assault, which had been scheduled for dusk. The troopers loaded up on ammunition, boarded the helicopters (without any newsmen) and headed to the enemy's supposed location. The company debarked without receiving fire, formed a 360-degree perimeter, and moved out to search and cordon off the area. There was zero enemy contact that night and that was fine with them.

As in many units, rumors flourished in the rear. Once when Leo's company returned to be resupplied there was an exciting rumor that had raised morale: The 101st Airborne was preparing to parachute into Hanoi, secure the Hanoi Hilton, and evacuate all U.S. POWs to the beach area which would have been captured by the 82nd Airborne Division. The paratroopers were excited about the possibility of taking the fight to the enemy. They were disillusioned when the rumor was quashed by their battalion commander.

On two different occasions, Leo's unit operated in Cambodia for several weeks at a time. In late 1966, there were not supposed to be any border crossing operations into Cambodia. After the unit had entered Cambodia, the lieutenant gathered his troopers and told them if anyone ever asked them where they had been, they were to say "lost." Then he brought out a grease-penciled map, in a dirty plastic holder, that showed everyone they were absolutely in Cambodia.

There was no contact during their first crossing.

A short time later, on their second incursion, just after crossing a rickety jungle bridge, the unit began receiving small arms fire. The patrol leader presumed it came from "stay behinds," NVA soldiers chosen to remain behind to slow or disrupt the enemy's advance. With this in mind, and the contact being light, the troops continued to forge ahead. They were surprised to discover a large way station for NVA crossing from Cambodia into Vietnam.

The area had numerous bamboo huts, large stashes of rice, and curiously, on the side of a hill in a covered hole, a number of two-pound sacks which were initially thought to contain tea. After checking for booby traps, they lifted one of the bags, and while the writing was in Vietnamese it included a skull and crossbones, indicating a poisonous substance.

Leo is unsure if anyone brought a bag back, but he knew at the time the NVA was known to poison wells. The platoon burnt down all the huts, destroyed the rice and remaining bags of poison, and briskly returned to the border.

Another time high in the Central Highlands, close to the Cambodian border, Leo's Company was moving to another area and in the process told to provide security for a 4.2 mortar platoon.

Usually a headquarters platoon provided security, versus a line unit, but Leo's happened to be nearby. The area was mountainous, and as they approached a Montagnard village, they noticed the residents were using elephants to transport the mortars. The disassembled field pieces were tied to the elephants, there were about 12 in all, and they were ridden by Montagnards (indigenous mountain tribesmen, so named by the French, allied with the U.S.), armed with crossbows. The platoon found themselves walking between two rows of the lumbering giants while the Montagnard women and children watched their strange procession. Leo said he "felt a little like Hannibal crossing the Alps."

At one point the lead elephant veered off the trail, and the rest of the group followed him for a short distance and then returned to the trail. Checking the spot where he veered off, the troopers discovered a giant scorpion "as big as a crayfish."

On one occasion, Leo's company had been airlifted into an area in the Central Highlands during the dry part of the year. For the first few days, there had been no clouds, the sun shone fiercely, and there was little extra water as they walked alongside a stony mountain with huge boulders. The next morning when they arose, a fog had set in, making visibility a problem. As they followed a path going down the hill, the NVA sprang an ambush announced by incoming mortar rounds. Leo's company couldn't locate the enemy so they moved into a rocky area to avoid the bombardment.

The lieutenant called in artillery and asked the company to mark their position so nearby helicopters could aid them with rockets and machine gun fire. They marked their location with a purple smoke grenade. For some unknown reason, the helicopters targeted the purple smoke and fired CS gas (tear gas) on Leo's company. The group, who did not carry gas masks, ran screaming up the hill and over the other side to escape the gas. They were reluctant after that episode to call for assistance.

During Leo's tour of duty in Vietnam, he went to a field hospital three times, always experiencing a high, 102-degree fever with sweats and chills. He presumed it was malaria, but the hospital said it was not malaria, just a fever of unknown origin (FUO). Leo presumed their continuous operations, in many different locales, exposed troopers to many unfamiliar viruses. After seven days in the hospital, the condition always improved, and he was sent back to his unit.

Leo was scheduled to rotate back to the United States at the end of November 1966. After being detached from his unit, he flew to Camp Alpha where he was given orders to go home. He grabbed a bunk in one of the transit buildings and planned to depart in the morning. The transit area had hundreds of men like himself waiting to go home. Just by happenstance, in the mass of people sitting on the dirt, back-to-back, near one of the buildings he recognized two soldiers who had been part of the replacement group he came into country with a year ago.

Thirty-six troopers started out in their group. They'd been to jump school together, sent to Vietnam as a cohort, and then disbursed to different units across country. The three soldiers began a rough accounting of the different individuals and found, of the group of 36, 10 had been killed-in-action, another 10 been grievously wounded but alive when they left the field. The remaining soldiers were alive, although some had been wounded repeatedly.

Their conversation lasted a while, then they went to chow and never saw each other again.

Coming Home

The brief flight from Camp Alpha brought Leo to Tuy Hoa then onto Phan Rang and had him departing from Bien Hoa Airfield, 16 miles outside of Saigon. Leo's plane refueled in Hawaii, arrived at Travis Air Force Base, and then ultimately at Fort Dix, New Jersey, for processing. The next morning, he took a bus to Albany, New York, and his friend Jim picked him up and brought him home to North Adams. Leo had two weeks' leave before reporting to Fort Bragg. His dad was still alive, but Leo spent much of the leave "in and out of the house," visiting friends.

Next, Leo was bused to Fort Bragg, North Carolina, where the Army decided to train a number of infantrymen, mostly Vietnam veterans, in the specialty of field med-

At Fort Sam's medic school, 1967 (courtesy Leo Chaput).

icine. Leo worked as a temporary medic for six months at Bragg, then went to Fort Sam Houston's excellent eight-week medic school. Shortly after Leo returned to Bragg, his father passed away and he was given an early out in January 1968 to care for his brother and sister.

Leo stayed in North Adams for several years and then decided it was time to see more of the United States. His travel began with "thumbing" to Seattle, working along the way as a trucker's assistant for room and board. In Seattle, he worked as a breakfast chef for a local hotel and as a security guard for an apartment complex.

His post–Vietnam trek then took him and a friend through the states of Utah, Wyoming, Colorado, and the Dakotas, ending up back on the East Coast in Philadelphia where they worked temporarily cleaning up a machine shop.

Next stop for the friends was Los Angeles and then on to the San Francisco Bay Area working as armed guards at a plasma center. He found this funny: "We wore lab coats, a tie, a stethoscope, and carried .38 revolvers," helping with screening services as well as providing security.

In the early seventies, Leo met his wife-to-be, Jane, at a party in Oakland. They dated for several years and were married in 1975. Both Jane and Leo worked while he attended San Francisco State College, and he obtained a degree in biogeography in 1979.

Interestingly, Jane was from Framingham, Massachusetts, so shortly after Leo's graduation they decided to move eastward to get closer to their families. Both outdoors people, they chose to live in Vermont, and while there Leo obtained a master's degree in social ecology from Goddard College. Leo went on to work for the USDA Soil Conservation Service and at an experimental farm for the college.

When the college closed, the couple began their next adventure and found themselves in Anchorage, Alaska. Leo worked for the State Land Office and the Bureau of Land Management as a biologist and a cartographer. He then was hired by the Postal

East Oakland, 1972, enjoying civilian life (courtesy Leo Chaput).

Service and worked as an electro/mechanical technician for 15 years, retiring in 2000. Upon retirement, the couple moved to Lexington, Kentucky, where they now live in a brick and vinyl tri-level home in a modest neighborhood with their dog Bella.

Over six feet tall, with white brush-cut hair and accompanying beard, Leo keeps fit, exercising at a gym and hiking in the nearby national forest. He also paints landscapes, enjoys woodworking, and together he and Jane listen to classical music and seek out live performances. Leo also makes stringed musical instruments in his spare time, such as mandolins and dulcimers. Quite handy, he crafts small metal items such as baskets and figurines and still finds time to target shoot, hunt, and fish. Just like the childhood version of himself, shoveling snow at dawn in North Adams, he keeps busy.

Leo, who has been self-supporting since the age of 10, is still fiercely independent, blunt talking, and self-assured. From the time he "thumbed" out of North Adams almost 50 years ago, with a few dollars in his pocket, he has been reliant solely on his own abilities. He earned both a bachelor's and a master's degree, worked at several long-term jobs and has been married for 44 years as of this writing. Leo is aptly described by his friends as solid, dependable, fit, at times quiet, trustworthy, and a lover of the outdoors.

Leo receives veterans disability for his arthritic knees (a result of parachuting), a heart-related condition, and hearing difficulties, and for a diagnosis of PTSD. His personal decorations include: Combat Infantryman Badge, Parachutist Wings, Presidential Unit Citation, Valorous Unit Citation, Meritorious Unit Citation, Republic of Vietnam—Cross of Gallantry, Republic of Vietnam—Civic Action Medal, Good Conduct Medal, Republic of Vietnam Service Medal with three stars, Republic of Vietnam Campaign Medal, and the National Defense Medal. Leo also wore the infantry blue-cord fourragère on his shoulder designating him as a qualified infantryman assigned to a U.S. Army infantry unit.

Even today Leo can describe the picturesque mountains in Vietnam, the abandoned, Mediterranean-style, stuccoed French buildings with red-tiled roofs, and the systematically designed rubber and tea plantations. On occasion when working in his garden, the smell of overturned dirt will whisk him back to the pungent odors of the jungle.

Having arrived to the theater of battle earlier than most, in 1965, Leo emphasizes how the soldiers in his unit often did not know where they had been, where they were, and where they were going—nor for how long they would be gone. Leo has "no regrets" about his service, but he admits, "there could have been a better time to serve." He has a 101st Airborne tattoo on his right shoulder and has been a stalwart supporter of the U.S. Army, and so when he is critical of the disingenuous leadership, both political and military, that led the country during the Vietnam War and cost the lives of many brave men, he comes by that opinion honestly. He earned it.

13

Mike Chalifoux—Army Mechanized Infantryman

Recipient of Combat Infantryman Badge,
Bronze Star, Army Commendation Medal

Mike's unit had one primary responsibility: keep Route 19 open between An Khe and Qui Nhon. They used 24,000-pound behemoths called APCs (armored personnel carriers) to keep the roads clear of enemy troops and mines. These tank-like, tracked vehicles, 16 feet by nine feet, were highly adaptable and considered the backbone of the armored cavalry, like a taxicab with guns. The two-member crew of this assault vehicle (the taxi drivers) ferried troops into battle, providing them some protection. Often troopers would ride on the top of it. The vehicle with its diesel engines could attain a speed of 40 miles per hour. All had top-mounted .50-caliber machine guns with armored shields. Some APCs added two additional machine guns.

The Panthers, Mike's unit, conducted early-morning road sweeps which were both methodical and boring, but nonetheless essential to keeping Route 19 open as a viable resupply connection to troops operating in the western part of II Corps, close to the Cambodian border. It had been awhile since they had uncovered an anti-tank mine but the commander continued to stress vigilance.

The two APCs on this morning's patrol operated one behind the other in mutual support. Sometimes a soldier with a metal detector would precede the two massive vehicles. Often the detector picked up false signals from the detritus of war: spent ammunition shells, broken pieces of military equipment, etc. This morning, the soldiers were not using a detector even though lately the Viet Cong had begun to "plant" metal pieces in the road to slow detection. The troopers were in a hurry to get back to base camp.

The Viet Cong, while unsophisticated in their bomb-making efforts, very effectively re-deployed discarded or unexploded U.S. ordnance, normally duds that were from artillery barrages or airstrikes. The enemy sent teams into bombed areas to retrieve unexploded ordnance. Lately, they had also started using Soviet mines constructed of black or brown tar-impregnated cardboard that made detection much more difficult.

The troopers on Mike's vehicle knew the anti-tank mines were detonated by 100 to 400 pounds of pressure, or (in more densely populated areas) by a nearby insurgent who electronically activated the mine. This particular morning, the APC crews were carefully scanning in front of their vehicle and on both sides of the road asking themselves, "if I were Charlie, where would I put the boobytrap?"

The troopers all knew the obvious places to look: approaches to road junctions, near bridges, in potholes, and anyplace where there was a possibility of tunneling underneath the road. The enemy's ingenuity even had them placing mines under old wheel and tread tracks in the road, then duplicating the tracks after the mine was placed. This tactic was almost impossible to uncover without a sophisticated detection system.

The APCs needed to cover 15 miles this morning and, at a cautious pace of less than five miles per hour, it was going to take hours to complete their mission. The morning's road traffic was beginning to get congested with motor bikes and mini-buses using the road. There was no indication that the VC had been busy the previous night.

As they approached a major intersection and negotiated a slight left turn, Mike was airborne. He soared twenty feet straight up in the air before he realized what was happening, and almost at the same time became aware of a huge explosion. Seconds later he found himself flat on his back in a large hole where the APC had been located. After all these years, Mike still remembers the landing and the softness of the dirt. It was like talcum powder.

Regaining his senses, he observed that he was sitting alone in a massive hole with dust swirling about. The hole was maybe eight feet deep and ten yards in diameter. Scrambling out, he found the 24,000-pound APC on its side and the other four crew members scattered across the road. Most were moving after several moments, and with the help of the other APC crew, all of the dazed crew members collected themselves and moved away from the destroyed vehicle.

The sister APC continued to provide security and radioed in for a "dustoff" (medevac) helicopter for the crew members. Mike seemed to be the least affected and remained with the destroyed APC. His four friends were evacuated to a local field hospital for medical observation and to treat their minor wounds. Later in the day they would all be reunited at base camp, and eventually four more Purple Hearts would be awarded. Mike declined medical treatment (and a Purple Heart), believing his abrasions were too superficial.

Mike's wrecked APC on the left, being towed to salvage (courtesy Chalifoux family).

Hours later, an armored recovery vehicle righted the APC, chained itself to the massive hulk, and towed it back to the salvage yard. The troops concluded that the explosion was caused by an improvised anti-tank bomb that had detonated at the front of the vehicle, ripping up the treads on both sides and twisting the heavy road wheels out-of-shape. The crew counted themselves lucky that the bomb had not set fire to the fuel tank.

The following morning they were back on the road headed to their next operation.

Early Life

Mike was born on June 22, 1947, at St. Luke's Hospital in Pittsfield, Massachusetts. He grew up at 445 Church Street in North Adams with his dad, mom, three younger siblings, and Aunt Mary. Mike's youngest sister Catherine, named after his mom, was diagnosed with Down syndrome at birth and was carried everywhere by the family until she began walking at age five. She had a particularly close relationship with her grandfather.

His house on Church Street was a sprawling white clapboard home located at the corner with Davenport Street, encircled by a white picket fence. This was the original farmhouse for the entire area, bordered by tall pine trees on Davenport Street and enormous, unclimbable beech trees in front and back of the home. The rambling house had a two-car garage, several additions from over the years, and a large backyard. Aunt Mary lived in several rooms at the front of the house. The family's kitchen was in the back.

Mike's dad, Jean Major Chalifoux, was an Army World War II veteran who fought in the European Theater and was wounded by shrapnel on D-day. Family lore says that

Jean's grandmother had wanted a girl when he was born, and had already encouraged using the name Jeanne. Not to be diverted when her grandson was born, she encouraged her daughter-in-law to use the male form, Jean. Jean's ancestors were from French and Scottish backgrounds. He was a quiet, gentle man, dark-skinned, tall, and slender with combed-back hair and dark, horn-rimmed glasses. He worked 30-plus years as a machinist at the local James Hunter Machine Company, involved in the construction of garnetting machines, large mechanized apparatuses used in the textile industry to process cotton. At home, he was "always moving," often working on a projects list created by his wife, Kitty. When not working, he could be found listening to the radio in a small room in the center of the house where the phone and wood stove were located. From his vantage point in "the wood stove room," he could see the TV in the front room (although not hear it) and be slightly removed if conversations became too boisterous.

Jean, while laid-back and easygoing, struggled most of his life from his World War II combat experiences. He continued to pick shrapnel from his damaged leg 25 years after the war had ended. Jean died from cancer when he was 71 years old.

Mike's mom's name was Catherine, although everyone called her Kitty. She was 100 percent Irish; her maiden name was Coyne. Kitty attended Elms College in Chicopee, Massachusetts, and graduated from St. Luke's Nursing School in Pittsfield in 1942. She promptly joined the Navy, was stationed at Chelsea Naval Hospital in Boston, and had the distinction of serving as nurse for the future President Kennedy when he returned home to recover from his injuries after being torpedoed on PT-109. Kitty has been described by her children as strong-willed, caring, and the family's disciplinarian.

She ran the Chalifoux Nursery School from her home for many years. A central point for her charges was the side-yard playground complemented by a large, old, blue-and-white motorboat resting on cinder blocks. Kitty attended, graduated from, and worked for North Adams State College as the Director of Health Services. As busy as Kitty was, she always made sure the family ate supper together and caught up on each others' daily activities. As her children grew older and married, Kitty continued to host Thursday night dinners for the entire family that everyone was expected (and wanted) to attend. The conversations were loud and raucous as the family debated local and national topics. All holidays were celebrated extravagantly at Grandma's, including each family member's birthday: parties included handmade finger-rolls, soda, and a grand birthday cake with candles. As the kids grew older, wine and beer were substituted for soda.

The birthday tradition included lights out and sister Cathy with her nieces Nora and Caitlin delivering the cake to the lucky recipient. Only Cathy had the exclusive right to use her finger to scoop out a chunk of cake from the side. Cathy, who was doted on by the family, used to sit in the "big room" and listen to bluegrass music for several hours a day.

Kitty is credited with maintaining the family's closeness until her death in 2010, at the age of 89. The family had a long-standing tradition of vacationing at Lake Saint Catherine's in southern Vermont, and at one point they purchased a lakeside cabin. When Kitty worked for the college, she and the kids would stay at the lake all of July and August. Jean would join them during his company's vacation shutdown.

As a youngster, Mike rode his bike everywhere, often ending up with his cronies at the Mark Hopkins School playground playing pickup baseball or football. Mike, skinny like his dad, was athletic and played on one of the better Little League teams, the Police

Department. When not playing ball, he and his friends could be found up at the Fish Pond (Windsor Pond) playing in the woods or at one of their favorite gathering spots, the railroad tracks. The tracks were at the bottom of a hill so the boys would split into two groups: one group would hide in the bushes at the bottom, while the group at the top would bombard them with rocks. After a while the groups would switch places. Surprisingly, no one was seriously hurt during these fusillades of fun.

Always the entrepreneur, at an early age Mike would canvas his neighborhood looking for lawns to mow or walkways to shovel, and at one point delivered the *Transcript* newspaper to a long list of customers. While in high school, he and his friend Bobby worked at J.C. Penney's as stock boys. His jobs provided spending money and, in the winter, supported his skiing passion. From an early age, Mike skied most weekends at Dutch Hill Ski Area in nearby Heartwellville, Vermont. Mike was an excellent skier, and even as a teenager, better than most adults.

Mike and his siblings attended Saint Joseph's grammar and high school. In high school, Mike participated in the Speech Club and, later in life, was considered a polished and gifted speaker. At one point, happy-go-lucky Mike and several friends created a bogus "Discussion Group" that provided a cover for their class absences and allowed them to smoke outside or leave school grounds. At some point, Sister Superior had Mike make morning and afternoon intercom announcements. Initially perceiving the new responsibilities as an earned distinction, Mike came to realize that Sister just wanted to keep track of him.

After high school graduation, Mike attended Saint Anselm College in Manchester, New Hampshire, for two and a half years, transferred to a local community college, and eventually became subject to the draft. After several notices from the draft board and passing a physical, Mike entered the Army on August 8, 1968. He boarded a bus in front of the North Adams Post Office and left for eight weeks of basic training at Fort Jackson, South Carolina. There, he received his Military Occupational Specialty (MOS) of 11-Bravo-infantryman. Mike's next stop was the eight-week Advanced Infantry Training course. Shortly after AIT, he was selected to attend a 10-week non-commissioned officers course at Fort Benning, Georgia. Mike enjoyed the course challenges and became especially skilled in the art of calling-in of artillery fire, which would serve him well in the future.

Senior catechist, Michael Chalifoux, becomes a twentieth century apostle.

Captured in time, with a caption from St. Joe's 1965 high school yearbook.

After a 30-day home leave, his entire family accompanied him to the Bradley International Airport just over the state line in Connecticut, and said their tearful goodbyes as he departed for Vietnam. Mike flew from Connecticut to Fort Lewis in Washington, then to Alaska and Japan, finally landing in Cam Ranh Bay.

Vietnam

After several days in-country, Mike was assigned to Company C, 2nd Battalion (mechanized), 8th Infantry Regiment, 4th Infantry Division (known as the Panthers) which had 17 mammoth APCs. There was one carrier per squad, four carriers per platoon, and 16 per company with an APC for the commanding officer as well. All were equipped with .50-caliber machine guns.

Mike's unit operated in II Corps and moved between the cities of Pleiku, An Khe, and Qui Nhong, all located in the center of the country. Pleiku is on the western side of Vietnam and borders Cambodia at a point where Mike said his platoon made several incursions into that country.

Over the course of Mike's one-year tour of duty, his unit conducted patrols, set up ambushes, and provided bridge, road, and fire base perimeter security. When Mike's platoon was outside the fire base they would laager (an Afrikaans term meaning, essentially, "circle the wagons" or entrench) for the night and his squad would move out a kilometer or more, and set up listening posts and/or ambushes. Although the Panthers went to war on APCs, they were infantrymen, albeit mechanized ones.

During the unit's time in Vietnam, it participated in 11 campaigns. Some of the operational names were Sam Houston, Francis Marion, Don Quin, and Paul Revere III and IV. The battalion so distinguished itself that it received the Vietnamese Cross of Gallantry and the Civic Action Medal First Class.

Preparing for a short-term patrol (courtesy Chalifoux family).

Keeping Route 19 open for convoys moving supplies and equipment inland from the coast was a daily chore. Mike, as the newbie, was often volunteered to "sweep" the roads with a metal detector, walking in front of the APCs almost as a sacrificial early warning device should a mine be detected or explode. It was nerve-racking: spent cartridges, old soda, C ration cans, too many things to list, would set off the sensitive detector. Then Mike used his bayonet and, digging with extreme caution, would uncover and identify the source of the alarm.

Some of the VC mines used explosives stuffed in a sandbag primed with an explosive actuator, and because of the lack of metal these were more difficult to detect. Once a mine was detected, the accompanying combat engineers would normally blow it up right where it was found. Magnifying his perilous responsibility and escalating Mike's anxiety were the platoon sergeant's brisk commands: "get the lead out of your ass" and move faster.

Mike, somewhere along Route 19 (courtesy Chalifoux family).

One dark night after several months in-country, while on perimeter watch, Mike detected movement just outside the protective barbed wire. He thought the shadows and faint sounds were caused by the wind and didn't want to raise an alarm and look like a fool. Waiting several minutes, and after close scrutiny, he could see tiny flashlights blinking softly and approaching the perimeter. At this point he became alarmed and called in pre-registered artillery fire all along the perimeter. The resulting bombardment extinguished the lights and halted a ground attack on their isolated encampment.

The next day a brief search found only a few pieces of flesh and some blood trails where it appeared bodies had been dragged off. As a result of Mike's quick actions, he was awarded the Army Commendation Medal, and given three days off-the-line, sent to the Vung Tau R&R center which was located on the coast southeast of Saigon.

While Mike was at Vung Tau, tragedy struck his unit. Viet Cong, using B40 rockets (rocket propelled grenades), ambushed his APC platoon, killing his best friend Dave and another trooper. The powerful, four-foot launchers, using a high explosive anti-tank (HEAT) warhead, can easily penetrate up to seven inches of armor from a distance of 150 yards. The APCs had one and a half inches of armor.

Mike heard that the rocket melted one of the soldiers directly into his seat so even the strongest man in their squad couldn't pull him out. Eventually they separated the man from the seat and some of the material was fused with the body. The soldiers tried to get the corpse into the body bag as quickly as possible. Mike never saw either man again and it bothers him to this day.

A rubbing of Dave's name from the Vietnam Veterans Memorial in Washington, D.C., is prominently displayed in Mike's living room, but it doesn't negate the pain: "I wasn't there ... I was on R&R.... I should have been there," he says.

After six months in-country, Mike was looked on as one of the senior squad members and assigned to lead nighttime patrols. The dangerous patrols usually involved Mike and between five and seven troopers. Prior to leaving their laager, the squad would replenish supplies of ammo, grenades, popup flares, and Claymore mines. They applied facial camouflage paint and, most importantly, closely studied the grease-penciled maps, familiarizing themselves with the terrain that they would be traveling through. While only a mile from their encampment, the squad would be alone, lacking immediate support and deep in dangerous territory.

One particular night, the platoon leader had decided the mission would be to lie in ambush along the berm of a distant rice paddy. The group departed after dusk and cautiously took a circuitous path to their ambush site. The night was of deepest black, lacking the kindness of moonlight, and deadly quiet with the exception of a distant barking village dog. The squad was crossing a field, fairly certain they were undetected, when they began hearing numerous Vietnamese voices. Realizing the sound was coming from a nearby tree line, and most likely Viet Cong searching for his squad, Mike had to make a quick decision: Either push forward, surprise and engage the unseen enemy hidden in the tree line, or find a "hide" and hope the threat would pass.

From the careless nature of the Viet Cong's chatter, Mike gambled that the approaching VC had not seen his squad and decided the group would conceal itself in a small, single cluster of bamboo right in the center of the field. He shepherded the group into this tiniest of shelters. The six anxious troopers barely fit inside the small island clump and found themselves trapped in the thicket, surrounded by voices. The VC continued talking as they searched around the tiny bamboo grove. Pulses quickened when the enemy unit took a break right against their bamboo hideout. Several of the VC began urinating near the hideout without realizing the Americans were ten feet away.

After hours of exaggerated, motionless, and deafening silence, the enemy decided there were no Americans nearby and moved on to search the next field. Mike, just before dawn, led the lucky and relieved troopers back to their encampment.

On a more relaxed occasion, while guarding a bridge, Mike and his squad would entertain Vietnamese children that were attracted to their large vehicles, looking for handouts. The dark-skinned, dark-haired, shoeless kids wore hand-me-down gauze shirts and oversized shorts. The kids were favorites of the soldiers. Their ages ranged from two or three years old to mid-teens. The troopers, rich by their standards, would share cigarettes and C rations with the friendly urchins and even help them catch fish.

The troopers' "fishing" would involve throwing hand grenades into the water, creating deadly and impressive explosions. The children would gleefully dive in and retrieve the stunned or dead fish. Even though cautioned by the troopers, they wouldn't wait for the grenade to explode before beginning to leap. As everyone got accustomed to "grenade fishing," the troopers decided to amplify their efforts and began using grenades, wrapped in C-4, a plastic explosive, and a detonator cap. These improvised depth charges created gigantic explosions, increasing the killing radius and harvesting many more fish. The troopers would again warn their little friends about waiting

Returning to the relative safety of his APC after a nighttime patrol (courtesy Chalifoux family).

for the explosion to finish before jumping in the water, but they weren't to be deterred and jumped in almost simultaneously.

Cigarettes or candy always bring smiles (courtesy Chalifoux family).

As his tour of duty was coming to a close, Mike was transferred to a small base near Pleiku and given miscellaneous duties including training rear-echelon soldiers in the art of patrolling.

When his tour ended, Mike flew from Tan Son Nhat Airport to Chicago and ultimately arrived in Albany, New York, as a civilian. He hitched a ride to North Adams, arriving unexpectedly at 2:00 a.m. Duke, the family's German shepherd, woke Tom, who warmly welcomed his older brother home.

Mike was drafted into the Army in August 1968, served for 20 months ("and five days"), and was released from active duty on April 11, 1970. Mike had attained the rank of sergeant and been awarded the Combat Infantryman's Badge and the Bronze Star for Meritorious Service.

Post-Vietnam

After his honorable discharge, Mike returned to North Adams and worked at the Mary Jezyk Sunshine Camp for children with special needs—the same day camp long attended by his sister Cathy. During the early 1970s, Mike also returned to college and graduated from the University of Massachusetts with a bachelor's degree in economics and politics.

He met Mary, who would become his wife, while they were working at Sunshine Camp. They were married in 1975 at the Notre Dame Church in Adams, Mary's home parish, and they would have two children, Nora and Caitlin. Early on, the family lived in one of Mike's rental houses on Furnace Street, known as "the big house." The slate-roofed, dark green asphalt-shingled apartment house was located on the side of a hill and had a finished attic space where the family resided. The building, with four apartments on each level, looked huge and ominous to Mike's little girls.

Every Christmas Mike would, with his devil-may-care attitude, climb to the highest part of the roof and affix a peace sign to the peak, decorated with Christmas lights.

The family then bought a home on Monroe Street on the edge of town, dead-ending into woods with a nearby stream and natural habitat. The family also acquired 10 acres of land in Stamford, Vermont, and over time built a rustic cabin, road, and a bridge. They all loved this getaway, known as "the land in Stamford," and frequently hiked, snowshoed, and even set up a small maple-sugar operation on the property. Eventually the property was sold.

As the Vietnam War continued on, Mike was always willing to speak out on issues he believed strongly in, what he thought were the unnecessary sacrifices by servicemen. With this in mind, he joined the Vietnam Veterans Against the War (VVAW) and participated in protest marches in Washington, D.C. Mike and thousands of veterans demonstrated against the war and threw their medals on the White House lawn. After seven days of protest and a final demonstration in front of the Supreme Court, Mike hitched a ride home with friends.

Always the entrepreneur, Mike partnered with his sister Mary Ann in opening a number of apparel stores serving the North Adams and Williamstown areas. They specialized in imports from India and China. During the late 1970s and 1980s, the young partners also began buying and selling apartment houses and at one point owned 26 units.

During the 1980s and '90s, Mike held various positions helping veterans. He was named the Veterans Outreach Specialist for the city of North Adams—one of only 12 such positions throughout the Commonwealth of Massachusetts. He focused on helping Vietnam-era and disabled veterans find employment and made referrals for housing, counseling, and general services; and provided assistance to those veterans seeking Small Business Administration (SBA) loans to start their own businesses.

Mike also served multiple terms as the head of the Vietnam Veterans Association in Massachusetts. Next, he served on the Massachusetts Governor's Advisory Committee on Veterans' Affairs. He was one of 23 statewide representatives making recommendations on legislative issues affecting veterans. The committee was central in working on housing for elderly veterans and expanding the state-run outreach centers for veterans suffering Post-Traumatic Stress Disorder (PTSD). Occasionally, Mike wrote speeches concerning VA issues for Governor Dukakis. Mike and his family had their picture taken with the governor during one of these occasions.

As his expertise grew, he was elected the first New England Regional Director of the Vietnam Veterans of America (VVA). His new responsibilities included managing the 28 VVA chapters in New England and lobbying for veterans' legislation in Washington, D.C. Locally, Mike's personal goal was to increase VVA membership and the number of state chapters.

As time passed, people began to notice that Mike's logical, commonsense approach to situations was being edged aside by symptoms of anxiety, agitation, impatience, and impulsivity. After extended visits to the VA Medical Center he was diagnosed with a severe case of PTSD. Mike would fight these relentless symptoms for the rest of his life, and in many cases channel them to his advantage, railing against bureaucracies he thought thwarted veterans from receiving their earned benefits. There are some who believe Mike's sensitivity made him especially vulnerable to the ravages of the war, somewhat similar to his dad's experiences.

Mike, who was an accomplished skier before going to Vietnam, came home, skied once, and gave up the sport. While he often demonstrated risky behavior, friends believed, skiing no longer provided the "rush" that he sought after his tour-of-duty in Vietnam. Family and friends became more convinced that Mike's PTSD had worsened and seriously affected his ability to keep a job, and more importantly, preserve a marriage. His daughters, Nora and Caitlin, were (and continued to be) close to Mike.

Mike eventually co-founded the North Adams Vietnam Veterans Chapter #54 known as Fire Base Trentino at 30 River Street. It was one of the first centers in the country with a liquor license and proved to be a popular gathering spot for local veterans and their families. They created an adjoining memorial garden, with special flag–medallions honoring the nine Berkshire County veterans who died in the War (among them, Russell Roulier).

The self-funded center and its women's auxiliary developed scholarships for the children of Vietnam-era veterans; decorated local cemeteries; hosted teen nights, Christmas, and birthday parties for children; and provided honor guards for parades. The center also manned a crisis hotline and sponsored in-house counseling sessions.

One of Mike's later initiatives was creating a pantry that raised and distributed food items to the needy. Through a state subsidy, and with the help of veteran volunteers, they sponsored, collected, and donated more than $1,000,000 in food. After four years, the program lost funding and gradually ended.

Not one to remain inactive, Mike began and managed, through generous donations, daily cleanup initiatives that had crews picking up litter on Route 2 from the Mohawk Trail to Williamstown and alternatively along Route 8, Curran Highway. Mike could be seen in his scruffy sport coat and flat, charcoal, herringbone cap covering his wild mop of curly white hair, using a broom and long handled dustpan to sweep up litter near the local Veterans Memorial Wall, always accompanied by Monty, his chocolate Labrador. Cathy, his constant companion, would be sitting close by in his car.

At one point, Mike worked several years for a local funeral home, primarily picking up and transporting bodies. As veterans have aged, become infirm, or died off, Fire Base Trentino now sees little activity but will always be remembered as a haven of support and solace for over thirty years.

Mike was patriotic, pro-community, and business-minded; he could also be blunt, earthy, and quarrelsome especially when he thought veterans were being disadvantaged. His familiarity with veterans' needs and issues enabled him to demand help for them, confidently and emphatically. Mike was often asked to speak to veterans' groups and occasionally on federal holidays. His impassioned, heartfelt, and well delivered speeches were appreciated by all.

There are many stories of Mike's tireless efforts to help veterans, from transporting them to medical appointments to visiting them during extended hospital stays. Mike drove hundreds of miles at his own expense. He doggedly helped veterans secure adequate housing, then would help them move their personal goods. In one particular case, Mike and Monty began visiting a wheelchair-bound, noncommunicative veteran at a local nursing home. After many visits, Mike began taking the man for car rides, and his condition began to improve. The veteran's speech returned and he became more independent. After years of Mike's attention, the veteran was released and now lives with his son.

Mike's good nature and easygoing personality, combined with his cynicism about politics and the VA, made him easily relatable to most vets. Personally, he was the first person to actually welcome me home from Vietnam (in 2009: it took that long for someone to say those words), and encouraged me to successfully apply for VA medical assistance.

Few people knew how sensitive Mike was when it came to caring for nature's creatures. He would capture bugs and let them go rather than squashing them. Early in his life, he carried a shovel in the trunk of his car to pick up dead roadside animals so he could bury them later. He and Monty were always together, and his independent cat never far away. (The cats were always named "crazy cats," a French pun from his last name, Chalifoux.)

In addition to his good works, in the last years of his life he became the sole custodian of Cathy, his 59-year-old sister afflicted with Down syndrome. Cathy was a gentle soul, petite and innocent with a baby-face appearance. The family had personally cared for Cathy her entire life, and her childlike nature softened the hearts of anyone around her. Her innocence made people more accepting, giving, and considerate. Early in 2018, Cathy's capabilities began to diminish, and Mike took on the tasks of feeding, bathing, and moving her up and down stairs. He also carried her to his car for their daily downtown trips. Mike pledged that Cathy, as she became weaker, would remain at home and not be hospitalized.

As Cathy's condition worsened, Mike found out on Valentine's Day through a brain scan that he had cancer. It had metastasized and involved his brain, lungs, and lymph nodes. His immediate concern was not for his critical circumstances, but who would take care of Cathy.

As Mike began treatments, Cathy became less communicative, eating very little. Unresponsive, she died in her bed on April 9, 2018, attended to by her nieces, Nora and Caitlin. Mike's condition continued to worsen. After brief stays at the nursing home and the hospital, Mike insisted on returning home to Monroe Street where he slept in a hospital bed in the living room.

Mike, who helped so many people, was now aided and supported by his daughters and fellow veterans. They provided transportation, visited him, and fed his dog, Monty, and the current "crazy cat."

His daughters maintained a sorrowful vigilance. At one point, the girls slept on an air mattress near his bed; he remarked how it was like having a sleepover. Mike slipped away around 9 a.m. on June 25, 2018. His funeral service and military burial were attended by family, friends, and the many veterans he had helped over the years. The honor guard presented the American flag to his daughters and fired three volleys from their rifles, a fitting tribute to a great veteran.

His family remembers that on the day of his passing, a large black bear visited his garage almost like he was saying goodbye, and several days later Mike's devoted dog, Monty, died.

14

William "Bill" Buzzell—
Army Artillery Unit

Recipient of Army Commendation Medal

In-Country

Bill was pleased as he could be, stationed in Vietnam and designated to support a mobile artillery unit with its headquarters located near Saigon. The assignment seemed relatively serene, compared to being an 11-Bravo Army Infantryman.

It didn't take long for someone to tell Bill, the newbie, that there weren't any safe places in Vietnam. Just two weeks prior to his arrival, several of the unit's troopers were patrolling back roads when their Jeep tripped a wire and triggered the explosion of several Claymore mines located on each side of the road.

The troopers had fabricated and welded from angle iron steel eight-foot metal arms with a crossbar that extended out in front of their Jeep. They thought the extended apparatus would find, expose, and trigger any booby trap wires before the Jeep ran over them.

The two troopers in the reconfigured Jeep had left just an hour after sunrise, before the deadening heat had established its presence, and began patrolling the back roads.

Unbeknownst to them, as they drove slowly out of one village, the local Viet Cong had strung a slack wire across the road, attached to Claymore mines. The wire when pulled would trigger the Claymore mines allowing the blast to occur on both sides of the Jeep. Never realizing what was about to happen, the Jeep hit the wire, setting off both Claymores and shattering the back road stillness. The troopers died instantly. They and their vehicle were shredded by 1,400 one-eighth-inch steel pellets that exploded from the mines.

Shortly afterwards, a foot patrol came upon the site, realized it was too late for first aid, and radioed back about the ambush. A tow truck dragged the Jeep to base, and several medics and an ambulance brought back the shattered bodies.

The story was a sobering initiation for Bill. It drove home the dangerousness of his new assignment. The dead troopers had been part of his battery and had slept in a nearby hootch.

Family

Bill's paternal grandfather, Edmund Buzzell, was an itinerant preacher who lived behind a local church and held revivals as far away as West Virginia. Family lore is that he was of French extraction and he may have intentionally dropped the "e" from Buzzelle.

His maternal grandparents, Mary and Anthony Klawitter, worked and met at a logging camp in Wisconsin. She was the camp's cook and he worked as a logger. They were both of European descent, possibly Slovak or Czech. After they married, Anthony eventually worked as a bricklayer and Mary as a seamstress working from their home.

Bill's parents, Harold and Genevieve, met in the unlikeliest of places: at the Marine Corps Recruit Depot in Parris Island, South Carolina, during World War II. Both were Marines. Sergeant Harold Buzzell was just back from the Philippines, where he provided technical support for Marine air groups. Corporal Genevieve Klawitter was stationed at Parris Island in an administration role. Earlier pictures, location unknown, show Harold and Genevieve, in uniform, with a group of squadron personnel posing in front of a B-25 Mitchell bomber. This twin-engine, medium-sized bomber was used by the Marines in the Pacific theater.

After a number of dates, the handsome couple were married in a simple ceremony in Genevieve's hometown, Mosinee, Wisconsin. A photo of the attractive, smiling couple shows them in their Marine Corps dress uniforms—Genevieve, with her dark curly hair and immaculate Women Marines uniform, and Harold wearing his dress blues and overseas campaign ribbons. Shortly after the picture was taken, they were both discharged from the Corps and after several moves landed in North Adams.

The energetic young couple waited not at all to start a family: Bill and his sister Faye were born in Wausau, Wisconsin, and his brother Gary was born shortly after their move to North Adams. Each was born one year apart in 1946, 1947, and 1948. They initially lived in North Adams and, with help from Harold's brother and friends, built a house on Notch Road.

Both parents were patriotic and proud of their military service, especially in the vaunted Marine Corps. The bulldog tattoo on Harold's right arm was a daily reminder of his service to his country.

Early Years

It was the late 1950s, and Greylock School auditorium was filed with adults and children enjoying the performance by the Braytonville–Greylock Minstrels. The small crowd was delighted with the hometown minstrel show. Harold and Genevieve were part of the popular troupe that sponsored weekend entertainment for many North Adams residents.

In a less aware time, the all-white troupe composed of six women, known as the Surfside-Six, and seven men with blackened faces, performed songs and music with origins in black American culture. The troupe danced on the makeshift stage to raucous applause. They also exchanged jokes, cajoled the audience, and sang popularized jazz, ragtime, and blues songs.

Harold Buzzell, theatrically outfitted in a patterned coat with tails and a dark scarf, played the trumpet and sang popular Al Jolson songs. He had a deep baritone, and the crowd loved his rendition of "Oh! Susanna." Genevieve, in a multicolored dress with a large bow on her head, performed with the chorus girls. Their three-night performances delighted the cheering crowd.

At one point, Harold converted to Catholicism, Genevieve's religion, and became active in church activities, achieving Grand Knight status with the popular Knights of Columbus. Harold was also the civic-minded campaign manager for Lou Diamond's successful mayoral race and both parents were actively involved in the Parent Teacher Association.

Harold put his organizational skills to work as the office manager for the Gypsum company, located in Cheshire. Genevieve worked full time in an administration role at a local manufacturing company. After she got home from work she would prepare the family's supper. As an accomplished cook, her main entrees were usually a combination of meat and potatoes, or a tasty lasagna, and always fish sticks on Friday night.

Genevieve was creative, thrifty, and had the knack of making great meals with leftovers. For weekend picnics she was known for her delicious "camp" salad in which she would substitute hot dogs for ham. The family also relished her home-baked pies and cookies. With both parents working, the family treated itself several times a month to eating out at Florini's Italian restaurant. Genevieve was also a skilled seamstress and in her free time made clothes for her children. Though kind, Bill's parents were firm, and shared in the responsibility of disciplining the children. An adage popular at the time was "spare the rod and spoil the child."

The family vacationed every summer in Mosinee, staying with their grandmother and playing with their cousins. The routine was to take the three children to Grandma's for several weeks each summer and be back in North Adams by late August just before school started. They often took a fun-filled, circuitous route to Grandma's via Niagara Falls, Canada, and a Lake Michigan ferry that landed in Wisconsin.

During the school year, the family often had Sunday picnics at Mausert's Pond, located at the Clarksburg State Park or at Windsor Lake in North Adams (a.k.a. the Fish Pond). Usually their Uncle Bill's family would accompany them, often playing car tag with his brother. One of them would pull behind a building and hide, and when discovered, it was the other person's turn to drive away and hide his vehicle behind a building. The kids loved this adult version of tag.

Bill attended local public grammar schools and Saint Joseph's high school. He held a variety of different jobs while in school. He served as a busboy at a local restaurant, worked with high school friends at the downtown J.C. Penney's, delivered milk and ice cream for Modern Dairy, and also delivered bread to local stores. As he grew older, Bill worked as a laborer at a local lime plant owned and operated by the Gypsum company.

At school, although tall for his age, basketball was not his natural talent. Realizing this, he became the training manager for the basketball team. Bill was also a member of the ski club, and worked hard as a backstage hand in the school play *Paris*. He found moving stage sets much more satisfying than trying to sing with his low-pitched voice. The year Bill graduated, he had perfect attendance but was most remembered for getting in a skateboard accident and attending his senior prom with both arms in slings.

Calamity touched the family when his father, Harold, died of a cerebral hemorrhage in the early 1960s at the age of 40. Bill and his siblings were still in high school. At the time, the kids were unaware their dad had persistent trouble with high blood pressure. The loss of their happy-go-lucky, fun-loving father had a great effect on family and friends. Genevieve went on to live to 93.

Many of St. Joe's high school boys, on occasion, traveled covertly over-the-line to Hoosick Falls, New York, where the drinking age was 18 and picture-less identification cards were seldom checked. On one of their treks, Bill and his brother got into a fight with several local men. As the situation escalated, they went outside to leave but someone had taken their car's distributor cap. By this time, local authorities had arrived, and Bill and his brother spent the night in jail. Their uncle bailed them out in the morning.

Bill's friends in high school included fellow future veterans Mike Chalifoux and Mike Gorman. The three frequented New York establishments, the Clarksburg Fair, and sometimes Little's Pool Hall located above J.J. Newberry's department store, a hangout for St. Joe's boys.

Graduating in 1965, Bill matriculated to North Adams State College and remained there through his junior year. While studies may not have been his top priority, he did make a number of close friends who often gathered for discussions at Unis's bar on State Street, and on weekends could easily end up at the Merry-Go-Round or Three-Way bars in New York State, a mere 40-minute jaunt through nearby Pownal, Vermont, and then a left off Route 7 onto Route 346.

When he left school, Bill worked a year in Boston for a publishing company and received his draft notice in December 1968. He chose a three-year enlistment period, one more than the draft required, to ensure he would be trained in the MOS (military occupational specialty) of his choice.

The Army

Bill attended basic training at Fort Jackson, South Carolina. Then he trained five more weeks at Fort Lee, Virginia, in his military occupation as a Stock Control and Automotive Repair Parts Specialist. Bill was assigned to a unit in Baumholder, Germany, and worked there for almost two years in a support role at a large supply battalion which supported the base's infantry and tracked-vehicle groups. Typically, he'd have stayed only one, but it was generally believed that Bill's deferred orders to Vietnam were a result of his brother Gary's having suffered a grievous wound as a Marine in Vietnam. Once Gary recovered and was safely out-of-country, Bill received his orders. After a brief leave and two weeks of infantry training at Fort Lewis, Washington, Bill flew to Fairbanks, Alaska, then on to Japan to refuel, eventually landing at the large U.S. air base in Bien Hoa, Vietnam.

Bill remembers deplaning into an almost unbearable wall of heat as he walked down the mobile stairway. He next noticed the throngs of weaponized soldiers providing base security. Quite different from his duty station in Germany, everyone was on high alert, carrying a loaded weapon, and anticipating trouble.

His group was transported to Long Binh, the largest Army base in Vietnam. It was located 12 miles northeast of Saigon and functioned as a major logistics center as well as a command headquarters. While awaiting assignment, the group underwent additional weapons training with M-16 rifles, grenade launchers, and the M-60 and M-50 machine guns. Bill was promoted to Specialist 5 at his first in-country morning formation. His responsibilities increased, and he quickly learned more about tracked vehicles.

Bill was assigned to D Battery, 5th Battalion, 2nd Artillery. This rapid-response mobilized unit was based at nearby Camp Frenzell-Jones, named after two earlier combat casualties, heroes Herbert Frenzell and Billy Jones.

The main responsibility of his unit was conducting early-morning road sweeps of Route 1, a major roadway between Xuan Loc and Saigon/Long Binh, just like his friend

A pause in an early morning road-sweep (courtesy William Buzzell).

Mike Chalifoux over on Route 19. This assignment was dirty and dangerous, as Bill tried to anticipate where enemy mines had been laid, and provided convoy and tactical support for other units in their area of operation.

The battery consisted of two platoons, each having four "dusters." The dusters were tank-like vehicles named "dusters" due to the large amount of dust they created speeding across the dirt roads of Vietnam. The machines carried two 40mm cannons spouting from the front of its turret and often included a M-60 machine gun. The Viet Cong called them "Fire Dragons" thanks to their high volume of devastating fire. Each machine was manned by a crew of four to six soldiers. All 40mm ammunition was tracer, allowing gunners to see the effect of their firing. The young duster crews often painted bravado slogans on the front of their vehicles. One of the dusters in Bill's platoon displayed the following words: "The Fearsome Foursome Kicking Ass. Rest-in-peace Charlie—May your bones rot in hell!"

(Courtesy William Buzzell.)

Often accompanying the "dusters" were "quad .50s"—four .50-caliber machine guns mounted on a self-propelled electrically powered turret, known as the "Whispering Death." In Bill's platoon, the turrets were mounted on five-ton trucks. The quads were anti-aircraft weapons, but in Vietnam, they were used against enemy personnel and operated by two loaders and a gunner. The guns would provide devastating, concentrated firepower in any direction.

The "dusters" and the "quad .50s" were accompanied by a searchlight unit with infrared capabilities. The searchlights would scan base perimeters in an infrared mode, then switch to visible light once the enemy was located, and bring a terrifying fusillade from the "dusters" and "quad .50s."

Shielded .50-caliber machine gun ready for action (courtesy William Buzzell).

The battery provided highway security for resupply convoys along contested highways and could be very effective in breaking up ambushes. The units were especially desirable in providing additional firepower for remote fire bases.

The "dusters" and "quads" were old pieces of equipment and required considerable maintenance such as removing and re-installing engines and repairing armament. Bill often found himself retrieving spare parts from the supply depot in Long Binh, and, using a duster with another armed soldier for security, delivering the parts to remote fire bases.

The deliveries were never made in the early morning because the roads needed to be swept for mines. It was a good indication if local Vietnamese traffic showed up; they'd often hear through the grapevine if a mine had been laid the night before. There were also times when the Military Police would alert Bill that he would be driving through contested roadways, and he was glad he had learned to drive an APC (armored personnel carrier) and could appropriate it for his delivery truck.

Bill, as a Specialist 5, also had nighttime sergeant-of-the-guard responsibilities where he was required to drive the base's perimeter in a Jeep with black-out-lights, and check each guard tower to ensure at least one person in the two-man outpost was alert and actively scanning the perimeter.

Occasionally when operating without vehicle lights, Bill would veer off the roadway. One particular night, on a bad stretch of road with a sharp corner, he turned on his headlights revealing an MP and his scout dog who were silently patrolling. The sudden headlights had caused the MP to lose his night vision and potentially exposed him and his scout dog to danger. The MP was irate and asked Bill to step out of the vehicle so they

Bill and his "delivery truck." The duster was originally designed as an anti-aircraft weapon but quickly found use against enemy ground forces (courtesy William Buzzell).

could settle this issue. The handler started the conversation by instructing Bill to be still or the dog would react viciously. After some calmer conversation and the handler realizing Bill was new to this job, they parted friendly without resorting to fists. Bill realized he had made a mistake.

The sleeping accommodations were austere. The troopers lived in two-man perimeter bunkers surrounded by degraded and leaky olive-green sandbags. As at other bases, the bunkers had heavy timbers for corner posts and roofs, dirt-filled ammo boxes for the walls, and the entire structure was surrounded with sandbags, usually two or three deep. The walls were six feet high with a two-foot 360-degree aperture, allowing for defensive firing. The roof was layered in sandbags. Their beds were dilapidated, filthy, faded-green cots used by many, many heavy-booted predecessors. The interiors might be enhanced if plywood or paint could be heisted or diverted from the nearby supply center. As always, the bunkers were irritatingly rat- and roach-infested. Fortunately, the nearby enlisted club would hold occasional promotions: two dead rats for a warm beer. With the increasing and easy availability, Bill and his friends were able to take fine advantage of this redemption system.

Bill considered taking R&R in Australia or Hawaii, but as his time passed he lost the opportunity. Between assignments he was able to take a three day in-country R&R at Vung Tau.

Several members of Battery D, including Bill, came to realize the importance of transportation and how it would enhance opportunities to visit nearby Saigon. American drivers would normally chain and padlock the steering wheel on Jeeps, knowing how

Vung Tau Center, an in-country R&R spot popular for its beaches and its close proximity to Saigon.

easy they were to steal. In this case, the troopers saw an ARVN soldier (Army of the Republic of Vietnam, our ally) stop briefly and go inside a building, leaving the vehicle unlocked. Following an old Army adage, "if you can't get it through normal channels, steal it," D Battery struck with swiftness and commandeered their first vehicle.

Next step was repainting the Jeep's markings on the bumper, hood, side panels, and rear, making it an "official" D Battery Jeep. Once the painting was completed, the vehicle was available to troopers for resupply missions or at night to those sneaking out to meet with lady friends in nearby villages. During one weekend, Bill and a group of soldiers drove the Jeep to Saigon and parked it inside their hotel lobby for safekeeping. The next morning, when joy-riding in Saigon, the Military Police stopped the vehicle. With no proper registration papers, the Jeep was swiftly confiscated. The five troopers needed to hitchhike back to their fire base. Surprisingly, nothing happened to them.

Bill's commanding officer allowed his unit to attend the Bob Hope Show at Christmastime 1970 in Long Binh, three years after I saw the same show in Da Nang. Thousands of troopers from other units were also at the raucous event, with numerous wounded soldiers occupying the front seats. As always, Bob and his entourage cracked jokes, performed skits, and danced with beautiful women. The troops loved it.

Bill worked several months with D Battery, 5th battalion, 2nd Artillery, until the unit was ordered to "stand down" and return to the States for deactivation. Since Bill had been in-country for a short period of time, he was reassigned to D Battery, 5th Battalion of the 42nd artillery, for the remainder of his tour. This heavy-gun unit employed 155mm howitzers, which were airlifted or towed to fire bases. The individual howitzer weighed 12,000 pounds, had a crew of 11, and could send a projectile nine miles. Capable of using high explosive, illumination, and smoke rounds, howitzers were involved in many types of missions, ranging from infantry support to fire base security.

Bill again found himself in the important role of finding, securing, and transporting supplies and repair parts from the Long Binh supply center to the main fire base located near Xuan Loc. This base, located near Highway 1 just outside of Saigon, was at a critical junction in the III Corps area.

Right: Stage set for the show. *Below:* Thousands of happy troopers attended. Bill smiles in lower right hand corner (both photographs courtesy William Buzzell).

Above: Bob Hope's regulars, the Golddiggers dancing troupe. *Below:* Prepping for his next delivery, or maybe just joking around (both photographs courtesy William Buzzell).

Coming Home

Bill left Vietnam in late August 1971, and was flown to Oakland, California, where he was discharged. His decorations include the Army Commendation Medal, the Vietnamese Service and Campaign Medals, and the National Defense Medal. During the waning months of his Vietnam tour-of-duty, Bill had applied for and been granted an early release to return to North Adams State College in September for his senior year. Bill remembers one of his first civilian purchases: bell-bottomed pants and flowered shirts for his first set of "real world" clothes in more than three years.

With only one year of school remaining, Bill resided with friends and then found himself an apartment. He was surprised upon his return by non-veterans thinking he was a baby-killer or, even worse, un–American. Bill considered their opinions at best naive, especially from people who had not given of their time or ever been in harm's way. Fortunately, he did find a nucleus of college veterans who were supportive and helped make his transition back to college life easier.

Upon graduation in 1972, Bill was hired by the Veterans Canteen Service, a division within the Veterans Administration, and was pleased to be an active participant in helping veterans. Bill met his wife Leanne while working at the VA Medical Center in Lyons, New Jersey, and they were married in 1976. For the next 34 years, while working for the Canteen Service, they moved 11 times. Bill was assigned to and managed different locations in New York, New Jersey, Pennsylvania, West Virginia, Maryland, and Washington, D.C.

Initially, Bill worked as a retail specialist within the organization. Over the years, as his knowledge increased, so did his responsibilities. They included managing and budgeting for all retail services, food courts, and vending operations located in VA Medical Centers. In the 1990s, Bill was promoted to regional director and, as a senior executive, began managing a staff of district managers who had operational oversight of 20 medical units. For the last year of his employment, Bill finished his career working in Puerto Rico.

He retired in 2006 and lives with Leanne in Maryland, where he works part-time as the manager of operations for a nearby golf course. He enjoys golfing, wildlife photography, and, on occasion, fishing. Leanne raises and shows Australian shepherd dogs. Their son, daughter, and grandchildren live nearby for easy family get-togethers.

Bill felt an obligation to serve his country. At the time he was drafted, he had no political affiliations, although he was anxious about joining the military and being sent to Vietnam. Once in the military, while not liking the strict rules and regulations, he became knowledgeable in his job and served under some outstanding commanding officers.

Bill feels a kinship with those who have served, and found it a maturing experience. It was "all part of doing what your country asked of you." The ensuing years have also made him question the politics, rationale, and sacrifices behind our involvement in that far-away land.

Regardless, Bill is most pleased with his life's work as a canteen manager, providing support to the tens of thousands of veterans who use, and rely on, VA Medical Centers.

15

Gary DeMastrie—Navy, Brown Water Sailor

Vietnamese Service Medal with seven Campaign Stars

Gary sat in the recruiter's second-floor office at the North Adams Post Office, a young man with a big decision to make. He and his friends, Joe and Russ, were tired of school. They were looking for excitement and realized the specter of being drafted was looming in their future. They wanted to enlist in the military's buddy program. This would send them to boot camp together. Joe and Russ took little convincing: The Marine Corps was the only way to go. Joe's dad had been in the Corps, and both he and Russ thought the Marines would be a great challenge. Gary thought otherwise.

He did not want to join the Marine Corps or the Army, even though their two-year enlistment was more appealing than the Navy's four-year requirement. It was late spring 1966 and United States involvement in Vietnam was expanding weekly, along with lengthening casualty lists, usually of Marine or Army infantrymen.

Gary chose the Navy. His enlistment was slightly deferred from Russ and Joe's, and he began Navy boot camp in July 1966. If you'd told him that day in North Adams that he would be, just several months later, assigned to sail to Vietnam aboard the USS *Seminole*, an attack cargo ship (AKA), he would have been more than surprised.

But there he was, reporting-in to the *Seminole's* homeport in San Diego. The master-at-arms informed him the ship was in Long Beach being re-fitted. Grabbing a cab, he made his way to his new ship. As a junior sailor, he was put to work right away in the weeks-long, arduous process of preparing a ship for war.

And then, there he was again, standing on deck of the *Seminole*, just offshore from Da Nang, watching fighter jets bomb and drop napalm on the nearby mountainsides. When he noticed splashes in the water from incoming fire, he thought nostalgically of the recruiter's office and his desire to find a safer haven for his enlistment. Being on an attack cargo ship resupplying the 1st and 3rd Marine Divisions up and down the coast from Da Nang to Hue was not where he expected to be.

He was now a "brown-water" sailor, a term he had never heard before enlistment. In Vietnam, brown-water sailors operated close to shore, either supporting resupply missions or patrolling Vietnam's 5,000 miles of intercoastal waterways and canals. The *Seminole's* mission was to resupply Marines and, consequently, the vessel had to remain just offshore and rely on eight LCMs (Landing Craft Mechanized) to provision the Marine Corps battalions.

Landing craft in the water, waiting to be loaded (courtesy Gary DeMastrie).

Vietnam's lack of dependable highways and rail systems enhanced the importance of the *Seminole*'s crucial resupply efforts. While operating close to shore, they would battle the natural environment of Vietnam, enduring punishing heat and pounding monsoons, ever alert for the threat of enemy divers and mines.

Gary would serve his entire enlistment on the USS *Seminole*, most of this time off the coast of Vietnam. He would end up with three nine-month Vietnam tours, and his ship would earn eleven Vietnam campaign stars. He went where the ship went, and when they returned from the Pacific to San Diego, he was released two weeks early.

Early Years

Gary's story begins in March 1947 at the North Adams hospital where his parents, Lawrence and Anastasia DeMastrie, welcomed their only baby boy. His sister Cynthia had been born four years earlier, and Madeline, a special-needs child, a year before his birth.

Gary's paternal grandparents immigrated from Sondrio, Italy, a small Alpine town known for its vineyards, located in northern Italy, close to Switzerland. It is said that the grandfather Americanized the family's name from Demaestri to DeMastrie—capitalizing the "M" and moving the "e" to the end of his name. They arrived in the United States as so many did, via Ellis Island.

Gary's maternal grandparents, George and Anna Januska, immigrated to the United States from Vilnius, the capital of Lithuania. George arrived first, found work as a shoe repairman, and sent for Anna, who was much younger than him. They raised a boy and three girls, one of whom was Gary's mom, Anastasia. For a short time, Gary and his family lived in the same block as his grandparents.

Gary still has vivid memories of his grandmother Januska's wood burning kitchen stove, and standing in line in the tiny kitchen waiting for potato pancakes, pierogies, and apple turnovers. He also remembers his grandparents' taste for salty herrings that they purchased in small wooden boxes. George and Anna considered the little fish delectable, and Gary was always surprised to see them eat the entire fish including the eyes. To this day, Gary enjoys herring filets—properly prepared, that is (less the fins, eyes, and tail).

Lawrence, Gary's father, enlisted in the Army at the beginning of World War II, only to be discharged from boot camp for angry behavior, and returned to his family in Adams. After his release, Lawrence met Anastasia, who was from North Adams, and they were married. Lawrence did not stay with the family long, and the children's few memories of dad are not warm. He was a professional painter, both commercially and residentially, and worked much of his life painting steel I beams on skyscrapers in Chicago and Florida. Due to the father's detachment, they saw little of the DeMastrie side of the family.

Gary has heard that when his dad was younger, before his illnesses, he was in a music combo with his two brothers. Lawrence was reportedly masterful with the bass fiddle, playing skillfully with either his fingers or a bow. In the 1940s, the group played in upstate New York at Catskill mountain resorts. Lawrence had the honor of making a special appearance playing with the Philharmonic Orchestra. Gary was mesmerized the few times he heard his dad play the fiddle; the large, restored fiddle now sits prominently, on display, in Gary's living room.

Over the years, the kids determined that their dad's dramatic personality changes were attributable to his job as a commercial painter and being exposed to significant amounts of lead-based paint and damaging solvents. In order to clean paint from his arms, he would immerse them in strong-smelling solvents. Lawrence suffered from many symptoms of lead exposure: irritability, headaches, mood disorders. Ultimately, he died at a young age, from cancerous throat tumors.

The family struggled with the absence of the father's income, and Anastasia, Gary's mom, worked three different cleaning jobs trying to support them. Even with her own nagging migraines and spinal column issues, she was seldom *not* working. Anastasia is remembered as being patient and caring with her children. She was also neat and meticulous, and made frugal but delicious meals, consisting of hamburger, salt pork, onions, and cream of celery soup poured over mashed potatoes. Another variation was chopped hot dogs with stewed tomatoes poured onto potatoes. Occasionally, Anastasia would make her "special" spaghetti sauce or her roasted chicken supper.

Once a year as a treat, she would make the family a "killer" apple pie. She had no time to make it more frequently. Anastasia never had a driver's license and, consequently, the family walked everywhere they went. A big treat for them was when Uncle John would take them once or twice a year to McDonald's in Pittsfield, a sojourn of forty miles round trip. The kids loved the hamburgers and fries.

When Gary was eight years old, Anastasia moved the family to a nicer apartment owned by her brother. They lived on the third floor, then moved to the first. The apartment was small: it had a living room, kitchen and two bedrooms. Anastasia and a female boarder shared one bedroom, his sisters the other, and Gary converted the cellar to his room.

Gary attended kindergarten and first grade at Johnson Elementary and moved to Saint Joseph's schools for second grade through senior year of high school. He was shy in high school and, while bright, found his studies boring. More than once, a nun pinched him by the nape of his neck for daydreaming. In spite of all this, and with little time for studying, Gary remained on the honor roll most of his high school years.

In the seventh grade, Gary got his first job, stocking shelves at Bruno's grocery store. In high school, he worked at Jack & Harry's Auto Store from 3:00 until 8:00 p.m. every weeknight and eight hours on Saturday. The store sold an eclectic group of items: tires and shock absorbers, appliances and guns, plus toys for Christmas. Gary could often be found under a car replacing shock absorbers or exhaust systems. With his earnings, he bought his mom a dented refrigerator that was on sale.

Gary's long work hours enabled him to buy his first vehicle, a Bridgestone 60cc Sport motorcycle, beginning his lifelong affection for cycles. Before graduating from high school, he traded in the smaller bike for a larger 1400 cc 1949 Indian motorcycle, which he eventually sold while he was in the Navy.

At one point, Gary was playing at the YMCA, and fell off the high bar, breaking his arm. With no available transportation, he walked over two miles to the hospital. He remembers calling his mom from the hospital and how worried she was about being able to pay the bill. The family tells the story of how she went to the hospital and told the administrator she needed a job to pay the debt. She was hired as a cleaning lady, and worked there for 15 years. Anastasia told her family it was the best job she ever had, with paid vacation, holidays, and benefits.

Outside of school, Gary hung around with Ernie, Leo, Joe Daigneault and Russ Roulier. When they had time, the boys hiked, fished, and hunted. They fished at Cheshire

Lake, which is to say they'd rent a rowboat, stock it with beer and bait, and have a great time "wetting" their fishing lines. Gary did not care if they caught anything; he just enjoyed being with his friends and having his first cold beers. Gary fondly remembers this time period as his "Tom Sawyer" days.

With life at home being uncomfortable, Gary spent many nights, weekends, and holidays with Ernie and his family. There were five boys in Ernie's family and they "officially" adopted Gary as their sixth. The boys played continually outside on the 150 acres of family land. They hunted for deer and small game and spent considerable time target shooting. Usually on Monday nights, after dark, the boys would fish at Bog or Mausert's ponds. Using a rowboat, or fishing from shore, they would try to catch bullhead, also known as horn pout, a hardy member of the catfish family.

Saturday night was card night at Ernie's. The game was Rook, and his mom and dad would take on all challengers. Usually, Gary would team up with Ernie or his brother Dave. Ernie's dad played the game seriously, and more often than not, his team won.

The boys created and often played a game called "manhunt." The rules allowed one participant to hide somewhere on three and a half acres of woods. Special hiding spots were usually in trees, down a hole, in some bushes, or behind rocks. Once situated, the other players tried to find him, and once discovered, it would be someone else's turn to hide. The games often would go on all afternoon until dark.

Ernie's house was the last one on a country road that continued for some distance, and in the winter the boys would make huge, long tunnels in deep snow drifts. The tunnels would extend across the hardly-used road. One time, Ernie's mom ran outside frantically screaming at the burrowed boys to abandon their tunnels. She had seen a huge public-works snow-grader clearing the road. They evacuated just in time.

As part of the local rite-of-passage, Gary made a number of Friday night drinking trips with his high school buddies "going over the line" to nearby New York State where he was easily admitted to Johnny Winarski's bar. Gary was tall for his age, and this worked to his advantage.

After graduation, for a short period of time, Gary worked at the Sprague Electric Company on Union Street in North Adams. His job was to pack and ship manufactured parts. He hadn't worked there long when he, Joe, and Russ made their trip to the recruiter's office.

In the Navy

After enlisting, Gary was placed on a deferred program, and was officially inducted into the Navy in July of 1966. He spent the next 12 weeks in recruit training, at the Great Lakes Naval Station, about 35 miles north of Chicago. Once his training was completed, and after two weeks' leave, he flew to San Diego to join the *Seminole*.

The *Seminole* had been launched in 1944, in support of World War II operations, and then spent considerable time in the Far East during the Korean War. The ship was 459 feet long and had a crew of 400 officers and sailors. After refitting, it was ready for the Vietnam War.

Re-designated as a Landing Cargo Attack Ship (LKA) in 1969, the *Seminole* was part of the Amphibious Squadron #9 of the Seventh Fleet, with its overseas home port located at Subic Bay, in the Philippines. The *Seminole* carried on its deck eight landing crafts 75 feet in length, 20 feet across, and powered by their own twin diesel engines. When hauled onboard, they were cradled and locked down over four large hatches on the main deck. The captain's boat and a liberty shuttle rested on the first hatch. The other four hatches had two LCMs per hatch, and each hatch had several booms, allowing sailors to lift or lower the crafts in and out of the water. Once loaded, they had the capability of delivering 60 tons of supplies to shore.

The *Seminole* was a slow-mover at 18 knots per hour and, while operating around the clock, took over two weeks for Gary and crew to travel the 8,000 miles from San Diego to the South China Sea. Gary never experienced seasickness nor had to get his sea legs. He loved sailing and enjoyed being underway. In typhoons, the ship would yaw 30 degrees from one side to the other, and it never bothered him. There were sailors so sick that in one case they medevaced a sailor and discharged him from the Navy.

The enlisted crew's uniforms, called dungarees, were light blue denim shirts and dark blue bell-bottom trousers. While working on deck, they wore hard hats, and on liberty the white hat known as a "Dixie cup" was worn. Always looking for opportunities to make a little extra money, Gary discovered and re-activated several dilapidated sewing

December '67, relaxing onboard the *Seminole* (courtesy Gary DeMastrie).

machines, and began tailoring his uniforms. Before long, he had an active business alter-ing shipmates' clothing.

The oily booms and winches dirtied the ship from bow to stern. The crew's daily routine was physically demanding and began with roll call, then sweeping and swabbing the decks, morning chow, then six-hour watches both fore and aft, and any other duties assigned by their petty officers. At the end of the day, the decks were again swept and swabbed. The ship needed perpetual maintenance, and there was little free time on board. In their scant time off, the sailors wrote letters, played cards, or listened to the radio.

Sleeping accommodations aboard the *Seminole* were challenging. All enlisted sailors slept below deck, and their berths consisted of four or five aluminum racks (beds), 18 inches apart, stacked from the floor to the ceiling. Their tiered beds were secured against the bulkheads (walls) and adjacent to many other tiers, adding to the claustrophobic, noxious, and damp environment. The racks were made of canvas material, corded to an aluminum frame, topped by a dirty, two-inch mattress.

The most difficult issue for Gary was trying to turn over in a rack so close to the one above him. Gary, who was personally longer than the six-foot rack, had to negotiate with the abutting sailor so they could sleep feet-to-feet. Adding to the congestion were hundreds of individual aluminum foot lockers.

Seminole sailors ate well. Gary enjoyed the all-you-can-eat buffet, around-the-clock

Gary (right) and a shipmate, less than steady on their feet (courtesy Gary DeMastrie).

availability of chow, and huge urns of black coffee. At times, there was even a cook who would make your eggs to-order. The ship would often secure provisions from the port where she was anchored; thus in Guam, they enjoyed mangoes and bananas, and in Hawaii it was pineapples and melons. When the ship transported land-based Marines, they were surprised how good the chow was on board.

During the ship's travels in and out of combat zones, Gary enjoyed liberty in many different foreign ports. While some sailors characterized shore liberty as I & I (intercourse and intoxication), Gary would often take the opportunity to nurture his interest in geography and history. In the Philippines, he toured the tunnels of Corregidor, viewed the many Japanese artillery pieces long ago abandoned, and drove along the exact route of the Bataan Death March. He visited the Pearl Harbor Memorial in Hawaii; the Atomic Bomb Park and Peace exhibit in Hiroshima; as well as Madame Butterfly's house in Nagasaki. In Hong Kong, he saw a cultured pearl factory, the famous Tiger Balm Gardens, and enjoyed the beautiful view from atop Victoria Peak, the highest mountain in Hong Kong. The crew also spent time on liberty or resupplying its warehouse stores in Okinawa, Guam, and Sasebo Naval Base in Japan.

One of his favorite haunts was Mom's Bar located at Subic Bay in the Philippines. The popular watering hole had a great Filipino band and, while unable to converse in English, they would perfectly mimic the latest country-western songs. The crew would also visit nearby Grande Island, an R&R center for thousands of sailors. In later years, it became a resettlement stop for Vietnamese and Cambodian refugees. During one of his liberties on the island, Gary checked out scuba gear and, with no instruction, taught himself how to dive, enjoying the challenges of spearfishing.

Once "on station" in Vietnam, the entire crew worked continuously, loading, directing and unloading LCMs, providing desperately needed logistical support for Marines fighting in I Corps, the northernmost Vietnamese provinces. The LCMs transported tons of C rations, large quantities of ammunition, Jeeps, and, on one occasion, even a tank. Most of the crew did not realize they were supporting critical offensive campaigns against the enemy. The *Seminole* was credited with supplying Operations Beaver Cage, Beau Charger, Beacon Torch, Bear Track, Bear Chain, Belt Drive, and Keystone Bluejay.

The work was demanding, dirty, and, at times, dangerous. The armored LCMs would be unshackled from the hatch and booms would lift them over the side of the ship. The two-man crews, consisting of a coxswain and a technician/engineer known as a "snipe," would test the diesel engines while the boats were in the air, to ensure they would work when lowered into the water. Once the LCM was in the water, the *Seminole* crew would lower supplies to its bed or storage area.

His superiors recognized Gary's abilities, even though he was a junior enlisted man. He was assigned the designation of hatch captain for the #5 hatch, a role normally reserved for senior Petty Officers. Gary had absolute authority for all activities related to hatch #5, and because of the continual din of operations, would often use hand and arm signals to direct a crew of eight sailors. The sailors launched and retrieved the LCMs using guiding ropes and boom controls. Individual loads for each LCM were pre-staged on the three lower levels beneath each hatch, ensuring the most important supplies were offloaded first. Once on shore, the craft were off-loaded by giant all-terrain forklifts.

Ever watchful, Gary knew the three sets of cables per boom would eventually wear out and break, causing the LCM that was being retrieved or off-loaded to swing dangerously out of control. With his constant vigilance of hatch #5's equipment, he avoided any

LCM being lifted off the *Seminole* (courtesy Gary DeMastrie).

dangerous situations, such as happened when the winch cable broke, in a near-disaster to all those nearby, including his crew.

The *Seminole* would operate anywhere from a half-mile to a mile offshore. Her 16-foot draft determined the minimum depth in which she could safely navigate. When off-loading LCMs, the Seminole would be in 1-Alpha alert status. The crew was called to "battle stations" status when threatened by enemy patrol boats. While the *Seminole* had four twin 40mm cannons, two on the bow and two aft, and its own radar system, usually American destroyers patrolling nearby would quickly eliminate any threats.

The *Seminole* had minimal medical and no dental staff. When Gary had a severe toothache, he was helicoptered to a LPH (Landing Platform Helicopter), a much larger vessel with dental services. Because time was of the essence, and he was needed on the *Seminole*, the dentist decided to pull four of his teeth in quick order, avoiding any future disruptions.

When its stocks needed replenishing, the *Seminole* would return to Subic Bay or, on occasion, to San Diego for resupply. As a hatch captain, Gary would have the opportunity to go ashore and barter for certain items. The five-gallon, shiny tins of Navy coffee he brought with him were a valuable commodity and could be lucratively traded for many different items, such as pallets of beer or grey deck paint.

Gary did have one disciplinary incident. He left the *Seminole* without authorization when he was denied a leave. The ship was home ported in San Diego and he wanted some time off before re-embarking for Vietnam. When he returned to the ship, and went before the captain to be disciplined, his exemplary past performance influenced the discipline meted out. He was restricted to the ship for 30 days and it sailed for Vietnam the next day!

One time the *Seminole* was dispatched to South Korea to help initiate Korean Marines in the art of "wet net" landings. These amphibious exercises allowed the Korean Marines to disembark from the *Seminole*, climb down wet landing nets wearing full packs

South Korean Marines practice disembarking from the *Seminole* (courtesy Gary DeMastrie).

into crafts that would then take them to shore, mimicking a sea assault. One Korean Marine, when climbing down, slipped and dropped his rifle in the ocean. The man was upbraided immediately and taken to shore. Gary's crew was advised that the Marine was summarily executed for losing his rifle. They weren't exactly sure the story was true, but never again saw the hapless Marine. The remainder of the assault exercise was conducted flawlessly.

On occasion, the *Seminole's* crew members could get overzealous about bartering. In Hong Kong, small sampans would greet the ship looking for brass items in exchange for silk shirts or sharkskin suits. Young, overeager sailors would exchange brass fire hose nozzles and ship fittings for apparel, much to the chagrin of the ship's officers. When all efforts of discouragement failed, the ship's water cannons were unleashed on the traders, dispersing the sodden bunch.

The *Seminole* served over four years off and on combat duty in Vietnam, from April 1965 until January 1970. Gary served on the vessel approximately three years and eight months, from late 1966 through July 1970.

Homecoming/Career

In mid–July 1970, the *Seminole* finally docked at its home port in San Diego and Gary was released from active duty. On the final sail to San Diego, Gary came to realize he liked shipboard life (less the close haircuts and spit shine rules) and enjoyed the camaraderie. He seriously considered joining the Merchant Marines. The more he thought about the idea, he reached the conclusion that the life and the absences of a civilian mariner would make marriage and raising a family too difficult. So, with his discharge pay, he decided to visit some Navy buddies living along the West Coast.

Gary promptly loaded all his possessions (a seabag and a stereo system) into his recently purchased 1966 tan, two-door Plymouth Barracuda and left San Diego, headed north. His first buddy-visit was in Sacramento and, after several more stops, he found himself in Provo, Utah. During his wanderings, he enjoyed Utah's weather, its majestic five National Parks, the picturesque Rocky Mountains, and a stronger job market than North Adams. With those things in mind he settled in Ogden, Utah—though, to this day, after fifty years settled, he acknowledges his natural wanderlust: "I'm just passing through."

Initially, Gary worked several years building mobile homes. Desiring more challenging work, he accepted a job with Pacific States Pipe Company as an ironworker. During this time period, he married and had three children. After some time, the marriage did not work out, and the couple split up.

Then Gary found a position with Hercules Aerospace, building rocket motors. He began his employment as a machine operator, was promoted to a technical writer, and later, worked as an engineering technologist. During his tenure with Hercules, Gary remarried and had two more children.

Tragedy struck his new family when his wife, diagnosed with breast cancer, rapidly succumbed to the disease, leaving Gary with two boys, six and eight, to raise by himself.

Gary became a member of the Utah Archeological Society and served a term as its president. After his wife died, Gary and the boys found an outlet for their sorrows, searching canyons, cliffs, and wooded areas for primitive artifacts. In their travels, they found rock fossils, petrified wood, grinding stones, arrowheads, and pottery shards left by Anasazi and Paiute tribes. One of their most significant finds was the skeleton of a young female in a long-dormant fire pit.

Gary loves the outdoors and worked for a short period as a lumberjack. He and the boys became avid campers and hikers. In winter, they snowmobiled and used almost any excuse to wander the canyons of Utah. At one point, they built a cabin in a remote section of the state and spent much of their free time exploring the outdoors.

As his next opportunity, Gary accepted a position at nearby Hill Air Force Base, applying multiple coats of paint to F-16 and F-22 fighter aircrafts. He worked there 11 years and received additional seniority credit for his four years in the Navy. He retired from Hill Air Force Base with 15 years of seniority in 2010. Ironically, Gary now displays some serious side effects from the painting, just like his dad. But his side effects are different, called "vitiligo," a disease that has caused loss of skin color on both his hands.

At this writing, his five children are grown and he has seven grandchildren. Gary still stands over six feet tall, although, in defiance of old Navy rules, he has shoulder-length grey hair with a scraggly beard and sports a loop earring in his left ear. He wears glasses and has recently had his sailor's tattoo on his right forearm re-colored and added to. Its skull tattoo sports a navy "Dixie cup" cap and rests on an anchor with a newly added rope.

He and his close friend Martha built a beautiful three-story cabin in the nearby mountains. Gary designed the cabin himself, and they often stay there for days at a time, nestled in some of the same areas he and his children explored.

Gary has a partial veteran's disability from hearing loss and more recently has had a spine operation at the local veterans hospital. He is also being evaluated for exposure to Agent Orange.

This easygoing, friendly man now enjoys the many visits from his children and grandchildren and finds pleasure working on thousand-piece jigsaw puzzles. He has framed his puzzles of Utah and Massachusetts in the cabin. After forty years of riding, Gary remains a diehard motorcycle enthusiast. He also enjoys talking about his many outdoor treks and local geography, geology, and history.

Gary earned the Vietnamese Service Medal with seven campaign stars, the Vietnamese Campaign Medal, the Armed Forces Expeditionary Medal, as well as the National Defense and Good Conduct Medals. During his service, he also received several captain's citations for exemplary conduct and job performance.

Gary can be cynical about the United States' efforts in Vietnam. Fifty-plus years later, he says, "common sense and rationale doesn't think we did any good." He is not even sure that if we had prevailed, it would have helped the South Vietnamese people. From his perspective, neither the politicians nor the military leaders gave "a rat's ass" about us as individuals.

After 25 years as a Navy ship, the *Seminole* was decommissioned in 1970 and scrapped in 1977, ending its long service through three wars.

16

Jim Luczynski—
Army Infantryman

Recipient of Combat Infantryman Badge,
Bronze Star, Army Commendation Medal

April 17, 1972

The small Vietnamese soldier was lying on his back close to the tracked vehicle. He looked like he was resting. His eyes were placid, although the irises had disappeared. With giant pupils, he was looking skyward with the sun reflecting in his eyes. For the briefest of moments, Jim wondered why he wasn't blinking. The man was dead, slain by a heavy volume of fire concentrated on their vehicle.

Jim, a first lieutenant and an Army Airborne Ranger, was assigned to Team 76, a group of 12 U.S. advisors, nine officers, and three senior non-commissioned-officers

(NCOs). The group were responsible for training junior officers of the Army of the Republic of Vietnam (ARVN). In addition, Team 76 provided direction and assistance when the ARVN went to the field. Over the course of 12 months, the team participated in 40 different missions with the ARVN, ranging from patrolling and ambushing to search and destroy. They operated in III Corps, above Saigon and close to the dangerous Cambodian border.

In mid–April 1972, Jim was halfway through his tour of duty when the team received an urgent transmission to proceed as fast as possible to An Loc, a small town under siege by three North Vietnamese Army (NVA) and Viet Cong divisions. An Loc was 20 miles from their current position and close to the Cambodian border, which meant the NVA would be well supplied and heavily armed, possibly with tanks. The relief column would be comprised of five U.S. advisors and 200 South Vietnamese officers-in-training.

This mechanized relief unit would be called Task Force Bravo and included 30 vehicles, including a Zippo APC (a flame-throwing Armored Personnel Carrier), a mortar APC, several Jeeps, and more than 20 APCs that would ferry the soldiers into battle. The group assembled hastily, their only focus getting to An Loc.

They had planned to cover the 20 miles in rapid fashion, but they were soon bogged down from sniper and mortar fire, making their progress maddeningly slow. They had to set in for the night, circling (laagering) the APCs. They continued to receive enemy probes and incoming small arms fire. Earlier that day, the task force came across a number of dead civilians whose minibus had hit a mine, scattering shattered people and animals across the roadway. They quickly cleared the human remains and debris from the road and moved on.

On Bravo's second day in the field, Jim's boss, a colonel, had him ride shotgun in their Jeep while reconnoitering in advance of their unit. The colonel was driving, Jim had area maps, and both were making terrain observations. For as far as they could see the land was flat, with some tall grasses, rice paddies, and woods that alternately grew close to the road and then opened back up. It made Jim think of an hourglass.

This day was unreasonably quiet as they drove their Jeep down a deeply rutted and dusty road, more of a path than a road. The action-oriented colonel, who had seen combat in Korea, wanted to visually assess where they would be taking their training cadre early the next morning.

After traveling some distance, both soldiers realized that, armed only with pistols, they had driven considerably beyond what could be called safe areas and were now in NVA territory. The quiet was now officially eerie and heightened their concerns. They turned around and sped back to the security of their group's encampment.

Early the next morning, Team 76 and the ARVN soldiers prepared to depart from their encampment. They were now located just south of Chon Tanh, about 40 miles north of Saigon, and 15 miles from An Loc, their destination.

As the anticipation of a fight hung heavy in the air, and enemy sightings became more frequent, the task force continued to circle their APCs at night in large semi-circles facing the direction in which they were headed. Often the 12-ton, 15-foot-long behemoths would use their powerful diesel engines and tracks to grind out two-foot-deep, oblong circles in the turf, creating temporary shallow bunkers. The APCs would then park over the scooped-out trenches, providing overhead coverage for the South Vietnamese soldiers, who continued to take casualties from snipers and indirect mortar fire. The soldiers learned to crack their APC hatches about two inches when they were inside, reducing the pressure caused by rocket hits, although this sometime allowed hot shrapnel to penetrate their vehicles, causing minor wounds.

The next morning, day three of their advance, a South Vietnamese lieutenant colonel, the deputy armored commander, flying in a Hughes OA-61 light observation helicopter (called a loach), was surveiling the area of march from several thousand feet. Suddenly his craft was fired upon by the NVA using a .51 heavy caliber machine gun. The small helicopter was hit and the colonel shot under the chin, the bullet passing through his head and spraying brain tissue throughout the helicopter, killing him instantly.

The loach, partly disabled from gunfire, struggled to land, and when it did, the pilot of the two-man craft ran from the machine and escaped capture. With the enemy so close, the colonel's body could not be recovered for several days.

Progress continued to be slow. The task force bumped into "one bees' nest after another," as Luczynski put it, especially as they closed the distance to An Loc. During one lull, Jim participated in a foot patrol, within a mile from their APCs, when a South Vietnamese soldier tripped a booby trap, seriously wounding himself and causing other casualties. The soldier's right foot had been obliterated, requiring multiple soldiers to carry him back to the APC in an impromptu poncho stretcher. The wounded were medevaced, and the patrol, realizing the enemy was close and in strength, turned around and returned to the night laager.

On the other side of the road, A-1 Skyraider jets manned by the South Vietnamese Air Force (SVAF) were air assaulting and bombing enemy bunkers. The attack aircraft would no sooner drop their bombs and pull up into the sky than the NVA machine guns (with green tracers) would fire right after them. Friendly forces would identify the gun locations, and the next flight of aircraft would destroy them. The NVA continued to replace annihilated gun crews until the bombing became so fierce it subdued their fire.

After the jets had finished their bombing runs, the task force discovered several Russian armored vehicles that had been destroyed by the air strikes. The vehicles were similar to APCs and had been hit repeatedly by armor piercing shells that put three inch holes in its sides and killed their NVA crews.

The laager was probed again that night by NVA continuing to look for weaknesses in the perimeter. The ARVN were responsible for night security, but all hands were alert, armed and ready for an attack.

The next morning the task force resumed its northward trek, still a considerable way from An Loc, and in their haste, the vehicles were lined up one behind the other with little thought given to spreading out. After several hours and just a few kilometers north of Chon Thanh, the group was assaulted by well-entrenched NVA soldiers. The APCs were now in a slightly staggered line, but the trap was sprung just where the road narrowed.

Jim was on the lead APC, and the enemy let his armored carrier pass through the ambush so they could focus on the commander's vehicle, several behind him. The task force's commander's vehicle was easily identified by the numerous radio antennae protruding from its hulk.

Using armor piercing shells and rocket propelled grenades (RPGs), the enemy opened fire, in an instant penetrating and disabling three APCs, including the task force commander's. The armor piercing barrage and ensuing small arms fire killed and wounded many of the South Vietnamese soldiers who had been riding atop the vehicles.

Enemy machine gun and rifle fire was also incessant, accurately raking the line of vehicles, adding to the toll of injured soldiers.

This was when Jim dismounted from his APC and his ally, the Vietnamese soldier, an arm's length from him, was slain. They had been silently communicating, both scanning the horizon trying to determine where the firing was coming from. When Jim turned to look back at the soldier, he was lying on his back, dead. Jim couldn't see a mark on him, but the small man was looking serenely at the sky.

Jim's next spontaneous thought was what a senior combat instructor had said to him at Norwich University, that someday in battle you will find yourself saying "better thee than me."

And while the thoughts were involuntary, Jim was convinced the NVA were aiming at him, the much bigger target, and had inadvertently hit the smaller soldier. Later, he would feel guilty about his thoughts, but right then he was in a fight for his life and quickly remounted the APC, leaving the dead man to be retrieved later.

The ensuing chaos temporarily halted the task force. Soldiers traveling atop the APCs were jumping or being shot off. Bodies were everywhere. The force was disoriented, and Jim was momentarily puzzled when he saw bloody soldiers running around in their underwear. It quickly dawned on him that their clothes had been blown off them in the initial barrage.

Jim, in the lead APC, continued to direct fire towards enemy strongpoints while the other APCs withdrew to a rallying point, several kilometers back along the road they had just traveled. Someone had lifted a wounded man atop Jim's APC. He was bleeding from wounds in his buttocks, feet, and arms. Jim applied compresses to the serious arm wound and his APC began to withdraw, still providing covering fire for the rest of the task force. Sometime later, Jim was recognized for his efforts and awarded a Bronze Star with "V" for Valor.

Jim (right), receiving his Bronze Star, in Saigon (courtesy Jim Luczynski).

The task force had desperately tried to recover their wounded while at the same time evacuating the ambush area. There were South Vietnamese bodies everywhere, some dead, others mortally wounded, and still other soldiers, alive and crying out for help. Gathering as many injured troopers as they could, the task force abandoned the disabled APCs, reversed their engines, and scrambled to a pre-designated rally point.

At the rally point, the enemy's fire subsided and the group began trying to account for everyone. In their retreat, wounded and dead soldiers were hastily thrown on any nearby APC. Someone estimated there were at least 30 dead South Vietnamese soldiers scattered over the field, some sprawled out and uncovered, others with ponchos covering their remains.

Medevac helicopters were radioed to transport the dead and the wounded. When the task force re-grouped, everyone was spent. They were dazed trying to understand what had just happened and reliving the events in slow motion. There was no energy left within the group.

Jim remembers the ambush as though it were yesterday. Of the Team 76 members assigned to Task Force Bravo, four had been superficially wounded and Jim, the fifth, escaped unscathed.

The Task Force Bravo relief column continued to be stubbornly resisted by the NVA and it never did reach An Loc.

Early Life

Jim's grandfather, named Thomas, was born in Lubin, Poland, an ancient, mid-sized town in southwestern Poland. Thomas immigrated to the United States in the early part of the twentieth century. Initially, he owned and operated a farm in Stamford, Vermont, and in later years became an accomplished weaver in the North Adams woolen mills.

Antonia Barlek, Jim's paternal grandmother, also immigrated from Europe and was of Polish and Russian descent. As a housewife, Antonia spent her time raising the couple's five children, including young Thomas, Jim's dad.

Thomas Luczynski, Jim's father, was born in the early 1920s, and during World War II, Jim's dad served in the U.S. Navy and was stationed in Brooklyn, at the New York Naval Yard. While there, he met and married Dorothy Mahar, Jim's mother.

Their first son was named after both Thomases, and year later their second son, James, was born in 1947 at a Pittsfield, Massachusetts, hospital.

Jim's dad and mom divorced when he was four years old, and Dorothy moved to California and remarried. Jim would see his mom four or five times a year, usually during holiday seasons.

Jim contracted polio at a very young age and spent three months immobilized in a hospital for infantile paralysis, as was the practice at the time. A caregiver decided to try the new "Sister Kenny" method to stimulate activity in his very skinny legs. The method required applying moist, hot compresses on his legs three times a day and gently exercising his leg muscles. Jim's dad approved of exercise and praised the "Kenny method."

Jim's dad, who had custody of both boys, placed them in successive boarding schools in Staten Island and Gladstone, New Jersey, while he looked for a job. The Luczynski boys, ages four and five, were separated and required to sleep in dorm rooms with boys their own age. Jim bunked with 12 other four year olds and can remember a lot of sniffling late at night, as little boys felt homesick.

Initially, Jim's dad found work in a bakery and subsequently found a better paying job as a long-haul trucker. When he could, Thomas would schedule overnight visits with the boys at the boarding schools. Jim remembers them playing endless games of Monopoly with their dad, who was permitted to sleep in a nearby room during his brief visits.

Looking for a more permanent solution, Thomas moved the boys to North Adams, where they would live with his father (Thomas), the boys' grandfather. Their grandmother had died years earlier. Initially, the all-male family rented an apartment on Ashland Street and, over time, Jim's father saved enough money to buy a house on Parker Street, where the boys and their grandfather lived.

Their father, with little formal education, was a voracious reader, and stocked the home with many books and magazines. He was also an early proponent of exercise, and when the boys were little, had them ride their bikes four miles every morning or, alternatively, run two miles. When their dad was home, he had the boys drink horrible tasting cod liver oil for vitamin A.

Although the grandfather was a strict disciplinarian, over the years he and the boys grew close. He kept a thick, black strap hanging by the cellar door as a visual warning of his method of punishment for any transgression. He nicknamed the belt his "dry kielbasa," after a common Polish sausage.

By strict dictate, there was no talking at the evening meal, grandfather following the maxim that children "should be seen and not be heard." There would always be time to talk after the meal.

One day, as a joke, Jim hid the "dry kielbasa" and began talking incessantly at the dinner table. It wasn't long before his grandfather reached for the strap and found it missing. He became irate that someone had moved his implement of punishment, and presuming Jim was the transgressor, chased him around the table until he finally threw his shoe and barely missed. Wisely, Jim ran out of the house (that exercise having come in handy) and was gone for hours, giving Grandpa enough time to cool off.

Grandpa was an excellent cook and served Polish meals like kapusta, a cabbage soup, or golumpki, a cabbage roll, and other dishes such as borscht or potato pancakes. He raised pigeons, so one of his evening dishes was meaty pigeon soup. Jim hated this meal.

The entire family could cook. At an early age, the boys prepared their own breakfasts. During their dad's visits, the boys would look forward to his specialty: excellent spaghetti sauce, pasta, three broiled chickens, and their own homemade wine.

The boys made wine with their dad in the cellar. Using two 25-gallon crocks, they put dandelions in boiling water, steeped the concoction for three days, removed the flowers, added yeast and sugar and let it ferment. They also made sherry and rhubarb wine.

The grandfather's favorite TV show was *Bonanza*, a western series that featured another all-male family. Their favorite movies usually involved John Wayne. The grandfather, who always wore a hat, was a proud American citizen, and repeatedly told the boys to remember that in the United States, "you don't have to tip your hats to anyone," as their family had to in Poland. At night, their heavily accented grandfather played poker with the boys, and sometimes Jim would catch him cheating, but as he might say, in America, you were free to do even that.

Other early influences in the boys' life were their Uncle Walter, who'd received a Bronze Star for his heroic actions during the World War II Battle of the Bulge, and Uncle

Edward, who was in the Merchant Marines. They regaled the boys with their stories and were unabashedly proud of their new country, the United States. They also shared family lore with the boys about a street named after them (Luczynski) somewhere in Poland and property long ago lost.

One of the earliest jobs the boys had was when they were in the seventh and eighth grades working three or four hours a day after school for the Berkshire Peeled Potato Company on Ashland Street. Semi-tractor trailer trucks would deliver 50-pound bags of potatoes, and the boys would unload the bags, cut them open, and dump them into a machine to be peeled. Sometimes they would need to closely inspect an entire bag prior to peeling to find a rotten potato that made the whole bag stink. The boys would then inspect the peeled potatoes and cut out any "eyes" or black spots.

Both Jim and his brother attended Saint Joseph's grammar and high schools, where they worked in the cafeteria from the eighth grade through high school, cleaning dishes in exchange for lunch. They spent an hour and a half each day eating their lunch, cleaning and racking plates and utensils, then stacking the clean plates after they had been through the dishwasher.

Jim also earned money mowing lawns in the summer and shoveling snow in the winter. He belonged to the North Adams YMCA and volunteered on Saturdays to operate a movie projector showing movies to little kids. As YMCA members, the boys and their friends exercised regularly by wrestling, playing basketball, or lifting weights.

The Luczynski boys and their friends enjoyed camping and fishing at Mausert's Pond at Clarksburg State Park. At a young age, with their grandfather's approval, they would hitch a ride to the pond, set up camp, start a fire, and spend several days fishing. They also climbed and camped on Mount Greylock numerous times. Their expeditions included hunting and target shooting with bows and arrows, rifles and pistols.

In high school, following after his brother, Jim served as the class photographer, taking pictures of the school's primary sport, basketball. Many of the pictures in the class yearbook were also taken by Jim. He was also an active debate club member. At home, he enjoyed making models of three-masted ships and of intercontinental missiles.

Every summer, Jim and his brother would take a Greyhound bus or fly to meet up with their dad in Albany, Pittsburgh, or some other rendezvous point. The boys would spend the entire summer traveling across the United States, helping their dad load and unload the 40-foot trailer. Jim remembers packing up and delivering many boxes of household goods for transferring military families. They also delivered a huge shipment of IBM mainframe computers to the original NASA Space Center in Houston, Texas.

The entire summer, the boys slept inside the cab, in the back of the truck, or camped nearby. By the time Jim was 12 years old, he had visited the lower 48 states, Mexico, and Canada. Jim's dad would often break up his long days of driving by stopping and showing the boys historical markers or points of interest, like the Alamo in Texas or the Air Force Academy in Colorado. He also wanted the boys to appreciate other cultures and they traveled to different locations in Mexico. Jim remembers seeing his first bullfight at a very early age. Jim loved the summers.

When Jim's dad was home for brief visits, he did not like to see the boys fighting. After one scrape, he took off his belt (as a warning) and directed them to keep fighting. The fight went on for twenty minutes until both were exhausted. They never fought with each other again.

Jim's dad was thrifty and saved enough money on his long-distance trucking job to

Shutterbug, James Luczynski finds himself on the opposite end of the lens this time.

From St. Joe's class of 1965 yearbook, *Retrospect*.

send Jim and his brother to Norwich University, a military academy located in Northfield, Vermont. At the university, freshmen known as Rooks spent their first months being "molded" into cadets.

Norwich, in existence for almost 200 years, emphasized small class sizes and instructed the future officers on subjects ranging from languages and science to field tactics.

At the university, uniforms were worn each day, and Rooks were frequently inspected by upperclassmen. The first year at Norwich was essentially a very long boot camp. The cadets were awoken by reveille each day at 6:30 a.m., except for Sundays. When they scrambled out of their beds, they answered roll call and were marched to breakfast. Freshmen cadets were antagonized by upperclassmen every day.

All rooms were the same: a double wardrobe for the two students, one table/desk with two chairs for studying, and a footlocker. First-year students could not have any other amenities except an alarm clock/clock radio. There were daily inspections of precisely folded underclothes and socks. Uniforms were required to hang all facing center of their wardrobes, buttoned and pressed.

Jim was in D Company, and he had some devious upperclassmen in supervisory roles, especially his platoon commander who continually harassed the platoon with actions above and beyond making any sense. The boy was appointed to the position because of his prowess at passing inspections, not for his leadership capabilities.

When not studying, Jim belonged to the Mountain Rescue Team, and the group of mountaineers were called out on several occasions to assist local authorities in searches. Jim also participated in the parachute, flying, and scuba clubs. He accumulated 70 parachute jumps while at Norwich. It was during this time period that Jim became a master parachutist, an expert classification, sanctioned by the U.S. Parachutist Association.

While at school, the brothers joined a sport parachute club, which is more familiarly known as skydiving. The club participated in competitive meets sponsored by the United States Parachute Association. At the national championships in 1968, Jim earned a gold medal for accuracy when landing within inches of a six-inch disc after free-falling from 10,000 feet and attaining speeds over 100 miles per hour. The medal is displayed, today, in his living room.

One school summer, when the boys were released from duty, their dad, always interested in education, paid for Jim to go to Europe where he visited a number of countries including Italy, France, Austria, Germany, and Greece.

Jim, a year behind his brother, graduated in 1969 with a bachelor of arts degree in government. His dad and brother presented him with a parachute for a graduation present.

Most graduates were participants in the Reserve Officer Training Program (ROTC), which required graduates to serve two to four years in the Army. Jim changed his commitment to "voluntary indefinite" in order to be assigned to Ranger/Airborne schools and Vietnam.

Jim, Norwich Parachute Club leader, participates in a parachute meet, late 1960s (courtesy Jim Luczynski).

Military Service

After graduation, Jim headed to Fort Benning, Georgia, where he completed a two-month Infantry Officer Basic School then spent two additional weeks at Fort Benning's jump school.

Next stop was Ranger School, considered by many to be the most physically and mentally demanding course in the entire U.S. Army. In 1969, the program was divided into three phases:

- Introduction at Camp Darby with a focus on achieving maximal fitness through long marches, and challenging obstacle courses.
- Mountain training at Camp Merrill in Georgia, which focused on platoon movements, arduous climbing, and sustaining oneself in the mountains.
- Jungle training at Camp Rudder in Florida, involving waterborne and small boat operations, living, patrolling, and orienteering in swamps.

Jim graduated after this "eight-week and two-day" program, proudly earning the right to wear the famous Ranger tab on his left shoulder for the rest of his Army career. It should be noted that graduation rates from Ranger School are 50 percent or lower.

His next assignment was the 82nd Airborne division at Fort Bragg, North Carolina. Jim was now part of one of the best trained infantry divisions, with a reputation for parachute assaults into contested areas. Shortly after arriving, he attended Jump Master school and completed military requirements, earning the coveted Jump Master status. At this point, Jim now had over 100 jumps and was qualified and responsible for inspecting soldiers' parachute equipment and giving jump commands to the parachutists. He became the company's Jump Master.

In an unusual turn of events, with no prior training, Jim, a parachute/infantry officer, was designated the battalion's Heavy Mortar Platoon leader. Instead of attending the five-month

Top to bottom: Jim's Ranger Tab, Airborne Wings, and Captain's Bars (courtesy Jim Luczynski).

mortar school, he was given a manual and told to "get up to speed" quickly on the mortar's capabilities. As the story unfolds, his qualifications as a mortar man will play into his next assignment—Vietnam.

Vietnam/Army Life

After a year at Fort Bragg, Jim received orders for Vietnam. Before traveling to this assignment, he was sent to a two-month Vietnamese language school located at Fort Bliss, Texas. It was too short a time to adequately assimilate the language, although he learned some basic commands and greetings.

Jim arrived in the Republic of Vietnam (RVN), after a brief stopover in Alaska, in November 1971. When he arrived at the replacement depot in Saigon, one of the first things he saw deplaning was a former ARVN soldier hustling about on a "rocker board" attached to the nubs of what were once was his legs. The sight gave him a feeling of impending doom.

At the replacement depot, a colonel stopped Jim and said he needed an officer on his advisor team with mortar experience. The next thing Jim knew, he grabbed his gear, jumped into the colonel's Jeep and they drove an hour and a half north of Saigon, where he joined Team 76.

While the team reported in to the Military Assistance Command–Vietnam, they were essentially on their own and expected to train South Vietnamese (ARVN) officer candidates in the handling of Armored Personnel Carriers (APCs) and mortars. There were nine advisors on the team: six officers and three senior enlisted men.

Jim, with an assigned interpreter (Sergeant Thom), was the designated instructor for training in the use of field mortars. As a first lieutenant, and the team's junior officer, Jim also had less glamorous duties, such as monthly trips to Saigon to fetch payroll in order to pay the civilians who worked on base, part of an old French bunker complex.

While at the complex, the team was rocketed a number of times, especially at night. It was an early, introductory exposure to living in a war zone where hours of boredom were punctuated with moments of terror, as explosions drove everyone to the nearest bunker.

As part of their responsibilities, team members accompanied their trainees to the field and conducted real life patrols, ambushes, and searches. Jim participated in 20 or more separate missions.

When the unit was not in the field, there were lighthearted moments at his base camp. Often bases would trade 16 mm films. Horror and vampire movies were popular at the time. ARVN officers and local Vietnamese women who worked on the base, would be entranced by the movies. At some point, a U.S. advisor would sneak out, move to the back of the crowd and at the appropriate moment scream just when the vampires were attacking someone. The screams scared and scattered the Vietnamese. Afterwards, with their gracious good nature, they would laugh at the silliness.

Usually advisors wore the sleeves of their uniform rolled up. The Vietnamese had little body hair and would often come up to Jim, look puzzled, and pat his hairy arms as if he were an ape. Some would pull at his hair to see if it was real.

One time driving back to base, Jim saw five boys clubbing something in the road. As he approached the boys he discovered them killing a giant cobra and, when done, carting the large reptile off for supper. On another occasion, Jim and Sergeant Thom, his Vietnamese interpreter and driver, went to Bien Hoa Air Base. The base was in the process of closing, and he and Sergeant Thom "liberated" five ice machines, a valuable item in this tropical environment. Four were returned to their base and one was left with Thom, who supported his family by operating a mini-convenience store that served Lucky 33 beer, grass-water shrimp, and knickknacks. Thom's business flourished with his new ice machine.

After months in-country, Jim qualified for an R&R in Bangkok, Thailand. Always interested in other cultures, he hired a taxi for the week and had the opportunity to visit the country's royal palace, an ancient university, the National Palace and a giant 150-foot-long Reclining Buddha, one of the largest statues in Thailand.

After Jim's 13 months in Vietnam as a single officer, he requested and was granted an inter-theater transfer to Korea. Following a brief flight to Kimbo Air Base in Seoul, he was appointed a headquarters battery commander. The Korean tour of duty, much less hectic and stressful than Vietnam, allowed him some time to travel about the country and satisfy his cultural desires.

He visited Admiral Yi-Sun-sin's monument, a famous sixteenth-century Korean naval commander who fought 23 naval engagements with the Japanese and never lost a battle or a ship. Yi is credited with inventing the turtle ship. The name is derived from a protective-like shell covering and is often recognized as the first armored ship in the world.

Jim, as a commander, had to deal with the abundance and availability of hemp grown by Korean farmers. Soldiers often used it as a poor substitute for marijuana and would illegally purchase and store their caches in their barracks. During barracks inspections, Jim often discovered hemp hidden in unique places, and one time he summoned the MPs to retrieve packages hidden in a barracks ceiling. The soldiers seemed upset, but no one acknowledged owning it.

After 25 months in Asia, Jim returned home, arriving in uniform at Travis Air Force Base. He was then bused to Los Angeles Airport for his final flight home. Just before departing, he was surprised and very demoralized to be harassed by people criticizing his uniform and service in Vietnam, confronting him with questions like "How many babies did you kill?" (This memory still gnaws at and haunts him today.)

After a brief home leave, Jim reported in to the 1/327th Battalion, 101st Airborne Division, an Air Assault Group located at Fort

At his desk, as a commanding officer in Korea (courtesy Jim Luczynski).

Campbell, Kentucky. He was assigned to the battalion's assistant S-3: The group planned operations, made sure necessary training took place, and disseminated information to the participants. Most importantly, at Fort Campbell, Jim was the skydiving club instructor; in his free time, he helped organize and train soldiers who had an interest in parachuting. It was at a club meeting where he met Jeanne Carpenter, a Specialist fourth class working in Personnel Management who wanted to learn how to parachute. She was attracted to the cute instructor, and some 60-plus jumps later, after perfecting the skydiver's "kiss-pass," Jim and Jeanne were engaged.

Towards the latter part of his stay at Fort Campbell, Jim was designated as the S-4 officer in charge of ensuring the line units were adequately budgeted and supplied to carry out their missions. Jim remained there until his service expired in 1976. With his Army career almost over, Jim realized staying in the Army would not be compatible with his traditional view of marriage, which involved being home every night. Jeanne left the Army about 30 days before he did. They had decided the Army wasn't supportive of family life, and they were getting married soon. The 101st Airborne had a hard-charging commander with a sign outside his office that read something like, "You're on duty 24/7. Job first, family second!"

Jim decided then and there family would be first in his life.

Homecoming/Career

Jim married Jeanne in 1976, and with his decision to exit the Army began his job search. Desiring to remain involved with parachuting and flying, he enrolled in Embry-Riddle Aeronautical University located in Daytona Beach, Florida. He graduated after three years of school, with an associate of science degree in mechanics.

While Jim attended Embry-Riddle, Jeanne was also attending nursing school. During this hectic period of their lives, they both found time to qualify for single-engine pilot's licenses.

In the late 1970s, Jim spent his first year after graduation working for Avco-Lycoming. As a tech rep., he traveled across the United States providing advice on turbine engines. His expertise enabled him to work on the Army's new, highly sophisticated main battle tank, the M1-Abrams, which was being qualified at the White Sands Testing Ground in Fort Bliss, Texas.

Jim next applied for and was hired as a mechanic for Delta Airlines, initially working one year in Atlanta, moving to Miami for several years, and then transferring to Tampa, where he completed 23 years of service as a lead mechanic and retired in 2000. Jim enjoyed his time at Delta, especially the family-friendly environment and travel opportunities, but during the 1990s the airlines were entering a vulnerable period with acquisitions and mergers, and job stability became a big question.

Planning ahead during his last years at Delta, Jim attended Hillsborough Community College, working nights at Delta and going to school during the day. It was an exhausting effort, but Jim graduated in 1999 with an associate degree in nursing, passed his certification, and worked at a major hospital in Tampa as a surgical nurse for the next seven years. The day after Jim retired from Delta Airlines, he started working at Tampa's St. Joseph's Hospital in the main OR.

For almost seven years, in tandem with his hospital schedule, Jim worked part time as a Certified Tissue Bank Specialist (CTBS), a diener, and a morgue assistant, helping a private company retrieve donated body parts. The work was tedious and exacting, requiring body parts to be carefully removed within 24 hours of the person's death, sterilization and handling being of the utmost importance. The retrievals would involve bones, tissue, and veinous systems.

After his stint with the hospital and the donor company, Jim and Jeanne, who was also a nurse, worked as part-time home health RNs and only recently retired.

They have lived in Wesley Chapel, in the Tampa area, for 36 years and raised three children in a beautiful country setting. Their A-frame house, located on two and a half acres, has a lanai with a pool and a nearby pond filled with fish. They are visited by local wildlife, including deer, egrets, and otters.

With Jim having made more than 600 parachute jumps (and Jeanne 65), they still have an affinity for all things aero. While they were still working, they bought a two-seater powered parachute. The motorized aircraft consisting of a parachute with wheels and a small motor allows people to reach altitudes as high as 10,000 feet. After receiving a sporting endorsement to his flying license, Jim and Jeanne have flown as high as 6,000 feet in the air. Jim strongly supports Army Airborne and several years ago participated in an Old Timers jump, where participants wearing parts of their old uniforms parachuted from Zephyrhills Municipal Airport.

The couple also loves travel and have been to England, Australia, New Zealand, Ice-

Jim (center) preparing for the Old Timers jump: Clothes don't fit quite like they did (courtesy Jim Luczynski).

land, Mexico, Canada, Poland, the Caribbean, and to Bora Bora for their 30th wedding anniversary. Jim and Jeanne continue to stay busy, attending yoga classes, occasionally assisting patients in their home health care jobs and traveling to see children. Jim himself writes poetry, has volunteered at the Wesley Chapel fire department for ten years, and he currently attends VA support group meetings. Jim's health has been affected by his wartime service, including symptoms of PTSD. His conditions were diagnosed about five years ago, and he was determined to have an Agent Orange disability attributed to the following conditions: Cardiac artery issues (he's had a quadruple bypass), diabetes, and peripheral neuropathy of hands and feet, but mostly his feet. There's tingling at times and feeling like they are burning or freezing at other times. Also, Jim has sensitive skin issues including basal cell carcinoma for which he's had operations to excise spots on his head, neck, ears, etc. When I visited him he showed no outward signs, and his chosen therapy is still parachuting.

Jim remains a stalwart supporter of the United States' efforts in Vietnam. His upbringing with relatives who experienced Communist suppression in Europe fortifies his thoughts and beliefs that our efforts in supporting the Vietnamese government were justified. He believes the war was winnable ("we never lost a battle"), but lacked the political will and leadership to accomplish our mission.

He remains ever proud of his military service, especially as an Army Airborne Ranger, and of his time in Vietnam.

17

Carol Bleau Boucher—
War Protester

Carol Bleau's dad, Norman, was part of the 503rd Parachute Regimental Combat Team that was one of the first airborne units to fight in the Pacific in World War II. The highly decorated unit fought primarily in New Guinea and the Philippines. After fierce fighting, the unit successfully captured Corregidor, an island known as the Rock, and was awarded a Presidential Unit Citation. Their unit's shoulder patch, an Airborne scroll with a plane and a parachute, was a badge of prestige and honor.

He also supported the war in Vietnam and, as most people were in the mid–1960s, was convinced that Communist aggression needed to be stopped, and that the United States needed to intervene before the contagion spread to other countries. The Bleau household's supper conversations about Vietnam were lively. Carol and her dad were at loggerheads about the Vietnam War. Her maternal grandfather, a World War I Army veteran, seemed to support Carol's position, which questioned the whole purpose of the war.

On one occasion, Carol was wearing her dad's long, wool Airborne coat, with the unit's patch on it, when she and her friends were protesting the Vietnam War. On this cold fall evening, the group of protesters proceeded down Main Street in North Adams, chanting anti-war slogans and carrying placards denouncing the war. Out of the corner of her eye, Carol noticed her dad up ahead, parked near the curb, sitting in his car. He motioned for her to come to him. Norman, realizing Carol was actively engaged with the group, didn't offer any immediate criticism. He just asked her to give him his wool coat. He brought her a warm coat in exchange.

Carol's story begins, like that of many of her classmates, as a welcomed post–World War II baby, a member of the so-called Baby Boomer Generation. She was born in 1948, on her dad's birthday, February 18. Carol was the oldest of four children, two girls and two boys.

For Carol's paternal grandparents, Zenaphil and Alma Bleau, it was their second marriage. Family lore has it that Zenaphil proposed to Alma when she was very young, but her mother prohibited the marriage and insisted Alma return his ring. Years later, after their first spouses' deaths to illnesses, they were married. The couple raised four children: one girl and three boys, one of whom was Norman, Carol's dad.

Zenaphil's ancestors had emigrated from Canada in the 1800s and, as a young man, he enlisted in the Army and fought in the First World War. Upon his return home, he worked the rest of his life as a barber in Williamstown, Massachusetts. He was known for giving free haircuts at Christmastime. Alma was a seamstress for the Lurie department store, and also ran a small grocery on an East Quincy Street corner.

Her maternal grandparents, Leonard and Mabel Dowling, were also U.S. citizens. Leonard worked as a foreman for the Boston and Maine railroad, spending most of his time at the company's then famous Hoosac Tunnel. He was proud of being a part of the crew that ran North America's largest transportation tunnel. Leonard, who was nicknamed "Pepper" by Carol as a young child and every grandchild thereafter, had unlimited, lifetime privileges for train transportation, compliments of B+M Railroad. He often took Carol to the depot station for train watching. The couple had three children, all girls, one of whom was Margaret, Carol's mother. Mabel also worked as a homemaker, enabling her granddaughter Carol to walk home for lunch when she was in grammar school.

Carol's parents met and married in 1946, right after the war. Norman, born in 1920, was from Williamstown and before the war worked as a butcher. Once married, he and Margaret moved to North Adams. Norman was described by most as an even-tempered, gentle soul who was five feet eight inches tall, in good shape, his dark hair well managed by Brylcreem, made popular during the war and initially sold exclusively by barbers.

He was always busy with house repairs, helping with the ironing, or doing whatever chores needed to be done. Norman settled on a trade as a barber, and worked in Williamstown and North Adams his entire life. For work, he always wore starched white barber's coats and white shirts, cleaned for him by the Chinese laundry located in the flatiron building on Eagle Street. It's interesting to note that Norman, his father, and his brother Eddie were all barbers, sometimes even working in the same shop. All were gregarious and genuinely enjoyed conversations with their customers. They had only one informal rule they tried to live by: "don't talk politics or religion." Many of Carol's friends would later tell her that they had their hair cut by one of the family's barbers.

Norman and his family faithfully attended the local Saint Francis Church. They always went as a family to 4:00 p.m. Christmas Eve Mass, and Norman helped out by ushering at Sunday masses for more than 30 years. He was a loyal member of the Knights of Columbus.

Carol's mother, Margaret, born in 1921, was a petite woman with long brown hair. She spent much of her time raising her four children, two boys and two girls. As the children got older, and Carol went off to college, Margaret worked the 5-to-11 shift at the local Sprague Electric Company and then as a housekeeper at Tyler House residence hall of Williams College. She was short in stature, five feet three inches, but long on kindness and always willing to help others. She had a subtle Irish temper, and when she asked her children to do something, she meant right now. Carol's mom was also serious about her children getting a good education. She was adamant that her children achieve As or Bs in school. Nevertheless, Margaret had a "Lucille Ball" sense of humor, and her contagious laugh brightened those around her.

One beloved family tale was when Norman drove to Williamstown to pick up Margaret, who had been working 8:00 to noon at the Tyler House. Norman often brought and picked up Margaret, especially when road conditions were snowy and slippery. On one occasion, leaving the family car running for warmth, he went into the building in search of Margaret, while she exited from another door, saw the car, and drove it home, leaving Norman behind. Norman got a ride home and asked his wife what she was thinking. Margaret thought he had left the car for her. He was bewildered, asking how did she think the car got there.

Sometimes Margaret would tell Carol she wasn't going out until her chores were done, or not going out at all. Her father would give Carol a telltale nod, indicating he would "take care of Mom" and she could go out. Carol had a special bond with her dad and welcomed the frequent comment that she looked like her father.

The family moved from Cole Avenue in Williamstown and rented an apartment on Bracewell Avenue, ultimately buying a home on Liberty Street, where they would remain throughout Carol's high school years and well into their 80s. Carol attended Saint Joseph's elementary and high schools.

From the early age of 10, Carol enjoyed fishing. In the summer, she would ride her bike with neighborhood friends to the Hoosac Tunnel and fish, either at the dam itself or in one of the adjacent streams. It wouldn't take long, and soon she would be peddling home with her catch and cleaning fish in the kitchen sink. Her mom was not thrilled.

Carol has always been petite and looked much younger than her age. When she entered high school, weighing less than 100 pounds, her youthful appearance could be embarrassing at times, and her school uniforms needed to be special-ordered. On her first day of high school, the French teacher found her wandering the halls and, presuming she was lost, kindly redirected her to the grammar school rooms on the lower floors. She was mortified but laughs about it now.

She was often described as quiet, shy, and studious, although social with her girlfriends. They often attended the local Saint Stanislaus school dances. Carol was also involved in many of the St. Joe's musicals and attended almost every St. Joe's boys' basketball game.

In the mid–1960s, other than wiffle ball and softball there were few athletic opportunities for girls, so Carol focused on fishing. During high school, Carol would sleep over at her friend Linda's, whose dad would drop them off near Burlingame Hill in Adams to trout fish. Linda is now a mission sister working with widows and orphans in Burkina Faso, a small country in West Africa.

Norman would close his barber shop on Eagle Street at 5:00 p.m. and walk home for supper, always on time for the family's evening meal at 6:00. Margaret, who didn't particularly enjoy cooking, always had a filling meal on the table or in the pot ready for Norman's arrival. Meals could range from chipped beef on toast to roasts, pork chops, and hot dogs or spaghetti. She was known for Swedish meatballs and homemade banana bread.

After graduating from St. Joe's High School, Carol went to Saint Joseph College in neighboring Bennington, Vermont. It was during her college years, 1965 through 1967, that the Vietnam War grew in intensity and casualties mounted. Carol's awareness increased by 1968, and she began talking with her friends and other students who were questioning the war. The gatherings encouraged participation in silent stand-outs in Bennington, and she felt that she was making a contribution to ending the war.

When at home, discussions at the supper table were intense surrounding the Vietnam War. As it became a main news item in the mid– to late 1960s, Carol found herself and her dad on opposite sides. Norman thought the war was necessary to stop the spread of Communism and the ultimate effect it would have on nearby countries. Carol, on the other hand, saw nothing positive and found it demoralizing and wasteful. She was personally affected by the increasing number of coffins shown on the evening news, night after night after night.

Carol's stance on the war only solidified over the following months as friends and classmates were being killed or wounded in this place called Vietnam.

Sometime in late April 1967, one of her college friends told her that Joe Daigneault, a high school classmate, had been seriously wounded. The friend had read an article in the local paper that Joe's right arm had been shattered by an enemy "machine gun burst" while on a search-and-destroy mission. The news article said he had been medevaced and was undergoing a series of operations at the naval hospital in Chelsea, Massachusetts. Carol used to see Joe and his high school hallway buddies every morning as she made her way to class.

It was less than six weeks later, in June 1967, that Carol received the startling news of another classmate, Russell Roulier, who had been killed while on a patrol in Vietnam. Early one morning, while in a defensive position, Russell had been guarding the flank of his platoon, when Viet Cong released a fusillade of fire, killing him instantly.

She knew Russell in high school; he was a commuter from the nearby town of Adams. She didn't know him well, but often said "hi" to him at school. He was a close friend of Joe Daigneault's. Carol often saw them together, hanging out on the seniors' fourth floor at St. Joe's. Carol might have shared classes with Russell's sister, Cynthia. Then, after high school, Carol and Russell had both worked briefly at Sprague Electric.

Russell's funeral was held in late June 1967, and was prominently featured by the *Transcript,* their small-town newspaper. She felt awful for Cynthia and her family. The death increased her resolve about the wastefulness of the war.

While in college, Carol was offered a part-time job at a high-school construction site and managed the payroll process. Carol graduated from college with a business degree, and upon graduation, Carol followed her dad's advice: To show her earnestness in finding a job, she drove to Pittsfield in the summer of 1967 for two weeks straight, meeting with the General Electric Personnel Department each time. Her efforts were rewarded and she was hired by GE Naval Ordnance a month after graduating and worked there for the next 12 years. As time passed in the drafting department where she worked, and war needs increased, it became noticeable that most of the younger draftsmen had left, consumed by the military's manpower needs.

Carol was working at the Naval Ordnance Plant in Pittsfield when the news arrived that a popular hometown boy, Peter Foote, had been killed in Vietnam on January 30, 1968. Peter was killed by small arms fire while trying to aid another wounded soldier. Peter had graduated from Drury, the other local high school, and Carol was aware of him talking to her dad about being an Army Airborne soldier. Months after his death, Carol would work side-by-side with his dad, Ed, in GE's drafting department. Ed had just returned from an extended bereavement leave and was withdrawn. Ed, a former World War II Marine drill instructor, was shattered by the loss of his son.

Carol now had the distinction of knowing the first men (and it would turn out the only men) killed from the small towns of North Adams and Adams. The deaths and maiming of people she knew continued to strengthen her opinion that the war was a huge mistake, and her friends were paying too severe a price to participate.

Less than eight weeks after Peter's death she received the most devastating news of all.

Just before entering college in the fall of 1965, Carol had begun dating John P. Hartlage, III, a young man from the small town of Savoy, Massachusetts. His nickname was "Bootsie," and he was an avid sports fan. They met at an Armory Dance in Bennington, Vermont, where Carol would be going to school, and began dating. Their dates included trips to the Pittsfield McDonald's, miniature golf, and indoor and outdoor movies. When Carol turned 18, the couple celebrated by traveling to New York State, just 40 minutes away, where Carol could now legally drink.

John was short of stature like Carol, very personable, funny, and came from a close-knit family. He graduated from Adams High School in 1965 and wanted to travel and learn a trade just like his dad, a skilled electrician who taught at the local technical school. John joined the Navy, completed boot camp, and qualified for the Seabees, the Navy's vaunted construction battalion. After boot camp, he received electrical training as well as instruction in defensive combat tactics. The Seabees were known to fight alongside soldiers or Marines while they constructed combat bases in the most remote areas.

Shortly after his home leave expired, John received orders to Vietnam. While gone, he and Carol wrote letters daily. His unit was deployed to the Dong Ha Combat Base, in Quang Tri Province. The base was just a few kilometers from the demilitarized zone between North and South Vietnam. John was assigned to Naval Mobile Construction Battalion-FIVE (NMCB-5), and his group was tasked with constructing and reinforcing combat bases in this northern, most dangerous, province. The area was subject to repeated enemy assaults and artillery fire.

After the completion of one tour of duty, John extended his overseas tour, which allowed him to take a 30-day leave. He arrived back in the States just in time to see Carol graduate from college in June 1967. John seemed to be getting serious about the relationship; Carol loved John but had reservations about marrying too young. The topic was discussed during his leave but no decision was made and he returned to Vietnam to complete his extended tour.

On March 8, 1968, the Dong Ha Combat Base was bombarded by 80 rounds of enemy rocket fire. Ten soldiers were killed and three Seabees. One was John, who died 60 days before he was to return home.

At the time, Carol was in the hospital recovering from a minor automobile accident injury. Her parents rushed to visit her. Both her mom and dad were crying when they entered her hospital room, and Carol initially thought they were overwrought about her minor injury, until they told her the news.

Carol and John on her graduation day (courtesy Carol Boucher).

Carol next saw John at the McBride Funeral Home in Adams, when she viewed his remains through an 18-inch acrylic-glass window, embedded in his coffin. Her dad, mom, and other family members accompanied Carol during this very emotional send-off for a young man who was well known and liked throughout the area. The Seabees sent a six-person honor guard that accompanied the body to Saint Thomas Church in Adams, directly across the street from the well-known Val's Variety store. After a Catholic funeral mass, the honor guard escorted the body to Bellevue Cemetery, played "Taps," and fired three volleys of shots as a final salute to John. The family was presented with the United States flag that had been draped on his coffin.

For years afterwards, Carol had a Mass offered at her church, Saint Francis in North Adams, on the anniversary of John's death. Usually his parents would accompany her.

In less than 12 months, her boyfriend of two and a half years, a classmate, and a family friend had been killed, and another classmate grievously wounded. These casualties occurred in three small abutting towns and brought the Vietnam War much closer than the coffins pictured on the six o'clock news. Even at work, where Carol worked alongside Ed Foote, grief followed her. She found it was easy to relate to him now, since she had lost Bootsie, and he had lost Peter.

The deaths and injuries of people close to her solidified Carol's resolve and renewed her efforts to help end the war. She began meeting with a group of friends, discussing ways to protest against the war. In North Adams, where many people of her father's generation were World War II veterans, the group's efforts were not popular but the young people remained resolute that they needed to speak up.

Carol had already participated in silent protests in Vermont in 1968. Now back home in North Adams, she and a group of twenty or so young people began discussing the war locally. Their efforts, while small on a national scale, helped to increase local awareness about the disastrous effects of the war.

Carol in 1969 with her first car, a 1967 Ford LTD sports coupe (courtesy Carol Boucher).

During national days of protest, Carol wore a black armband to work at GE, wondering if the "statement" would jeopardize her employment, or affect her secret clearance at Naval Ordnance Division, a stalwart defense contractor. It did not.

Around this same time, one of Carol's friends was dating Mike Gorman, another classmate, who went to Vietnam to work as a crew chief on attack helicopters. During his tour of duty, he was catastrophically wounded and paralyzed on January 23, 1969.

She and her fellow protesters continued meeting at different homes, discussing and carrying-out public protests. Without permits, the committed group would walk the length of Main Street in North Adams, carrying placards and chanting, calling for the end of the war. The placards would read "End the War Now!," "Make Love, Not War," "All We Are Saying Is Give Peace a Chance," or "Hell No, We Won't Go."

Carol also had the chance to participate in the Woodstock Music and Art Festival held in the Catskill Mountains of New York in August 1969. More than 400,000 people gathered at a dairy farm to celebrate three days of "Peace and Music." Carol bought a ticket for the first day, but the remaining days were free, as the number of participants greatly exceeded expectations and tickets became pointless.

And she kept the ticket! Shown front and back (courtesy Carol Boucher).

Just several months later, Carol and the North Adams group participated in the nationwide "Moratorium to End the War in Vietnam" on October 15, 1969. It was a massive demonstration across the United States, involving hundreds of thousands of people, and followed up a month later by an even larger group of protesters.

With these very public demonstrations, the small towns in western Massachusetts grew more accepting of protests, seeing firsthand the devastation the war was causing through the killing and maiming of their young men. As time passed, the towns' citizens became seriously disenchanted with the war.

On May 1, 1971 (May Day), some of Carol's friends participated in the March on Washington. She didn't go because she couldn't risk arrest and lose her government job. They camped in nearby West Potomac Park near the Washington Monument and marched with thousands of other protesters. Several were arrested and detained in one of the largest mass arrests in U.S. history. The detainees numbered over 12,000. After several days in detention, in an eight-foot enclosure near RFK Stadium, protesters were released and returned to North Adams and Williamstown.

The anti-war protests continued for years and eventually waned as the United States began withdrawing substantial numbers of troops from Vietnam. The lists of casualties began to abate, and the protesters, seeing the end at hand, decided to move on with their lives.

After the War

During the early seventies, Carol met Mike Boucher. Carol, a passionate softball player, was the only girl on a men's city league softball team, playing as their short fielder. Mike was the team's catcher. After a number of games, Mike asked Carol for a date and although she usually said no, she agreed to go to the local drive-in. They rode in Carol's Saab and parked near the concession stand, giving her some sense of control and security. Shortly after they arrived, the couple was surprised when the rest of their team decided to attend the movie and parked on both sides of them. It was a memorable ending to their first date.

Carol and Mike dated for some time and eventually were married in 1974. Carol remained at GE until their first child was born. She decided to stay at home when two more children were born to the happy family. Later in life, she used her business administration skills to work for a mental health system, for a CPA, for a local psychiatrist, and at a federal credit union. When the children were young she waitressed at the local fish market and loved the sociability.

Carol has maintained many interests, some from her childhood, like fishing. When first married, she helped outfit Mike with a fishing pole and waders, and they continued to fish at area spots around North Adams.

Carol has played women's softball since 1975, lately on senior teams with names like "Forever Young." That team made it all the way to the Senior Softball Olympics in 2007.

She never sits still for very long. Carol enjoys cards and plays "pitch" and "cribbage" in a local league. She is a traveler, and when not visiting grandchildren, she can be found at the beach, at Red Sox home games, gambling at a casino, or visiting the race track in Saratoga, New York. Ever the protester, Carol made sure to be in D.C. on January 21,

2017, with her sister Diane in tow, to attend the Women's March which brought hundreds of thousands of women together.

Carol continues to be involved with the St. Joe's Class of 1965, helping to organize alumni get-togethers or just spontaneous luncheons when out-of-town classmates visit. To this day, her engaging and outgoing personality finds her visiting former classmates, friends, and family. When the local weather is nice, you may see Carol happily driving her sporty, two-seater Mazda Miata, sporting a Boston Red Sox hat.

Epilogue

Some 58,000 names are etched deeply into the polished black granite of the Vietnam Wall. It's a soul-wrenching monument to America's war dead. No one can precisely know the shattering effects on the families and friends connected to each one of those names, not to mention the 300,000 wounded not named. Of the nearly three million Americans who served in Vietnam, this book focuses on just 11 young men and one young woman, all from the same high school class, and from two small adjoining towns in the Berkshires. The war called on our conflicted generation and demanded personal sacrifices. One died in combat, another was paralyzed, others were wounded, and some suffer from debilitating conditions, five decades later.

An etching from the Vietnam Memorial, provided by Russ's best friend Joe Daigneault.

Stories like these are so very common with the thousands of people who served in-country. Many were from small, close-knit communities like ours, with little exposure to a bigger world. Initially, for the early enlistees, the place called Vietnam was not much of a concern, a minor struggle in a small country thousands of miles away. Most couldn't, or wouldn't, even bother finding it on a map.

As the United States' commitment to the war grew, most of my St. Joe's classmates believed what they were told by our government—that the South Vietnamese's emerging democracy needed our support; that the country needed to be protected from the scourge of Communism; that if South Vietnam fell, nearby countries were destined to fall under Communist influence.

217

The book's participants, my classmates, were all born around 1947 to parents who lived in Adams or North Adams, Massachusetts. All the dads were World War II vets returning home to a robust economy that ensured employment and helped them build or buy homes, and in one case start a farm. Many worked two jobs, and the common places of employment were at Arnold Print Works; Sprague Electric Company; or the ultimate job opportunity, General Electric in Pittsfield.

Growing up in the 1950s, we played war games with military-surplus equipment and listened to our dads and uncles talk about the greatest adventure of their lives, World War II. We watched *Combat!* on television, loved John Wayne films, and marched with the Boy Scouts on national holidays. We enjoyed the outdoors. We said the Pledge of Allegiance every day in school. And many of us would receive our first gun as a birthday gift or find it under the Christmas tree. Until the Vietnam War, for many of us, the major event in high school was "going over-the-line" to New York State for a bit of underage drinking.

Vietnam altered the trajectory of our lives, no matter in what capacity we served. Young, courageous, naive, and trusting—we went. Some volunteered, and others, as school and job aspirations waned, were drafted. Some enlisted because of the threat of being drafted. They enlisted so they could at least select their branch of the service, choose the number of years of enlistment, or receive specific training—anything other than becoming infantry. For some, enlisting would be a patriotic issue. For others, it would present a thrilling challenge, a test to physical courage or toughness. For still others, it was a job opportunity. It also meant emancipation—a chance to get out of the house or to get away from legal troubles.

While college was an option, too often middle-class kids couldn't afford it, and either dropped out of school to earn money or changed to part-time student status. In either case, dropping out or going part-time left them immediately draft-eligible.

Seven of us served in the Army, three in the Marine Corps, and one in the Navy. All were cited for exemplary performance or heroism and honorably discharged. Many trusted the government, knew little about the war, and presumed it was a righteous thing to do because their government said so. No one had any idea of the future physical and psychological challenges we would face as a result of just a couple quick years' service.

Of the 11 men, nine received or are receiving some type of disability income—due to gunshot wounds, a hard landing, the effects of Agent Orange, or Post Traumatic Stress Disorder (PTSD). The length of time in-country before being shot, in most cases, was just months. Mike Gorman was paralyzed four months after arriving, Pat Lupo was shot within three months, Joe Daigneault was wounded seven months after arrival in-country, and Russell Roulier was killed after nine months, less than a hundred days before he was to go home.

It was almost universal among classmates that, when in Vietnam, they seldom knew where they were, where they had been, or where they were going. Usually, they just followed their leader's orders for the day, or the hour.

Sometimes fighting would be so furious and lengthy that the troops looked forward to being wounded just to get out of the field. Some would toss their malaria pills, knowing malarial fevers would get them sent to the rear for a respite. Most of us were just trying to "beat the calendar"—to survive a 12- or 13-month tour of duty and get home. (The Marines added a month for ship transport.)

Keeping time became a sort of mantra. Some just crossed off months until they qualified for a 100-day calendar (that's when you'd become a *double-digit midget*: "99 days and a wake-up"). The soldiers and Marines in the rear would usually color daily one of the blank spots on the picture of a naked woman. It tended to hang over their rack or in their office, divided into days with days 3, 2, and 1 being personal areas. Some used Playmate calendars and circled their actual departure date.

The Army and Marine grunts in the field usually did not carry a calendar. They had no room and it would get sodden in the elements. They knew their month, and they just tried to survive until then. Some grunts wrote on their helmets and flak jackets, listing the months and crossing each off as it was completed.

All of the St. Joe's veterans profiled herein were raised Catholic, although in adulthood most have changed their faith beliefs. They own their homes, and most are in long-term relationships, with children and grandchildren. After the war, some attended and graduated from college. Others were entrepreneurs, managers, or worked hard at skilled-labor positions. They were glad to be out of the service and anxious to catch up with their peers who had not been sidetracked by serving in the military. One was unable to work because of his injuries and struggled the rest of his life in pain. Another's inability to hold a job was due to PTSD. All of them now, in their early seventies, find their disabilities becoming harder to cope with.

Some veterans were bothered by the vociferous anti-war protesters, although all realized it their right to do so. Others were bothered by the 1970 film *M*A*S*H*, because it created a comedy around war injuries at a Korean War medical unit. Even that was all too fresh for some.

Most of us look on our Vietnam memories as the most vivid moments of our lives, shaping the future. Even those of us with successful post-military careers, Vietnam remains our most significant experience. We are proud of our service and realize our sacrifices earned us membership in a unique group. Belonging to this "club" helps us talk and relate to other veterans. Many participants display their military ribbons, medals, or citations in various fashion: from shadow boxes or wall hangings, to license plates and bumper stickers.

Interestingly, almost all the participants are now involved in the arts or the outdoors, quiet pursuits: Ron weaves scarves and is teaching himself to play the violin. Pat works with stained glass and enjoys spending time at his cabin. Gary embraces the outdoors and is a student and collector of native Indian artifacts. Bill loves wildlife photography and is a golf enthusiast. Joe spends time outdoors on bird hunts, hikes, and fishing trips. Jim writes poetry and remains an aviation enthusiast. Leo builds and plays stringed instruments and uses any excuse to tromp in the woods. When Mike Gorman was alive, he was interested in astronomy and genealogy. Mike Chalifoux spent hours upon hours of his own time, and sometimes his own money, managing trash collection in areas of North Adams that were important to him.

Conducting interviews for this book had a wonderful side benefit. It has allowed me to reconnect with former classmates after a lapse of 50-plus years. At times the search became more rewarding than the writing, hearing about their careers, family lives, and what they were doing now. At other times, searches were sad: I found out that some classmates had died, although I was able to have great conversations with four others months before they, too, passed away.

I found myself knowing much more about people's family lives than I did as a teenager. They shared deeply with me, invited me into their houses, took me to their cabins,

showed me where they grew up, made supper for me, and introduced me to their families. Some even gave me personal gifts to remember them by. Repeatedly, everyone was gracious and kind.

Veterans were willing and open to talking about Vietnam, especially with me, another vet, another kid from the Berkshires. Most continue to think the war was winnable—e.g., "we never lost a battle"—although as the years have passed and more information has become available, many veterans have come to realize that their sacrifices, while personally noble, were based on misinformation or even lies by politicians and military leaders. Most of us believed our country would call us only in times of great necessity, and for many families, the expectation was that their son would serve. Many now believe the politicians or military leaders didn't know what they were doing.

"We may have been the last generation to trust politicians," one veteran said. "They didn't care about us." We also now realize that the South Vietnamese, tired of the strife, just wanted the conflict to end. They associated much of the violence with our presence and wanted us to leave.

For me there was an odd twist to the story.

For many years, I struggled being in large crowds, especially in shopping malls. I was always searching for the nearest exit and hypervigilant about any potentially threatening individuals. After returning from Vietnam, my sleeping was always restless. I ignored these signs, worked hard at my job, which included business travel, and helped to raise six children. Once I retired, the symptoms bothered me more, and I found myself becoming easily irritated at perceived slights and was often ready, willing, and eager to fight.

During the writing of this book, as I talked to my veteran friends, I came to realize that I needed to be examined by the Veterans Administration (VA). Subsequently I was evaluated in 2017, and have been part of a PTSD therapy group beginning in January 2019.

In the meantime, this book itself has been therapy for me, and I hope for others.

Opposite, top: **Dennis with Jim Luczynski (left) at his home in Florida. Researching is fun when it means reconnecting with old friends.** *Bottom:* **With Joe Daigneault at his home in Adams, having just finished off a couple of cigars.**

Appendix: Guide to Terms and Abbreviations

Agent Orange	Herbicide used to defoliate, so named for the color-coded stripe on the container
Air Medal	Awarded for meritorious achievement while participating in aerial operations
AIT	Advanced Individual Training; Advanced Infantry Training
AK-47	Standard VC/NVA weapon; Soviet-made 7.62 assault rifle
AKA	Attack cargo ship
APC	Armored personnel carrier
Army Commendation Medal	Awarded to soldiers who distinguish themselves by heroism, achievement, or service
ARVN	Army of the Republic of Vietnam
B-52	U.S. bomber aircraft
Base camp	Tactical field headquarters
Bronze Star	Military decoration awarded for heroic or meritorious achievement
Brown water sailor	Naval personnel operating inland or close to shore
C rations	Canned, boxed field rations
C-4	White, plastic high explosive
C-130	Cargo transport plane
Carbine	U.S. .30-caliber rifle
Cattle car	Tractor trailer converted to carry personnel
CH-34	Single-rotor transport helicopter
CH-46	Twin-rotor transport helicopter
Chain of command	Hierarchy of military authority
Charlie Med	Place for field medical treatment
Chicken plate	Chest protector worn by helicopter crews
Chieu Hoi	"Open Arms" program to repatriate enemy soldiers and encourage defection, "Chieu" meaning "Welcome"
Claymore	U.S. antipersonnel mine
Close-order drill	Training on movements used in marching, parades, and ceremonies

CO	Commanding officer
COBRA	Heavily armed helicopter gunship
Combat Action Ribbon	Awarded to Marine Corps or Naval personnel who participated in ground or surface combat
Combat Infantryman Badge	Awarded to soldiers who fought in active ground combat
Corpsman	U.S. Navy medical personnel
Cumshaw	Naval slang for borrowing/misappropriating
DI	Drill instructor
DMZ	Demilitarized zone
Duster	Track-mounted armored vehicle with dual 40mm cannons
Dustoff	Medical evacuation by helicopter
11-Bravo	Army infantryman
FDC	Fire Direction Center; command center for tactical firing orders
.50-caliber	Machine gun used on helicopters, trucks, tracked vehicles, etc.
Fire base	Temporary artillery base
Fire watch	Night security watch
Firing lanes	Cleared areas for unobstructed firing
Flak jacket	Bulky, vest-like body armor intended to protect U.S. Armed Forces from low-velocity projectiles
Footlocker	Wooden storage box, typically for personal items
.45-caliber pistol	Sidearm used by officers, senior NCOs, radio operators, tankers, etc.
Four deuce	Slang for U.S. 4.2–107mm heavy mortar
Gook	Derisive slang for VC/NVA, or Vietnamese in general
Grunt	Infantryman
Gun team	Group of soldiers/Marines operating a firing system, e.g., machine gun, mortar
Halazone tablets	Used in the field for water purification
Heat tabs	Tablets used to heat C rations
HMM-263	Helicopter Marine Medium Squadron 263
Hootch	Wooden, screened, metal roofed billet for U.S. Forces
House mouse	Recruit selected to serve a drill instructor
Huey	Slang for UH-1 helicopter, also called a slick
Hump	Slang meaning to walk, usually while carrying a burden
Immersion foot	Fungal disease, also called jungle rot
In-country	In Vietnam
Jungle penetrator	Device used by helicopters for personnel extractions
Laager	Night defensive position, often armored vehicles in a defensive circle
LAW	Light anti-tank weapon, shoulder-fired, single-shot, disposable
Listening post (LP)	A position outside of the perimeter intended to detect enemy movements and provide advanced warning
LKA	Landing cargo attack ship
LOH	Light observation helicopter OH-6A

LPH	Landing platform helicopter
LZ	Landing zone, spot where helicopters could land
M-14	Standard 7.62mm U.S. infantry rifle, replaced by M-16
M-16	Standard 5.56mm U.S. infantry rifle
M-26	U.S. fragmentation hand grenade
M-60	U.S. 7.62mm machine gun
M-79	U.S. 40mm grenade launcher, breech-loaded, single shot
Manual of arms	Instruction on the handling of weapons
Marble Mountain	Marine helicopter base
MARS Station	Military Auxiliary Radio System
MCB	Marine Corps Base
Medevac	Medical evacuation
Medic	Army medical personnel
MOS	Military occupational specialty
MP	Military police
Napalm	A highly flammable sticky jelly used in bombs
Navy/Marine Corps Medal	Highest non-combat medal for heroism
NCO	Non-commissioned officer
Nuoc mam	Fermented fish sauce
NVA	North Vietnamese Army
122mm rocket	Ground-to-ground Soviet missile
Perimeter	Boundary around a fire base where defenses are established
Perimeter watch	Base security vigilance
Permanent routines	Bodies of those killed in action
PFs	Popular Forces of the South Vietnamese Army, much like a local militia
Poncho liner	Lightweight quilt, used as blanket
Pop-up flares	Handheld parachute flare
PTSD	Post-traumatic stress disorder
Purple Heart	Decoration awarded to U.S. Armed Forces personnel wounded or killed-in-action
PX	Post Exchange, essentially a retail store on base
Quad 50s	Vehicle-mounted, 4-barreled .50-caliber machine guns
R & R	Military slang for rest & relaxation, recreation, or recuperation; often an out-of-country seven-day leave
Razor wire	Large-coiled sharp wire used for defensive purposes
Recoilless rifle	Lightweight artillery (105mm), single shot, breech-loading
Road sweep	Checking a road for mines
RPG	Rocket propelled grenade, Soviet/Chinese produced, shoulder-fired
RVN	Republic of Vietnam
Sapper	Enemy soldier trained in explosives
Shelter-half	Partial tent, often combined with another section to make a complete tent

Shrapnel	Fragments expelled from an exploding bomb or shell
Snapping in	Familiarization with different shooting positions
SVAF	South Vietnam Air Force
TAOR/AOR	Tactical Area of Responsibility, or Area of Responsibility
Task Force	Field Command Center
Thermite grenade	Incendiary used to destroy metal objects, e.g., weapons, vehicles, etc.
.38-caliber pistol	Common sidearm for aircrew personnel
Tracer	Bullet with luminous trail: Viet Cong used green; U.S. Forces used red
Trip flare	Flare rigged with a trip wire; ignites when triggered, warning of enemy troops approaching
USO	United Service Organizations; provides recreation-like services to U.S. Armed Forces personnel
VC	Viet Cong
Vietnamization	Transitioning combat operations to the Vietnamese ahead of U.S. withdrawal
Ville	Village
Water "Buffalo"	Portable water tank
Zippo APC	Flame-throwing Armored Personnel Carrier

Index

Numbers in **bold italics** indicate pages with illustrations